The Tuscan Poet Giuseppe Giusti, and His Times
by Susan Horner

Address:
HardPress
8345 NW 66TH ST #2561
MIAMI FL 33166-2626
USA
Email: info@hardpress.net

Horner
(Giusti.)

WORKS BEARING ON ITALY.

Crown 8vo. cloth.   6s. 6d.

ROME IN 1860.

By EDWARD DICEY.

" The writing of the whole book is terse, direct, and because of sound judgment in selection of details and the total absence of waste writing, very graphic.   Written in plain unaffected English, intent everywhere upon its subject."—*Examiner*.

" It is the Rome of real life that is here depicted."—*Spectator*.

" Written in a very agreeable and unaffected manner, and shows throughout a creditable anxiety to get at the most reliable sources of information and to tell the exact truth, which is nowhere less easily attained than among the sensitive, excited, and unveracious population whose chronicler he undertakes to be."—*Saturday Review*.

Crown 8vo. cloth.   6s. 6d.

THE ITALIAN WAR, 1848–9, AND THE LAST ITALIAN POET (GIUSTI).

By the late HENRY LUSHINGTON, Chief Secretary to the Government of Malta.

WITH A BIOGRAPHICAL NOTICE.

" This book is of incontestable excellence.   Mr. Lushington's sympathies with oppressed and priest-ridden Italy were keen, and his acquaintance with the social and political condition of that country seems to have been unusually profound."—*The Press*

" Told with great clearness and remarkable vividness."—*The Economist*.

Two Vols. 12s.

THE BROKEN TROTH.

A TALE OF TUSCAN LIFE.

"A genuine Italian tale—a true picture of the Tuscan peasant population . . . . It is the best Italian tale that has been published since the 'Promessi Sposi,' of Manzoni."
—*London Review.*

Fcap. 8vo. 3s. 6d.

GARIBALDI AT CAPRERA.

By COLONEL VECCHJ.

With a Preface by Mrs. GASKELL, author of "Mary Barton," &c.

"After all that has been told of Garibaldi, there was something wanting to the full and true impression of the patriot's character and mode of life, as every one who reads this artless and enthusiastic narration will certainly admit. . . . It has an air of truth that commends it, even when it is most extravagant in its admiration."—*Nonconformist.*

"It gives the fullest and most minute account of the life of Garibaldi at Caprera yet published. Many of the reflections and remarks of Garibaldi in this little volume will give most readers a new view of his general character."—*Morning Star.*

Two Vols. 8vo. 32s.

HISTORY OF FREDERICK THE SECOND, EMPEROR OF THE ROMANS.

By T. L. KINGTON, M.A.

"A detailed life of the greatest man of his age. . . . The book shows an understanding of the time with which it has immediately to do. The narrative is always clear and straightforward."—*Saturday Review.*

MACMILLAN AND CO. LONDON AND CAMBRIDGE.

GIUSEPPE GIUSTI,

AND HIS TIMES.

THE TUSCAN POET

GIUSEPPE GIUSTI,

AND HIS TIMES.

BY SUSAN HORNER.

London and Cambridge:

MACMILLAN AND CO.

1864.

g. n. 247

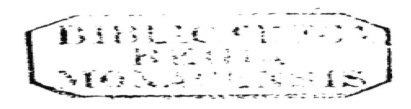
LONDON:
R. CLAY, SON, AND TAYLOR, PRINTERS,
BREAD STREET HILL.

INTRODUCTION.

THE writings, character, and example of the Poet and Satirist, GIUSEPPE GIUSTI, are acknowledged throughout Italy, to have had no inconsiderable share in leading to the realization of the hopes of all true Italian hearts. The idea of a United Italy, so long treated with contempt or ridicule, as the dream of ambitious usurpers or of restless political exiles, has at length attained a substantial form, and has been acquiesced in and approved since successfully achieved. The hot-headed and inexperienced youth, as well as the masses of the Italian people, have, now for a succession of years, maintained an attitude which has won for them the respect and admiration of nations glorying, like the Israelites of old, in their superiority: The source of this rapid moral growth in a whole people may be chiefly traced to the direct as well as indirect influence exercised by writers such as the modern Tuscan poet; and though now little known beyond the confines of Italy, the verses of Giusti may perhaps some day be read with those of Dante, as marking an epoch in the history of their common country.

Italy, degraded and corrupted by contamination from Spanish and Austrian nobles, and by a long course of systematic demoralization, first woke to obey the call of her guides and prophets, such as Alfieri and Parini, and to a consciousness of national existence, at the trumpet blast of the French Revolution. The French went forth as political missionaries to preach liberty abroad, and, in the spirit of their calling, to enforce what they preached; their pulpits were the thrones of fallen tyrants, but they at least gave Italy the benefit of material improvements and a more even administration of law and justice. The flattering appeal of the Archduke John once more held out the hope of regaining a national existence and independence, and the Italians hastened to join the Allies and drive out the French. But a worse form of foreign despotism followed, and the people, who had been duped and betrayed at the Congress of Vienna of 1815, have since then unceasingly offered every kind of resistance to Austria and to the other governments which were at that time forced upon them. The Liberals divided into two camps ; one, chiefly composed of young men, who met in secret to consult how to unite all Italians in the same aim, to soften the jealousies of the divided States of the Peninsula, to cherish the idea of a national existence, and to organize a force of volunteers to fight the battles of their country. Their watchword was Republicanism, and their leader Giuseppe Mazzini. Communism never found a place among the Liberals of Italy, and the republic they hoped to establish was a settled form of government, not anarchy. The spirit of patient endurance and courage which has led so many to fall willing martyrs to their cause, must more than apologise for errors in judgment and rash deeds.[1]

---

[1] The accusation of assassination having been permitted, and even encouraged, by the Society of Young Italy, is a calumny. That such had been the case with other secret societies, as the only restrictive

But another division of Liberals, equally honest, and including many of the wisest and best men of Italy, possessed more enlarged ideas of the future of their country, as well as of the means to be employed for its redemption. Those who adhered to these views rejected all secret means as unworthy of their end, besides, leading to useless bloodshed, more dangerous to morals than the measures adopted by their tyrants : with indomitable courage, patience, and hope, they have endeavoured to train the people to moral elevation of character. Among their ranks, indeed, are to be found many, even of the leaders, who in contradiction to the name which they have adopted, of Moderate, have displayed all the rancour and bitterness of party spirit towards those opposed to them ; whereas a calm appeal to the practical common-sense of the people is most needed to lead to the conviction that an idea traditional and unobjectionable in itself, may, under the circumstances of the present time, be impossible to realize.

measure of police for traitors among themselves, is true ; but Mazzini expunged this, and all which might lead to crime, when instituting the Society of Young Italy.

Among those who raised their voices in the cause of true moderation and Christian charity, and who with an earnest desire for political freedom and regeneration, have ventured to speak aloud when it was alike dangerous to brave the power of the oppressor and the opinion of the oppressed, was the Tuscan poet, Giusti; his writings stand forth pre-eminently among the patriots who have sown in the hearts of the Italian people the seeds of virtue, wisdom, and the love of true liberty.

The sketch of his life given in the following pages has been chiefly extracted from the biographies of Giovanni Frassi, Enrico Mayer, and Giosuè Carducci, whilst the contemporary history has been derived from *Le Istorie Italiane* of Ranalli, *Gli Ultimi Rivolgimenti Italiani* di F. W. Gualterio, *L'Italie est elle la terre des morts*, by Marc Monnier, and a pamphlet containing the evidence of some of the most honest as well as able of Tuscan statesmen, entitled *Toscana e Austria*. The chief attraction which this little volume can offer to the public, is a selection from Giusti's own correspondence, and from his most celebrated poems, whilst the narrative of the stirring events of this century, in which he played an important though unobtrusive part, may be read with interest at the beginning of a new and, it is to be trusted, a happier era for Italy.

CONTENTS.

CHAPTER XV.

CHAPTER XVI.

CHAPTER XVII.

CHAPTER XVIII.

CHAPTER XIX.

CHAPTER XX.

CHAPTER XXI.

CHAPTER XXII.

CHAPTER XXIII.

CHAPTER XXIV.

GIUSEPPE GIUSTI.

CHAPTER I.

MONSUMMANO is a little town of the Val di Nievole in the midst of the Apennines, situated on the road between Florence and Pescia, in a beautiful country, watered by many streams, and varied by hill and plain. Here, on the 13th May, 1809, was born Giuseppe Giusti, the only son of the Cavaliere Domenico Giusti, and of his wife, Ester Chiti. His paternal grandfather, another Giuseppe Giusti, had been the adviser and friend of the Grand Duke Leopold I., and had assisted him in his reforms, and in the compilation of the famous Code of Laws which gave Tuscany a pre-eminence over other Italian States. His maternal grandfather, Celestino Chiti, had attained a greater and as honourable a renown, by his adherence to the cause of liberty, in spite of obloquy and suffering. The son of a respectable

citizen of Pescia, and educated for an advocate, Chiti,
at the news of the first outbreak of the French Revolution in 1789, had shared the hopes of many, for the
liberation of his country ; but ten years later, these
hopes faded away, as the despotic character of the
great military leader showed itself in its true light,
whilst the alarm of French invasion caused the rule
of the petty sovereigns of Italy to become truly
reigns of terror.   The more enlightened portion of the
community, abandoned to their fate, fell victims to a
worse tyranny than before : Chiti was assailed by the
lowest of his fellow-citizens, torn from his wife and
children, and, under a burning July sun, with the
skeleton of an umbrella held over him in mockery, he
was dragged from his villa to a prison in Pescia.   In
this prison he found Sismondi, the future historian of
the Italian Republics, and they there formed a friendship which endured for life.   Some time later, Chiti
was not only set at liberty, but was appointed President
or Governor of the province, and he had then an opportunity of being nobly avenged upon those who had
so cruelly persecuted him.   A famine visited the land,
and the former leaders of the mob came to entreat for
forgiveness, and for aid.   Chiti's reply has been ever
since remembered with honour by his countrymen, and
with just pride by his descendants.   " I know you have
large families," he answered, " who are in want : at my
house you will be given the grain you require ; go,

take it, and be at peace." Such were the actions, and the men, whose memories young Giusti was trained to reverence from his childhood : and with a higher genius and more literary tastes, he appears to have inherited many of the qualities of his grandfather Chiti, who is described as having been dignified and courteous, yet violent when roused to anger ; affable, playful, frank, and of a social disposition.

In an autobiography, which has been preserved by the Marchese Gino Capponi, Giusti records that the first lesson taught him by his father was the famous description of Ugolino, set to music, and he thus early imbibed his passion for song, for poetry, and for Dante. His parents were anxious to make their child hardy in mind and body; the servants were accordingly forbidden to tell him ghost stories, and even fairy tales, and he was trained to bear falls and blows without tears or complaint. But systems of education formed to counteract, rather than guide nature, seldom succeed ; and notwithstanding his apparent hardihood as a child, Giusti grew up singularly sensitive, nervous, and imaginative, with a delicacy of constitution, unhappily ending only with his early death. At seven years of age he was sent to a priest to receive the rudiments of instruction. His master possessed a good library, and the boy was soon able to read with sufficient ease to enjoy " Plutarch's Lives," a history of the siege of Jerusalem, which—as he himself relates—he read over sixty times, and the memoirs of poets, painters and warriors, with the lives of saints and martyrs, over the description of whose torments he appears to have dwelt with that delight children always experience in tales of horror. The priest was in the habit of taking long walks, and was always accompanied by his pupil, and though often wearied mentally as well as bodily by these excursions, Giusti acquired a taste for distant rambles, which he retained throughout his life.   After an early dinner his tutor would take the usual siesta, or afternoon sleep, and the boy, shut up in darkness, though wide awake, indulged in castles in the air and idle thoughts, a bad habit, which once acquired, he found difficult to relinquish. In the evening his master frequently paid visits to other priests, with whom he would recite his breviary, whilst his pupil amused himself with his favourite books ; when he stayed at home, Giusti was compelled to go through the same exercise, which so disgusted him, that he afterwards declared he was only surprised it did not make him renounce the Roman Catholic faith. As his master was only acquainted with one system by which to instil knowledge, that of corporal punishment, his pupil made little progress during the five years in which he continued under his tuition.   In his twelfth year Giusti was removed to a school at Florence, where he arrived with little beyond the power of reading his native language, and a superficial knowledge of history, whilst entirely ignorant of Latin, and in a hopeless state of discouragement, the natural result of everything having been done to place before him the difficulties which beset the path of knowledge, and his own inability to conquer them.

Giusti was more fortunate in the instructors he met with at the school of Attilio Zuccagni of Florence. The assistant master, Andrea Francioni, inspired his pupils with the love of study and of virtue, and became, in after life, one of the poet's most attached friends. Francioni appears at once to have admitted him to terms of intimacy, if we may judge by a letter written to him by Giusti at thirteen years of age, in which he familiarly reproaches him with not having replied to another of his letters. A strong interest must have been awakened by their mutual love of poetry, as Francioni was an enthusiastic admirer of Virgil and of Petrarch, and many years later, Giusti thus speaks of his old master :

" To this man I owe all I am, the little I know, and all the pleasure I derived from study when a boy, which has accompanied me in riper years, and which will crown, with a happiness without satiety and without remorse, the age of wrinkles, white hair and paralysis.... Andrea Francioni is my first friend, my benefactor, the only one, among many, who has been to me both instructor and father. I have loved him heart and soul, I have studied, and ever study to do him honour, and to him I trace the source of all in which I have been most successful. I feel that were I to give him all I possess, I should only be paying a just debt. In his class-room, neither cries nor noise was to be heard; there was neither punishment nor favour, nor that perpetual and disgraceful conflict between the rage of the master, and the anger and humiliation of the scholar; but there was affectionate reproof, and emulation without caviling, whilst perfect harmony was stamped on the smooth, firm and calm brow of that excellent man; and ready and prompt attention was given on our side. Study had become a pleasure, including even Latin, with its bewildering terminations and difficulties. I was only ten months under him, but they were enough for a lifetime, as all depends on a good start."

Giusti had likewise the advantage of another valuable instructor in the Abate Lorenzo Tarli, an accomplished scholar, and a young man of high principles. In a correspondence carried on twenty years afterwards, the Poet writes to him : " I can never forget the time in which you were my guide and light, in the arduous path of life. Would that I had had no other guide in my first steps ! " With Tarli, Giusti visited the churches and galleries of Florence, where, without assuming the dictatorial manner of the schoolmaster, he drew the attention of his pupil to the wonderful and rich collections of works of art, only to be found in that most beautiful of cities.

Before Giusti had completed his thirteenth year, the

school of Attilio Zuccagni was unfortunately broken up, and he was sent to a Lyceum at Pistoia, and from thence was shortly afterwards removed to a college at Lucca. When at this college, one of his schoolfellows, who subsequently became his biographer, Giovanni Frassi, bears ample testimony to his precocious judgment on works of literature; whilst another schoolfellow, Giacomo Baratta, was the first to encourage his poetical muse. To him Giusti writes in 1844: "I have always remembered how much advantage I derived from your affectionate advice when I was at the college in Lucca, and how I may almost be said to have walked by your side in the path of letters; I have still the verses corrected by you, and an ode which you wrote for me when I was returning home." Giusti's was a nature easily guided by his affections, which were as steady and constant through life, as they were warm in their first impulses. The aid and stimulus of such influences were much needed by one, whose lively character rather inclined him to idleness than to study, and whom the system of education prevailing at that time was not likely to attach to books. He chose as a subject for his first attempt at poetry, the Tower of Babel, followed by an ode to Italy, both of which have been lost or destroyed; between the ages of twelve and fifteen he was constantly scribbling rhymes, though in other respects, his education, (as far as mere learning may be understood by this often

abused word,) made little progress. So imperfect was
the teaching at the college, that though, when he left
it, he carried off the prize for Italian Translations from
the Latin, and attained honours for his proficiency in
French; he was but superficially acquainted with either
language. After his return to the country residence of
his father, he gained some reputation among friends in
the neighbourhood, for verses written to given rhymes,
then a fashionable amusement. His education was
again confided to a priest, to prepare him for the Pisan
University, and, at the request of this tutor, he wrote a
poem in Commemoration of the day of the Crucifixion,
which was published, with a series by other authors,
on the same subject; that of Giusti, however, was preferred, and was declared the gem of the collection.
These compositions do not appear to have obtained
much favour in his own eyes, or even at the time to
have been thought by himself indications of genius;
for that which renders Giusti even more remarkable
as a man than as a poet, was his singular truthfulness
of character, and the clear and unbiassed judgment
with which, thus early in life, he could examine and
appreciate the value of his own productions, united
with that moral courage, which enabled him to rise and
strive again, after self-condemnation. Undazzled by
the praises of admiring friends, with too little vanity to
suffer from the paralysing effect of mortification, whilst
conscious of his own short comings, he ever looked

steadily at one aim in life, and pursued it unflinchingly through good and evil days. That aim, it will be seen, was twofold; first, to render the weapon with which he proposed to fight the battles of his country as perfect as in him lay; and secondly, to apply every effort of his genius to use it for her moral and political regeneration. As a youth he was more occupied with the first than the last, with the means rather than with the end in view; and it was only after he had completed his career as a student at the University, that we may date the earnest thought which decided the life-long direction of his labours. In 1826, after he had entered his eighteenth year, Giusti was sent to Pisa to study Jurisprudence. Easy, sociable, witty, and gay, he was little inclined to the drudgery of law, and he was more frequently to be seen at the Caffè del Ussero, among friends as idle as himself, than poring over law-books. His time was not, however, always spent frivolously, and the narrative of an evening of revels as it was remembered by Giovanni Frassi, then his fellow-collegian at the University, conveys some idea of what kind were the attractions which led Giusti away from his duties and graver studies. A friend, who was rather more of a scapegrace than himself, came to Pisa to pay him a visit. Late one evening of a day they had spent with Frassi, a proposal was made to adjourn to a tavern, to which the trio accordingly proceeded, singing and dancing through the streets. They had hardly been seated over their wine, when the conversation took a religious turn ; Giusti maintaining the necessity of a form of faith, and his friend disputing the point with him.   This subject led to another as serious, on the death of a young, beautiful, and virtuous girl, to whom Giusti had addressed a sonnet, in which he laments the low state of morals of the age.   After a time the wine began to take effect, and before they left the tavern none of the young men were perfectly sober. Frassi was living at his father's house in Pisa; but not choosing to return home in this condition, he accepted Giusti's invitation to pass the night at his lodging.   As the lodging consisted of one room, with one bed, capable at the utmost of holding two persons, Giusti, as the host, wrapped himself in his cloak, and sat down to write, whilst his friends slept.   When they rose in the morning, they found he had spent his time in the study of French authors, and in translating verses by Dumoustier.

It was at this period of his life that his satirical vein first displayed itself in a sonnet he wrote to a priest who had offended him by strictures on Ariosto, and whom he advises to confine himself to his Breviary. After three years, in which time he had made little or no progress in his legal studies, his father recalled him to his home.   He accordingly joined his family in Pescia, where he continued three more years, spending his life even more unprofitably than at the University, gambling and accumulating debts. The Cavaliere Domenico Giusti accordingly resolved to make another attempt to induce his son to study law, and to lead a more steady life : in November, 1832, he paid his debts, after obtaining from him a promise to refrain from incurring more, and to be more diligent in study ; and sent him again to the University. The promise was easier than the performance, especially when Giusti found himself exposed to all the temptations and associations of his former life ; he, however, contrived to pass an examination in Jurisprudence, in June, 1834 ; but he owed his success rather to the incompetency of his examiners and to his own ready wit, than to proficiency in study. It was shortly after this second return to Pisa that he wrote the first poem we find in his published works, entitled *La Guigliottina a vapore*, the Steam Guillotine. This poem is a satire on the prodigality with which patents were granted for the numberless inventions of the day ; and whilst supposing a machine to have been invented by a headsman of the Chinese Empire, by which a hundred thousand heads could be taken off in three hours, he proceeds to inform the reader, that the priests have seen in it a presage of the gradual civilization of China ; and he concludes by a verse in which Francis IV. the reigning duke of Modena,[1] is thus alluded to under

[1] Francis IV. Duke of Modena, son of the Archduke Ferdinand of Austria and of Beatrice d'Este.

the name of Tiberius, supposed to be addressing the
infamous Prince of Canosa : [1]

> Grida un frate ; O bella cosa !
> Gli va dato anco il battesimo.
> Ah ! perchè, dice al Canosa
> Un Tiberio in diciottesimo,
> Questo genio non m' è nato.
> NEL DUCATO !

[1] The *Prince of Canosa*, the instrument of many of the acts of
cruelty and tyranny under Ferdinand I. of Naples and Sicily, and who
when banished, was received at the court of the Duke of Modena.

CHAPTER II.

ITALY IN THE BEGINNING OF THE NINETEENTH CENTURY.

BEFORE time, age, and necessity had weakened hope, crushed aspirations, or corrupted purity of intention, young and ardent spirits like those of Giusti and his companions, with their patriotism nourished by the perusal of their best native authors, naturally turned to politics. The struggle appeared ripening between justice and injustice, freedom and oppression; between tradition, history, and lawful right on one side, and invasion and lawless usurpation on the other. Repeated, though vain, attempts to shake off the yoke had been the only signs of life given by the nation from the time when an iniquitous fiat of a congress of kings, or their representatives, at Vienna, had betrayed the hopes held out of a united Italy, and passed a sentence of condemnation on the liberties of every people in Continental Europe : but in order to understand the excited state of political feeling in Italy at the time when Giusti began his career in life, it is necessary to review the condition of the several States into which the Peninsula was, at this period, divided.

Among all the princes of Italy, none had exceeded, or perhaps equalled, the exactions and cruelty of Francis the Fourth, duke of Modena; but that which called down upon him peculiarly the execration of young and old, was, that a recent immature attempt at revolution, and its unhappy results, were attributed to his perfidy and double dealing. Before 1830 he had been engaged in a conspiracy with Louis Philippe, then Duke of Orleans; and under the pretence of sympathy with the cause of liberty, but really for the furtherance of their ambitious designs, they had encouraged and fostered the hopes of Italian patriots. No sooner, however, had unforeseen events placed Louis Philippe on a throne, than, desirous to secure the friendship and countenance of the other sovereigns of Europe, he renounced his share in the plots, which could no longer be of service to himself and would have imperilled his good fortune. Francis of Modena, abandoned to his fate, returned to seek the protection of Austria, with whose reigning family he was connected by blood.

The last Italian Duke of Modena had been Hercules D'Este, celebrated for his opposition to feudal and ecclesiastical tyranny, but likewise notorious for an excessive care and economy, which enabled him to amass an amount of treasure, eventually destined only to tempt French rapacity. He died in 1803, at the age of eighty-nine, leaving an only daughter, Beatrice, married to the Austrian Archduke Ferdinand. She survived her father three years; and her son, Francis, more Austrian than Italian, succeeded, in 1815, to the Duchy, with an accession of territory assigned to him by the Treaty of Vienna. He entered upon his government in the double character of heir to the throne and of conqueror. After the attempt at a revolution in Piedmont, in 1820, which had likewise infected the Italians of other States, no Italian sovereign was more severe than Francis in the persecution of the Liberals. The Modenese dungeons were filled with suspected persons, belonging to the Carbonari or other secret societies; and the Governor of Modena, though himself a member of these societies, drew up the prosecutions against the prisoners, and, under the cloak of compassion and kindness, extracted revelations which brought mourning and desolation into many families. Nothing, perhaps, is a stronger proof of the miserable state to which the Italian people were reduced than the eagerness with which they welcomed the faintest ray of hope, and trusted in the promises of a man so notorious for unscrupulous cruelty as Francis of Modena: not that they believed in his love of liberty, but they confided in their own means of tempting his ambition, and thought to secure his aid by his interest. Ciro Menotti, one of the purest and best of patriots, was among those who were misled by this idea, the suggestion of despair; he sought an interview with the Duke of Modena, and offered him the crown of the Italian kingdom, if he

would consent to put himself at the head of the projected movement. The Duke appeared to yield, and
Menotti communicated his success to the Liberals in
other parts of Italy, endeavouring to induce the leaders
in Romagna and in Tuscany to join in the scheme.
Many felt too invincible a repugnance to Francis of
Modena to concur in any enterprise in which he was
engaged ; but Menotti tried to overcome these scruples,
and reminded them that the Duke's wealth was required
to make their success secure. Francis still further contrived to deceive Menotti by lavishing favours and confidence on him : he frequently received him in a private
room of the Palace for secret conferences, when he exhorted him to continue the good work he had begun ;
and, on one occasion, he assured him that, whatever
might be the result of their plot, not only should his
life be safe, but the Duke pledged himself to obtain for
him immunity from even a sentence of condemnation.
Though public sympathy with the Italian cause had
been expressed in the French Chambers, the open de-
fection of Louis Philippe from the cause of the Italian
Liberals convinced the Duke of Modena that he, too,
must seek his safety in abandoning the project. Ciro
Menotti had foreseen this possiblity, and, in the hope
of preventing total failure, resolved to anticipate the
hour for the explosion of the conspiracy.

On the 3rd February, 1831, Ciro had collected in his
house several young men, to whom he was giving

directions for the work of the following day, when the Duke in person, with soldiers and artillery, presented himself before the door, and declared his intention of blowing up the house, if all within did not at once surrender. Ciro and his comrades, after a desperate conflict, yielded themselves prisoners, on condition of their lives being spared. Two days afterwards, news arrived of an insurrection in Bologna, when Francis fled from his own Duchy to seek the protection of Austria, carrying along with him in his flight, Ciro and his fellow-prisoners. The revolution then broke out all through Modena, and was only suppressed by Austrian arms, which restored the Duke on the 9th of March. Francis brought back with him the unhappy Menotti, who had meantime been confined in the prisons of Mantua, and the first act of the restored sovereign was to name the tribunal by which that man was to be tried and condemned, to whom he had promised that he should not be amenable to any sentence of condemnation. Ciro Menotti was condemned to die on the 21st, and was executed on the 26th of May.[1] The Prince of Canosa, of Neapolitan notoriety, was among the advisers of the Duke on this occasion, when many other victims were offered up to his vengeance. But tyrants seem to forget that if the life of an individual on this earth be mortal, nations are immortal, and that neither executions, nor exile, nor martial law, nor even the subtle poison of an

[1] I Martiri d'Italia da Atto Vannucci.

C

hierarchical Government can enable a single generation of despots to destroy the life of a people : the Society of Young Italy came into existence the year Menotti died, and its author, Giuseppe Mazzini, though opposed in many of his views by a large number of the liberal party in Italy, was at least one with them in his principal aim, that of liberating the nation from Austrian satellites.　The death of Francis of Modena opened the way for fresh hopes and expectations in his successor ; but doomed, as usual, to disappointment.

Modena was, however, not the only State groaning under that native tyranny and misrule which was supported directly or indirectly by Austria.　Piedmont had never been subjected to a more severe treatment than in the years intervening between 1820 and 1830, under Carlo Felice ; the Jesuits had become so powerful that they controlled the king himself, and upon the accession of Carlo Alberto, the liberals, who in spite of a Government of repression had increased in numbers, looked in vain for an amelioration of their condition.　The new king laboured under the imputation of having been a party in the Revolution of 1820, and he had not the courage, if he had the desire, to institute reforms which would have given an appearance of truth to this accusation, and roused a hornet's nest around him in his nobles, courtiers, army and clergy.　In the summer of 1833, active prosecutions were instituted against the Society of Young Italy, and incarcerations, and even executions followed. The irritation caused by these harsh measures, produced an attempt at another revolution: an expedition from Savoy, composed of Polish, German, and Italian exiles, and provided with arms, procured in Geneva and the Pays de Vaud, heralded their descent from the Alps by republican proclamations; but, ill organized, ill led and ill imagined, the end was utter failure, with the loss of more lives.

Attempts at revolution were likewise made in the Roman States, but here, as in Naples, the supremacy of the rulers over law as well as over their subjects, continued as before.

Tuscany had enjoyed a mild and comparatively good government ever since the days of the Grand Duke Leopold I. 1766–1790, whose code was cited as a model of wisdom and of justice. His son, the Grand Duke Ferdinand III. had the advantage of possessing a minister who was remarkable both as a statesman and patriot: Vittorio Fossombroni followed his sovereign into exile during the period of the French occupation of Italy, and returned with him when his dominions were restored in 1815. At the Congress of Vienna, Ferdinand, with the other princes of Italy, agreed to act, in all matters appertaining to war and peace, as subordinate to Austria, and received in return her guarantee for the possession of their thrones; he thus placed Tuscany in the condition of a fief of the Austrian Empire. It can hardly be supposed that Fossombroni

was cognizant of this act, or at any rate that he could
have approved of it, as we find all his efforts directed
to shake off the incubus of Austrian usurpations.
Foreign interference penetrated into every branch of
the administration, and, in spite of the mild nature of
the Tuscan Government, and of the people, who, in
1820, when all the rest of the Peninsula was disturbed,
remained comparatively tranquil, the dictation from
Austria was felt and resented. Fossombroni on that
occasion wrote to Vienna : " We wish to be masters in
our own homes ; we do not therefore want Austrian
soldiers to play the masters." But, in spite of this
remonstrance, Austrian troops were sent to occupy
Tuscany.

Leopold II. succeeded his father in 1824, when such
was the subservience to Austria, that it was considered
a bold and patriotic act on the part of Fossombroni,
when he refused to comply with the demand of the
Austrian Minister at the Tuscan Court, to wait for
orders from Vienna before proclaiming the new sovereign. Unfortunately for Tuscany, Fossombroni loved
power too much to allow of any internal reform which
might limit that which he enjoyed ; and he relied on
his own conciliatory manners and ingenuity to avoid
the evils resulting from the neglect and relaxation of
duty in the public officers. The Tuscan people, too
long accustomed to a paternal Government, could not
anticipate what might arise when the individual was

removed on whom they depended for a just administration of the laws. The laws themselves did not undergo the reforms they needed, and if bad, only remained in abeyance as long as Fossombroni maintained his power; when old age and infirmity forced him to resign, he was succeeded by Don Neri Corsini, who had the merit of showing respect to the retired minister, and turning to him for advice as long as he lived. He was a man of upright character, and guided by the same principles as his predecessor; and he continued, like Fossombroni, to resist papal encroachments, and to maintain toleration for political opinions. But whilst a censorship was continued in the press, and Tuscany was unable to carry reform into her internal administration, the admission of refugees from all parts of Italy, among whom were men of the highest virtue and ability, holding liberal opinions, was only to introduce the contagion her rulers wished most to avoid. New ideas of what Tuscany might become under a wiser government, and when delivered from a foreign dictation, ideas of growth and progress, were imported by patriots, who, besides being themselves Italian, had all the prestige of martyrdom to recommend their views. Such ideas found a congenial soil in the intelligent Tuscan mind, since the recollections of the history of their republican government could neither be obliterated by the vicious and effete rule of their Merchant Princes, nor of the Princes their successors, foreign in character as in race. As the people began to show signs of re-awakening life, and of becoming restive under their yoke, their rulers almost involuntarily increased their burdens, and the police became more vexatious and troublesome than ever; a fact readily explained by a despatch from the Aulic Councillor Mentz to Prince Metternich, written in 1836, which runs as follows :—" The Tuscan Government, led to reflect on the dangers which it has encountered from its former mode of conducting affairs, has assumed a firmer attitude, and its police is better constituted, and has become more vigilant and active. At all events, the respect for Austrian bayonets posted at the gates of Tuscany, will be sufficient to put a stop to illusions and revolutionary projects, and to prevent their realization or success."[1] The conduct of the police in interfering in trivial matters was so petty and vexatious as to expose them to ridicule and resentment, especially by the young men at the Universities. In an incident which occurred at Pisa, in 1833, Giusti was called to account, and took his revenge in his own way, as he relates himself in a subsequent letter to a friend.

"The summons of the police alludes to a fact which happened in 1833, when I was a student at Pisa, and when their excellencies smelt out something revolu-

---

[1] Toscana e Austria Cenni Storico-politici, published in Florence in 1859, and signed by Cosimo Ridolfi, Bettino Ricasoli, Ubaldino Peruzzi, Tommaso Corsi, Leopoldo Cempini, Celestino Bianchi.

tionary even in the applause at a theatre.   I was called up with a hundred others, as disturbers of the public peace, and after having been threatened with arrest, and with being expelled, if I did not regulate my taste for music by that of a Commissary of Police, they asked me if I had nothing to say.   'Nothing,' I replied, ' except that I was not in the theatre.'   ' How could you not be in the theatre, if I find your name on the list of accused?'   ' That may be,' I replied, ' police-agents and spies may have me so much in their heads as to see me where I happen not to be.'   At this the Commissary flew into a violent passion, but I remained cool, and cited as a witness Count Mastai, with whom the man was often in the habit of dining.   At this name the recollection of boiled and roast, eaten and to eat, rose up before him, and suddenly changing his tone, he said, 'Go ; but at all events take this summons as a paternal admonition.'"

Giusti immediately afterwards produced his poem of *La Rassegnazione* (Resignation), or a feigned repentance, and resolution to change his course of life, with a list of the advantages to be derived from playing the hypocrite, and bowing before those in authority.

The unsuccessful attempts at revolution in Modena in 1831, the treachery of the Duke, and the executions of Ciro Menotti, and of others who bore honoured and respected names, converted contempt and ridicule into intense hatred and indignation, and changed the thoughtless students of the University into grave and earnest-minded men. In place of romance and light literature, their favourite reading became the history of their country, and the patriotic verses of Berchet was the poetry most generally repeated. Frassi records how one evening, when Giusti was reading aloud to some of his companions, a part of Botta's History of Italy, relating to the years intervening between 1789 and 1814, one of his auditors was so much excited at the description of the defence made by the Calabrese against the French, that, in the vehemence of his feelings, he crushed to atoms the *scaldino,* or jar of hot ashes he was holding between his knees. Every emigrant who passed through Pisa was sure to meet with assistance from the students of the University, who each and all strained their slender means to the utmost, to contribute to the relief of those whom they regarded as martyrs to liberty and to their country. Though now and then deceived by an impostor, nothing could check the ardour of their generous spirits, and Giusti was justly proud of friends, who if not among the most diligent of students, were then, as in after life, true to the instincts of their hearts, and warm lovers of their country. When frequently regretting the misspent hours and idleness of his University life, the poet would console himself with the reflection, that in the choice of his companions he had always avoided what he called the germs of government officials and the worshippers of

those in authority, whilst selecting for his friends, men
who to the end of their lives proved themselves worthy
of the affection and admiration they then inspired.
With a heart glowing with love for his country, and
indignation at her wrongs, the Pisan student wrote the
following patriotic song:

> " Fratelli sorgete
> La patria vi chiama
> Snudate la lama
> Del libero acciar;
> Sussurran vendette
> Menotti e Borelli;
> Sorgete, fratelli,
> La patria a salvar.
> Dell' Itala tromba
> Rintroni lo squillo
> S' inalzi un vessillo
> Si tocchi l' altar;
> Ai forti l' alloro
> Infamia agl' imbelli
> Sorgete fratelli
> La patria a salvar."

CHAPTER III.

IN 1834, Giusti, at twenty-five years of age, came to Florence, to commence his professional career, under the Advocate Capoquadri ; but here, as at the University, his law studies were laid aside for his favourite Dante in the mornings, and for amusements in the evenings.

A society of literary men, admitting all shades of opinion, but chiefly consisting of liberals, was at this time in the habit of meeting at the house of M. Vieusseux, a Swiss by birth, but long an inhabitant of Florence, who himself presided at these meetings, to which distinguished foreigners, as well as Italians from all parts of Italy, were admitted. Vieusseux had travelled much in his youth, but in 1820 settled finally in the Tuscan capital, where he hired the old Palazzo Buondelmonti, and established a bookshop and lending library, or literary institute. He next started a periodical, which he called *L'Antologia*, and for which he collected articles from the pens of the most celebrated Italian writers. In 1833, the Grand Duke ordered its suppression, at the instance of the Czar Nicholas, who had been attacked in some of its pages.[1]   M. Vieusseux had besides edited a Journal on Agriculture since 1827, and he joined the Abate Lambruschini, one of the most eminent of Florentine philanthropists, in a work entitled *La Guida dell' Educatore.*   Among the remarkable men who assisted the *Antologia* by their writings, or met in the apartments of M. Vieusseux, were Professor Rosini of Pisa, the editor of the History of Guicciardini, and of the Apologia di Lorenzino dei Medici ; the mathematician Frullano ; the artists Bartolini, Dupré and Fantachiotti, the last two of whom are still living ; the Marchese Ridolfi, at that time tutor to the sons of the Grand Duke, and likewise eminent as an agriculturist and founder of model farms in Italy ; Mancini, the translator of Homer ; the Marchese Gino Capponi, who unites to high literary attainments, virtues which render him the worthy descendant of a long race of patriots ; Terenzo Mammiani, afterwards minister to Pius the Ninth ; the Livornese Guérazzi, celebrated first as a writer of romance, and afterwards as the leader of the Democratic party ; Montanelli, of Pisa, a musician, poet, and doctor of laws, and a Professor at the early age of nineteen ; Niccolo Tommaseo, of Venice, a Dalmatian poet and dis-

[1] The *Antologia* was succeeded by another periodical edited by M. Vieusseux, the *Archivio Storico,* an important work for the historian.   M. Vieusseux died at an advanced age in the summer of this year, 1863, lamented, as he was esteemed, in Florence.

tinguished patriot ; and Giuseppe Mazzini.   All these
had been, or were shortly afterwards, associated in
the same literary undertaking, when Giusti arrived in
Florence.[1]

The modern literature of Italy may be divided into
two distinct schools ; that over which Manzoni presides,
or the romantic school, whose doctrines encourage the
idea of temporal power united with the Papal supremacy ;
an idea so transcendental as almost to seem in anti-
thesis with the history of more than ten centuries of
ecclesiastical misrule and crime ; and the school of
Niccolini, the poet, who is best known as the author of
Arnaldo da Brescia, a historical drama, intended to set
forth his antagonism to the union of the authority of
this world with the authority of the next.   Manzoni, the
grandson of the Marchese Beccaria, born in Lombardy
in 1784, was the pupil of Monti ; Giovan Battista
Niccolini, a Tuscan, born a year later of poor but
respectable parents, was first patronised by Elisa Buonaparte, Queen of Etruria, who obtained for him the place
of Secretary of the Academy of the Fine Arts in
Florence.   In 1815, the restored Grand Duke Ferdinand
conferred on him the office of Librarian in the Palazzo
Pitti, but he soon afterwards gave in his resignation,
preferring a life of comparative poverty, to official de-
pendence.   Besides his plays and poems, on which his

---

[1] This chapter is chiefly taken from a little volume entitled, "L'Italie
est elle la terre des morts ?" by Marc Monnier, of Naples.

fame rests, he contributed several articles to the *Anto-logia* of Vieusseux. An anecdote illustrative of Nic-colini's character, is given in the introduction to Ugo Foscolo's *Lettera Apologetica*, lately published by Le Monnier, of Florence. Before reading this letter, Niccolini had doubted the strength of Foscolo's prin-ciples ; but when his doubts were removed, he exclaimed with delight : " Foscolo has here revealed himself, and whoever does not imitate him, and is not ready to die on a bed of straw rather than deny his principles, will not live to be blessed in the memory of mankind."

In the cultivated and refined society of men such as Florence then presented, a mind like Giusti's found itself in its true element. Italy needed all the moral influence of her sons to whom nature had been most prodigal in her gifts, to counterbalance, or remove the weight of ignorance and vice into which she had fallen, under centuries of despotism, and under the corruption caused by foreign importations in morals and manners. It was necessary that men of virtue, as well as of literary eminence, should, by their example and teaching, lead the way to political independence, and wipe out the stain left by others, like Monti, who had stooped to flatter the tyrant of the day. It was therefore to the literary men of Italy that Ugo Foscolo appealed when he lectured in the University of Pavia ; and he again appealed to them in the letter which so much delighted Niccolini, and in which he considers it their duty to instil the national literature : " opposed to foreign laws, language, and usages ;" whilst adding that, " the most indissoluble fetters have always been foreign fetters ; and you men of learning have, more than any, conspired to establish the universal servitude." Similar sentiments breathe through every line of Giusti's early compositions ; sentiments he imbibed at the very time when Tuscany was governed by a sovereign who lent himself to be the submissive tool of an Austrian Emperor.

Whilst Manzoni, Niccolini, and others produced works of a grave or romantic nature, Giusti's writings more peculiarly represented a type of the Tuscan mind. Tuscany had always been celebrated for satirical writers from the days of Horace, of Dante, and Macchiavelli, and young Giusti had been early encouraged in satire by a favourite uncle, himself noted for his wit, and beloved by his nephew as a second father. His first attempts at poetry intended to meet the public eye, cost him no small labour, and were discouraged even by his own father. But, in spite of acknowledged failure, he felt an inward conviction of his own powers, which stimulated him to persevere, and the result was a series of minor poems, which, though laid aside by himself, were published after his death, among his youthful productions.

It was about this time that he met with his first bitter sorrow in a severe disappointment in love, and he was only gradually able to resume his favourite studies. It was to the lady who subsequently forsook him, that he addressed the charming little poem, entitled *All'amica lontana,* to a distant friend; and when the sight of a statue by the Florentine sculptor Bartolini roused him from his state of depression caused by her inconstancy, he composed the still more beautiful verses *Fiducia in Dio,* "Trust in God."

The death of the Emperor Francis of Austria, in 1835, called forth the first satire by Giusti which attracted public notice. The *Dies Iræ* as he named it, celebrated this event as full of hope for the people, as of danger for the princes of Europe. He begins his poem by denouncing as a rebel the illness which laid Francis in his coffin, and adds his thanks to the physician who had not preserved the Emperor from this attack; the rebel disease had only followed the fashion of the day whilst acting the part of a liberal, or foe to tyranny, but liberty itself is yet distant and ideal, and therefore is called *Vanità del Secolo.* The poet proceeds to name all the great powers of this earth who had put on mourning for the occasion, and amongst them he places a Pisan of the name of Samminiatelli, well known as a tool of the Duke of Modena's, and alike hated and despised; this man is represented bleating forth the praises of the deceased. The liberals, who rejoice at the death of the Emperor Francis, are not confined to the Italian side of the Alps; even the tears of Poland are repaid by the end of her tyrant's friend;

the Czar, meantime, is looking with greedy eyes at the obsequies of his brother, hoping, like a hyæna smelling out a carcase, to derive some advantage from his death : Prussia plays the spy, and bides her time, in the expectation of attaining the boundaries she covets : in Spain, the people imagine they may now burst their ecclesiastical fetters, and already begin in thought to burn their friars, and rejoice in liberty : England, whose steam engines and mechanical inventions are to be found all over Europe, sends the Tories, the friends of tyrants, to the right about. In France, Louis Philippe, with his face like a pear (an allusion partly to its form, but also to a Tuscan term expressive of dulness), scratches his head in doubt how to act, but, with a failing heart, remembers the king he had so lately unseated. Italy laughs for joy that the despot is dead, and that she is relieved from his presence : but the poet bids her tyrants be of good courage ; the nation (here described as the maker of the boot) is asleep. But hush ! he hears the cannon—it is nothing new— only another master, who is proclaimed in the words customary at the election of a pope :—

> " Ma silenzio ! odo il cannone :
> Non è nulla : altro padrone
>   Habemus Pontificem."

This sketch of the state of public feeling in Europe was perhaps hardly exaggerated ; a strange fact in the constitution of human affairs, when the death of a single individual, of a man without genius or talents to raise him above the level of his fellow men, ignorant, despising knowledge in others, cold, cruel, and selfish, can excite the hopes and fears of millions, and that their lives, property, and social happiness, with that of generations yet unborn, should have depended upon his will! The *Dies Iræ* owes its attraction to its point, conciseness, and satire, to the bold enunciation of truths men had hardly ventured to speak aloud, and to the wit without venom with which the poet stings the enemies of his country, whilst not even sparing the foibles of Italy.

Giusti's poetry, as has been already said, is peculiarly Tuscan, both in its allusions, its humour, and language, and therefore extremely difficult for a foreigner, and even for an Italian, not a Tuscan, fully to comprehend and appreciate. The author of this biography, therefore, could hardly have ventured on an examination or analysis of his writings, without the assistance and sanction of a native Italian, educated in Tuscany, and the early friend of the poet. The charm of his compositions consists, partly in their musical metre, and the selection of words which, in elegant yet racy language, convey the meaning of the poet; they are indeed sometimes obsolete, or only employed by the peasantry, yet so forcible that no other could have as well expressed the intention of the author; grace of thought and expression, united with redundancy of wit and

playful humour, sparkling condensed in every line,
seem to soften the asperity of his denunciations against
political and ecclesiastical tyranny, against the cor-
ruptions of the age, and against those native Italians
who cringed before men in power ; and this was boldly
spoken, at a time when the agents of the government
were ready to seize on all such expressions as a ground
for persecution. His verses roused the most lethargic
to see the necessity of clearing away so great an accumulation of evil, and he delighted the ears of the wit-
loving Florentines, whilst avoiding everything which
could offend individuals, or degenerate into petty
scandal : they present a rare combination of the highest
moral tone and common sense, united with a lively
fancy and poetic flights ; the author never conde-
scending to puerile or insipid truisms, nor conceits, nor
carrying himself and his reader into a region of wild
and extravagant dreams.

His works were yet unpublished, because obnoxious
to the government, but they were nevertheless everywhere known and recited, even among the peasantry.
One of his biographers, Carducci, thus describes the
excitement they occasioned throughout the country :
" These verses met the comprehension, and were sought
after by the common people, and although still in
manuscript, were read along the smiling valley of the
Arno, amidst the forests of the mountains of Pistoia,
and on the plains of the Pisan coast. Friends passed

them jealously from one to another ; fathers pretended not to see them in the hands of their sons ; they were read in the watches of the winter evenings, and under the shade of the chestnut-trees in the lovely days of spring. The author of these pages can remember, when little more than a boy, being dragged into tailors' and carpenters' workshops in a remote village, to write down and comment on Giusti's poetry."

It was about this time that Giusti had his first interview with the historian Sismondi, the old friend of his grandfather Chiti, and for whom he appears to have early imbibed the greatest veneration. He thus describes the meeting in a letter to a friend :—

To Professor . . . .

"DEAR PROFESSOR,

"I have at last spoken with Sismondi, and have twice held long conversations with him. I am not by nature easily impressed with wonder at anything ; but whenever I do see or hear something extraordinary, I feel an inward agitation, which excites me to such a degree that for the instant I feel transported beyond my natural self. After a time my ideas flow more distinctly, and at such moments everything I have ever read or thought returns to my mind with greater distinctness. I experienced this sensation whilst conversing with this great man. I do not know that I ever felt more trepidation and nervous hesitation than

that day, on the road between my house and his
little villa, a few steps outside of Pescia. On my
arrival, I found two ladies before the house, one of
whom was the sister-in-law, the other the wife, of
Sismondi.[1] The latter gave me as courteous a reception
as ever, and introduced me to her husband. You must
know that he was the intimate friend of my mother's
father, and that in 1799 (as I gather from one of his
letters written to my grandfather as far back as 1802),
they were prisoners together here in Pescia, in the
monastery of San Giuseppe. You will not, therefore,
be surprised to hear that he received me with every
possible kindness. The conversation travelled over
various topics, chiefly history. Unfortunately, another
person was present who did not understand French,
and Sismondi, who is all politeness, always spoke
in Italian, but which language, from his long absence,
and the constant habit of speaking French, is not
so familiar to him, so that his words were occasionally a hindrance to his ideas. He told me that he
found Italy much improved from the time he left it ;
that, having had an opportunity of conversing with
persons attached to the Courts, he had perceived the
influence of the age even in them ; that, above all,
it appeared to him that a taste for the study of history
has been much diffused, and that he rejoiced in finding

[1] An English lady, Miss Jessie Allen, daughter of John Allen, Esq.
of Treselly, in Pembrokeshire.

Italians aware that the epoch of their glory lay in the Middle Ages.

"We spoke of Manzoni, and here the greatness of the man was peculiarly displayed. I introduced the subject with the utmost delicacy, but caught at the first opportunity which presented itself, as I wished to clear up a doubt which had arisen in my own mind, on reading that work of Manzoni, where he refutes the two first chapters of the "History of the Republics."[1] Sismondi spoke of the book in terms of admiration for the courteous manner in which it was worded; he praised the sincerity of the author, and lamented his late misfortunes, which, in his opinion, had had no small

---

[1] "Della morale Cattolica"—pub. Rome, 1826—translated and published in Paris 1834, under the title "Vindication of Catholic Morality, or a Refutation of the Charges brought against it by Sismondi."

In the 127th Chapter of the "Republiques Italiennes," Sismondi maintains that the corrupt state of Italy was partly to be attributed to the immoral system of the Roman Catholic Church. Manzoni, taking sentence by sentence as a text for refutation, examines into the truth of this assertion, and defending its rules and discipline, endeavours to prove that the evils complained of are abuses incident to everything human, and that the established laws of Catholicism are borne out by Scripture, and intended for the promotion of brotherly love and charity. Though the work must necessarily be open to objection by us, and be considered full of errors, no Protestant can read it without admiring the Christian spirit breathing throughout its pages, and feeling that he may meet the author on the common ground of religious sympathy, apart from disputed questions of theology and Church discipline. The work is more esteemed in Italy than Giusti believed when he wrote this letter, and Sismondi himself found reason later in life to modify his views. "Della morale Cattolica" may be considered the moral signification of the "Promessi Sposi."

influence in confirming him in his views; he then added (but always in a spirit of moderation) that he appeared to him to have started from an opposite point from himself, as *he* considered things as they are, Manzoni, as they should be. I cannot tell you how gratified I felt that I had not been deceived in my opinion of Sismondi. I thought it fair to acquaint him that the book had not been much praised by Italians, and, that, without at all diminishing the reverence due to Manzoni, it was considered a mistake, or, at least, as a work suggested by some one who had got round him for other ends, unsuspected by the upright, noble-minded author.

"French literature came on the *tapis*, and here he likewise displayed great moderation in his opinions, whilst asserting that which has been said by many, that the present style of writing cannot last. He warned me against trusting too much to newspapers, which only give exaggerated views of all parties, because, for the most part, written by young men, who do not look below the shallow wisdom of the day : most of the material which adds to the profits of the journalist being provided by ready writers, who engage in this branch of commerce, and only aim at satisfying the public with an appearance of truth, and obtaining an ephemeral reputation whilst flattering the passions of the day.

"I asked him if he were acquainted with Mazzini and

he told me he had been introduced to him some years ago, when he first left Genoa, and that he had perceived him to be a man of great ability. He had invited him to dinner, and had kept up a correspondence with him, until the time when the three hundred refugees attempted a revolution from Switzerland under his guidance. Mazzini's aim then appeared to him a dream, and the means by which he proposed to attain it by no means justifiable, as he intended to have seized the arsenal of Geneva, and to have made use of it in order to occupy Savoy; Sismondi, accordingly, broke off all relations with him, and has never since had anything to do with him. It was at that time he wrote the pamphlet, *Consigli d'un Amico ai refugiati politici* (Advice of a Friend to Political Refugees) which he has given me to read. On this subject also, however, this excellent Swiss never departed from candour and charity.

"He said much more, which my memory does not at this moment recall ; but all full of wisdom, and worthy of that mind which, under the external appearance of old age, preserves the fire of better years.

"He has brought down his work on the Annals of France to the Edict of Nantes inclusive, but, he says, he is tired of it, and needs repose. He is now writing on political economy, and he has a book in the press, on Free Constitutions, which he first thought of forty years ago.

"My veneration for great men increases, when I compare their modesty, integrity of purpose, and simplicity, with the vainglory, bad faith, and noisy loquacity of our rising hopefuls."

Giusti, without attaching himself to any political party, was a republican by conviction and sentiment, but he was averse to all underhand proceedings, and whilst in his writings he openly attacked rulers and systems of government, as well as the want of energy and the faults of the age he joined those who endeavoured to train the people by improving the systems of education and by establishing mutual aid societies, savings-banks, &c. He even considered conspiracy unjustifiable on the score of utility, because, quoting a saying of Macchiavelli : "i troppi le guastano, e i pochi non bastano" (Many mar the plot, and few do not suffice).

CHAPTER IV.

In the autumn of 1836 a violent flood caused considerable damage in the country. Giusti was then residing in Pescia, and he made an expedition into the mountains to visit the scene of the disaster, which he describes in a letter to his old friend and former schoolmaster, Andrea Francioni.

"DEAR FRANCIONI,   Pescia, 20th October, 1836.

"This *semi-serious* month is made for me, who am by nature half melancholy, half comic ; it drives me from my books, and gives me a rage for walking. I have rambled over all the neighbouring heights, I have again been through all the bye-paths across the fields, and in the woods of the country round, and I have spent long half-hours gazing at the fine points of view which present themselves at every turn, on the summits of these hills, covered with olives and chesnuts.

"So heavy a rain fell in the night of the first Sunday of October, that the shallowest brooks were converted into torrents, and there was such a storm of thunder and lightning, that it seemed as if the end of the world were near at hand. There was little or no injury done here, and we escaped, thank God, with no further damage than could be set to rights by some few repairs in the walls or in the sides of the ditches. Those who had to undergo the greatest damage and misfortunes were the poor Lucchese, for whose destruction the Lima and other torrents conspired, after the manner of the Holy Alliance.[1] The report of the terrible havoc caused by these rivers soon spread, and inspired many with a desire to go and see. There are some who blame this rage for sight-seeing which sent us to the scene of the calamity, as a savage and stupid curiosity; I think philanthropists ought not to shun the sight of pain, nor occasions which excite their feelings of pity. The solitary being who considers himself a centre and a pattern for the universe may refuse to know anything of ills which do not immediately concern himself; but the man who lives in the midst of his kind, and loves them, does not fly from the sight of public calamities, but rather, I should say, is ever on the spot where there is human suffering; and I am among those prepared to give their sympathy for a common misfortune.

[1] Giusti here alludes to Lucca having been assigned temporarily, by the treaty of Vienna, to the Spanish Bourbons of Parma, to enable Maria Louisa, the widow of Napoleon, to enjoy the sovereignty of Parma. The Constitution of Lucca, granted by Napoleon, was guaranteed; but, as might have been expected, had become a dead letter in the hands of the Duke of Lucca.

"With these and other reflections, I started a fortnight after the floods, in company with a dear friend, in the direction of the Baths of Lucca. For five hours we proceeded through forest and over a mountain road, till, by continual ascents, we reached the district we were in search of. Everywhere we saw signs of the storm, and everywhere heard a more or less tragical account of that night, according as the narrator had been himself more or less a sufferer. At the Baths, we found the fields devastated by the Lima ; houses, buildings of all kinds, walls and walks destroyed, and laid in ruins. Promenades, which a few days before had swarmed with the quintessence of the fashionable world, now choked up with sand, rubbish, and trunks of trees brought down by the torrent. A pedlar of the place acted as our guide ; and as he himself carried all his patrimony in his box, he looked on at this havoc with the most cool indifference. At Ponte a Serraglio, we were divided between admiration at the charms of the scenery, and horror at the devastation around us, when our worthy peripatetic guide, pointing out to us the house which used to serve for the meetings of the Literary Club, and calling our attention to the fact that the road there had been so injured by the deluge as to render all access impossible, said with a half sigh,

Ah ! that is indeed a remarkable fact, . . . in which one can see the hand of God Himself.' I was fool enough to interrupt him, and ask him what he meant, which was sufficiently plain, since he considered the ruin of that house to be a consequence of prohibited books having been read there. The bigoted Lucchese at once perceived the irony of my question, and like a true Jesuit, got off, with two or three of those interjections which are so expressive when spoken, and so meaningless when written. My companion, who understands architecture, mathematics, and I don't know what besides, explained to me the how and the why of these vacant spaces, ruins, and so forth, and looking complacently on the mounds of gravel, exclaimed, 'How beautiful! if I could only get a little of this in Florence!' Instead of looking at the gravel, I was admiring the pretty girls, who were passing, carrying wood, and made the same exclamation as my friend.

"After leaving the Baths, we took another direction, the high road from the Baths to the capital of the Empire of all the Lucchese. It is a most beautiful road, which, for a considerable distance, skirts the Lima, and upon which these waters lose their name in that of the larger river,[1] which united with them, accompanies the traveller through this part of the country. On the left bank of the stream bare rocks protrude, and the combination of light and of perspective is enough to enchant a painter, and all who are not painters, if they have eyes to see, and a soul to

[1] The Serchio.

feel with their eyes. That terrific night this beautiful road was covered, in its length and breadth, by great waves from the river, which had burst into the fields, carrying along with it beams, cottages, and the dead bodies of men and beasts, caught unawares by the fury of the waters. At Fornoli, a bridge was swept clean away; a few miles lower down, the road was broken up and engulphed by the stream for a quarter of a mile; everywhere high walls had been destroyed, and the parapets of bridges, with embankments, laid in ruins. The bridge of Decimo, which is new and very beautiful and elegant in structure, alone remains uninjured; that at Moriano was damaged, with the village of the same name, in which our guide pointed out to us where in one place lay the coping of the wall of a shop, in another the door of a house; here the fragment of a window, there a ground-floor under water, whilst all the household utensils had been washed away. The bridge of the Maddalena, celebrated for its antiquity, its singular construction, and for the legends attached to it, proved the fact that many centuries of existence cannot secure the poor work of mortal man from the insults of the storm.

"When my companion first caught sight of this bridge in the distance, he remarked, 'These low arches appear to have been added later; the last arch on the farther side is so much higher; perhaps that was the old bridge, and formed the principal curve for the whole.' He may perhaps have made other important observations, but my mind was engrossed by a comparison that suggested itself between the bridge and a giraffe, and whilst amused with this idea, I lost half my friend's lecture on architecture.   Meantime we reached the bridge, and discovered that the final arches on our side were all broken down, but had been since patched up as well as had been possible, with bands and joinings made from the roots of trees, so as to allow even carriages to pass over.   We proceeded onwards, until we had ascended the highest part of the curve, when looking over the bridge, we remembered to have heard that last year a crazy woman had thrown herself into the dry bed of the river.   'She must have been suffocated by the rapidity of her fall through the air,' we remarked to one another, assigning, whether right or wrong, a natural cause for this aerial death, whilst waiting until some one should pass by, to point out to us the 'Devil's Hole,' as it is called, which, for aught we knew, must have existed in the middle of the bridge, but which is not now to be found there.

"Before telling you how we learnt the history of the Hole, I must give you some idea of the character of the peasantry.

"The Lucchese peasant is industrious, patient under fatigue, accustomed to hardship ; as parsimonious, perhaps more so, than the Swiss, and for the most part, poor and oppressed by the system of labour in this part of the country.   He is a violent bigot, and would not omit the prayers for the dead, though he would murder his own brother; shy with a stranger, he is tamed with marvellous ease if he find the stranger gentle, and he is more ready to yield obedience to the despotism of the Priest than to the laws of the Duchy. In his countenance you may trace the dulness of superstition, with the embarrassment of a man unaccustomed to associate with other men; in its expression, the cunning of a friar, with the fear produced by sermons on hell: his limbs are usually robust, and almost impervious to fatigue and want. Benjamin Franklin would have found among them industrious agriculturists for a new colony; Cardinal Ruffo would have found a Fra Diavolo and Trentacapilli.[1]

"I accosted an old woman who was crossing the bridge, with—'Tell me, my good woman, where was the Devil's Hole?' She looked suspiciously at us, muttered something I could not hear, and went on her way without answering. We began to think we had been made fools of. A man with a load of wood on his back was somewhat more courteous, and stopping, when we repeated the question, pointed with his foot to where the hole had once been. 'And the history of it?' I asked. 'How should I know? What would you have of me?' he said in reply: 'they say that Saint Giugliano, when he built the bridge, asked *a friend* to help him to finish this arch, and they say that he did help him; but who can tell if it is true?' 'Why not—and what followed?'...

---

[1] Celebrated brigands.

'He asked aid of ... he asked aid ...' (here we perceived the good man had some scruple in naming the Devil), 'and he promised him the first soul which should pass over it. When it was finished, Saint Giugliano, to cheat him, provoked a dog to run at him from below, having placed a trap on the bridge; the dog pursued him—and here, where my foot touches, he was caught in the trap—he, who was waiting to see who would first cross the bridge, immediately hurried to seize on him, but when he found a dog in place of a Christian, he caught hold of him and dashed him with such violence on the ground that he made a hole, through which he passed.... But perhaps it is not true ... it is a legend—and who was there to see?' The man related all this to us, with that smile, and forced ease of manner, which men assume when they are afraid of hearing their opinions ridiculed, and therefore protest their innocence of belief; as if feeling their way not to fall. We thanked him, and continued our journey, without meeting with any further adventure till we reached a kind of inn, where travellers stop in an evening, to take a glass of something to drink.

"We entered the house; the entrance was a mixture of shop, cupboard, and kitchen. The only seat was, as usual, the table. We called below, we called above, and not a soul answered. We passed from that room into the next, as if we were masters of the house; though the darkness (arising as much from the time of day as the place itself) made it impossible for me to make out for what purpose these rooms were destined. At last we thought it wisest to sit down and wait for the host of this new kind of inn. My friend seated himself upon a tub, I on a broken bench. Suddenly, I heard the floor crack, and felt something move beneath my feet. 'By Jove,' I exclaimed, 'the house is falling!' and I attempted to rise, but was prevented by feeling a head between my legs, which proved to be that of the host himself rising out of the cellar. He was not at all surprised to see us, but smiled, and presented us with wine, which we had not asked for, but which he had drawn from the cask when he heard us call, though he had given no reply, either because too idle or because he thought shouting might increase our thirst.

" 'Were you alarmed on the night of the flood?'

" 'Well, to deny it would be to tell a lie.'

" 'Did you receive any injury?'

" 'What injury do you suppose it could do me? I do not possess a foot of land. I may even say it did me good, because in the midst of it I collected firing enough to last me three years.'

" 'From the pieces of wood brought down by the river? But of what kind?'

" 'What kind of wood? Wood from the cottages; beams, laths, broken stools.'

" 'Poor souls! Who knows to whom these articles might have belonged!'

E

"'Well, well; when it is God's will, what help is there? He who is down is down; to-day me, to-morrow you.' (Thus could this lucky fellow philosophise.)

"Just then a middle-aged man entered, and bade our host good evening, in a tone which expressed the reverse. The host, on his side, accosted him with 'Come, friend Bastiano, it is all past now, so don't let us think any more about it. Good luck to those who remain.'

"'Very fine talking,' he rejoined; 'you may be as merry as you like, you who are just as you were before the flood. Have you heard the last news? That part of the wall which remained standing has ended to-day by falling over the other three.'

"'What!' my friend inquired, 'has the river destroyed your house?'

"'My house and farm, and all I have besides.'

"'What besides?' The man did not answer, but sat with his head sunk on his breast, and one leg crossed over the other, as if lost in thought.

"'Poor Bastiano! I am sorry for you,' resumed our host. 'Tell these gentlemen how it all happened, and how the water carried everything away.' Then, as if half repenting what he had said, he turned to us, and continued: 'The morning of the flood, this poor man went to look at his fields to see if the river had broken in upon them. . . . The first flood was then advancing; for the rivers did not overflow together, as, had it pleased God that they should all have overflowed at the same moment, we should none of us have been here. It was during the first flood (and although we could see the damage it had done up higher, we had no fear for ourselves), this man—was it not so, Bastiano?—heard the bells, and went to mass without thinking of danger. Whilst at mass, and when all the congregation were about leaving the church, they first heard a noise—a sound of destruction—which terrified every one, and the people rushed out, shouting, "The river! the river! carry off all you can!" As they left the church they saw the whole plain under water. You see the water took its course over there, never farther from that house, and reached this place, where the mark is almost halfway up the window. This man was turning homewards, when all of a sudden he saw that his house and farm had disappeared, all swept away. Poor Caté! who knows at this moment where she and the baby may be!'

"'My God!' I exclaimed, 'were there people in the house?"

"'Indeed, there were, sir; the wife and a child eight months old she had at the breast.'

"The man never spoke, but having taken something from the host, went out, muttering to himself in a broken voice, interrupted by sighs—signs of overwhelming grief and the stupefaction caused by recent misfortunes.

"We then learnt, through the same channel as before,

that when a boy this unhappy man had earned his livelihood by selling little plaster figures, a peculiar branch
of trade confined to this part of the country, and he
had been employed to work in the fields, or cut wood,
in Corsica. His house and his little farm were the
fruits of this wandering and hard life, and of the little
dowry brought him by Caterina, whose name the host
had shortened to Caté. The river had again reduced
him to beggary and solitude, and to be a wanderer on
the face of the earth.

"Meantime, night had closed in, and the increasing
darkness depriving us of the view of the hills and of the
country round, left us cogitating over many thoughts.
The terrible stories we had just been listening to occupied both my friend and me, as every now and then
he or I kept exclaiming, 'What misfortunes!' 'Poor
people!' Fatigue gradually absorbed the feelings of
both pain and pleasure; and, to tell the truth, we
could not attend to anything except our steps, or to
seek to pass the time by other thoughts. I suggested to
my friend: 'Imagine to yourself that you have a commission to build a house according to your own fancy;
sketch your plan, and you will see how this will shorten
the distance.' 'You are right,' he replied; 'I was just
thinking the same.' After this ensued a silence of
some miles. My friend, however, stuck at his staircase,
and vainly rummaged his brain to discover where to
place the steps. I had arrived, happily, at the third

act of a tragedy, and had all the fifth ready, with the dramatis personæ arranged on the stage at the final scene—a splendid and horrible catastrophe ; I saw and heard the applause on every side, but I could not somehow contrive the fourth act, and I was endeavouring to find a classical reason for its omission altogether, my reputation being at stake, when the campanile of our city, seen in dark shadow, relieved us from our embarrassment. The idea of supper and a good bed absorbed all our intellectual faculties, and we swallowed the buskin and the plummet in a yawn.

CHAPTER V.

ONE of Giusti's most lively and remarkable poems of this year, 1836, was *Lo Stivale* (The Boot), a description of Italy. The Boot, supposed to be speaking, begins by stating that it is not made of common leather, nor by an unskilful hand ; that it is well adapted for the chase and for war ; that although always standing in water, it is uninjured, and that many fools who have tried it on can bear witness to its worth. It is compact and strong, with a rim to protect it at the top, and a seam down the centre.

It proceeds to say that it cannot be worn by the weak without fatigue and the danger of their becoming lame, and that there are not many who find it adapted to their feet. It is impossible to enumerate all who have attempted to put it on, and it is therefore contented with giving a list of the most celebrated, and the misfortunes brought upon them. Beginning with the time of the Romans, when Italy coursed over the world without restraint, and fell because she had aimed at too much, there followed the arrival of races from all parts to contend for the possession of the Boot. But the Priest wished to keep it to himself, and when he found it did not fit he let it out to others. A German disputed the possession, but was forced to return to his country, and for a whole century it was worn by simple merchants, Venetians, Genoese, and Florentines, who, occupied with commerce, kept it in good condition. But, after a time, the merchants became wealthy, and wished to make the Boot more ornamental, which thus gained in beauty, but became less serviceable. Charles of Anjou attempted to wear it, and was lamed in Sicily : and Charles VIII. of France, a certain king of pikes, next seized on it with feet and hands, but was menaced by Pier Capponi, and obliged to retreat. Giusti alludes to the family of the Medici, in those intrigues which lasted a hundred years, and who, by ointments and other medicines or impostures, flayed the country. Tossed from hand to hand, the Boot was alternately the prey of France and of Spain. The Spaniard introduced titles, and with the oil of courtesy was more destructive than all the rest. But in the centre of Italy, a lily (the emblem of Florence) reminded her of her ancient glories, until a Pope presented her to Alexander de' Medici, and created him Grand Duke. From that time forth, all have taken their pleasure with the Boot, until little has remained of its original condition, whilst it has lost all that vigour which once enabled Italy to compass the universe.

Now that it desires to be worn by a native, it is so weak and disheartened, it fears to move a step. Its greatest enemies are the Priests, and the Poet agrees with certain modern neo-catholic poets, that the Canon laws forbid Priests to wear boots. Neglected and torn to pieces the Boot waits to be restored and occupied by some leg which shall not belong to a foreigner. Alluding to Napoleon the First, Giusti declares that he intended to have made it stronger than ever, but, halfway, abandoned the enterprise, and that now it will be impossible to mend it without great expense. The Poet then gives a description of the various colours or banners of those ruling in Italy, and hopes that if the Boot be again repaired, it may be worn with tenderness and discretion, and be made all of one colour :—

> " E poi vedete un po' ! quà son turchino,
> Là rosso e bianco, o quassù giallo e nero ;
> Insomma a toppe come un arlecchino :
> Se volete rimettermi davvero,
> Fatemi con prudenza e con amore
> Tutto d' un pezzo e tutto d' un colore." [1]

---

[1] And look—this bit of blue—how ill it matches
With red and white, and black and yellow there ;
I'm a mere harlequin of shreds and patches.
If you would really put me in repair,
Make me, with loving zeal and sense to aid,
All of one piece and one prevailing shade.

This translation is by the late Henry Lushington, Esq., pub-

Giusti ends by the assurance that if once Italy is re-united under one man, provided that man be not a coward, she will never again allow herself to be tyrannized over as she has been.

The Poet, in this humorous sketch of the history of Italy, endeavours to rouse his countrymen to a sense of their past greatness, their past misfortunes, and their present state of degradation. He reminds them of its cause, and anticipates the union of the Italian nation under one head, foretelling that, profiting by past severe experience, such calamities will never recur. Such ideas could only have owed their ready acceptance to their having already existed, though dormant, in the hearts of the people : for the spirit of self-reliance and independence diffused throughout all classes, and in every petty State into which the Peninsula was divided, only needed the genius of their poets and great men to give it form and reality, whilst fixing the individual minds in the common centre of aspirations, towards which all were tending.

Giusti's mind appears to have been unceasingly occupied in considering the means for the social regeneration of the people, and education was therefore naturally among the first subjects which engaged his

lished in a review on the works of Giusti in the "British Quarterly Review," No. XXXIII., Feb. 1853. Another spirited translation of this poem may be found in "Macmillan's Magazine," vol. ii. p. 244.

attention.   Writing to a friend, in 1838, he thus expresses himself on that topic :—

" DEAR LORENZO,

" I delayed writing to you, because it was not enough to have seen the College of ——— ; I was anxious to think the matter over, and to make other inquiries about the method employed there.   I knew ——, and found him a clever man, a plausible speaker, one of the many who understand to which side his hearers lean, and, without having any bias to one opinion over another, understands how to take advantage of his knowledge of a man's mind, to advance his own ends. The rest of the friars, whether superiors of the monastery or masters in the school, follow more or less in his steps, and boast much, speaking up for —— and for the college : a bad beginning in my opinion, because what is really good recommends itself, whereas he who acts well from a love of excellence rarely strives to enhance his own merits by boasting.   But allowing for ambition and the desire of putting themselves forward, which is the malady of the species, that which made me most suspicious was the usual holding forth about Roma and Toma, the display of models of machinery, collections of stones, lessons in drawing, &c. &c. and afterwards learning that the lectures on these subjects were either given late in the season, or that they were required to be paid for as extras.   Little was said about the Italian language, and that little I thought more as a condescension to the popular wish on the subject, than from feeling its necessity. The best years of childhood and youth are absorbed by Latin and by trivial studies, frittering away time, filling their heads with many fragments of learning, without nourishing them with one solid piece of information. An example was given, in which a solemn display was made of emptiness and ostentation; and any one having a grain of sense or of heart must have gone away deploring the fate of these poor youths, who are delivered up into the hands of these fellows, who maim them under the pretence of training them. They are meantime persuaded of their own learning; and if they become conscious of their ignorance, or even worse, of the errors they have been taught, they are either disheartened, and remain where they are, or are obliged to begin all over again, the instruction received at the College serving as a warning what to avoid. A single instance among many will suffice. One of the themes given them to be turned off-hand into poetry was, 'Michael Angelo; or, the Revival of the Arts.' Now you are aware that Michael Angelo precisely marks the era of the decline, and that the true reign of the arts lies between the epochs which commence with Giotto and *end* with Michael Angelo.

"The locality is excellent, well situated, and kept clean; the food appeared to me to be good and sufficient; but all that was shown to us was prepared as for a holiday—that is, everything was prepared for the occasion : and who knows what it may be the rest of the year?

"My advice is, to do nothing. Let us record our own experience, and let our children, at any rate, profit by our misfortunes. One of our many mistakes is, to educate a man as if he were made in separate pieces. The head is separated from the heart, the heart from the head, and now one is neglected, now the other ; whereas these two faculties ought to act in perfect harmony, and to advance by equal steps towards perfection. Hence arises that perpetual struggle between the reason and the affections, between the real and the ideal—a struggle which accompanies us through life and often follows us to the grave."

That same year, Giusti writes to his friend Francesco Puccinotti, lately appointed Professor of Clinical Medicine at the University of Pisa. Puccinotti was one of the most eminent men of his profession in Italy ; the adversary of Bufalini, and the author of a history of the science of medicine.

"MY DEAR PUCCINOTTI,

" I must now fulfil an intention I have had from the moment I heard with certainty that you were appointed a Professor at Pisa, which was to rejoice with you on the occasion; and if I delayed fulfilling this intention, the wish was the same. I do not rejoice because I believe this confirmation of your talents necessary to raise you in public estimation, but because a Chair in the University is the most independent and honourable position which can afford shelter to an honest man under an absolute government. Besides, a heart so benevolent as yours must certainly feel enjoyment in being able to communicate to others the light you have acquired; wisdom is the light which increases and purifies its owner whilst propagating itself; so that the mind of the master is, as it were, rekindled by reflection from the rays he communicates to his disciples.

"The Tuscan Government has, indeed, honoured itself in choosing you, and has given hopes of better times; because when honours and remuneration are accorded to merit, by one in authority, there is room to believe things are not so bad. I hear you have opened your course of lectures with great and general approbation, which does not surprise me. Oh! how much I now regret that my youthful days are past, and how gladly would I return to them; not again to weave the gayest portion of our web of life, but to travel another way, under your guidance. Those legal studies dried up my heart and my brain: how much better had it been for me if, instead of tracing the capricious laws of man, I had been engaged in the contemplation of the wise, eternal, immutable laws of Nature. But it is too late now.

"Having paid my debt of congratulation, I must pay that of gratitude. You have kindly read and praised to Azzolino my sonnet upon Bartolini's statuette of Fiducia in Dio (Trust in God),[1] thrown upon paper two years ago, at a time when my heart sought, in literary study and in the works of the first artists, some consolation for the mental sufferings I was then enduring. That little statue consoled me, and inspired me with these fourteen lines, which perhaps breathe the first restoration to calmness of a mind until then over-shadowed by a long and deep sorrow. I accept the praise from you without further words ; and I derive strength, and the desire to compose better, from your approbation."

Among Giusti's Florentine friends was Count Piero Guicciardini, a descendant of the historian, a new edition of whose works he has edited, and who still inhabits the dwelling of his celebrated ancestor, at the corner of the Piazza dei Pitti and of the narrow street bearing his name. Since the period when the following letter was written, Count Guicciardini has become known as the head of a religious movement in Italy. About the year 1846, or a little earlier, he began to read the Bible, under the auspices of a Swiss gentleman visiting

[1] Composed when recovering from a severe disappointment. See p. 31.

Florence. He was the first to establish infant schools in Tuscany, assisted by the Signora Matilda Calandrini, who had already established a girls' school in Pisa, which she carried on, as nearly as was possible at that time, in the principles followed by the Evangelical or Protestant sects, though not allowed to introduce their doctrines. After the year 1848, Count Guicciardini ventured to make converts to his religious views, which drew upon him the persecution of the restored Grand Ducal Government, and about 1851, when one night reading the Bible in a house in the Borg' Ogni Santi, he and six persons who were with him were arrested and conveyed to the prisons of the Bargello. After eight days' confinement, they were condemned to six months' obligatory residence in the Maremma; but Count Guicciardini obtained a commutation of his sentence, and permission to go into exile. He chose England for his home, where he remained until 1859, when he was at liberty to return to Florence. He now is at the head of the most popular Italian Protestant sect in that city. At the time when Giusti addressed the following letter to him, Guicciardini was engaged in his educational schemes :—

To Count Piero Guicciardini.

"MY EXCELLENT FRIEND,

"I want your advice and aid in an affair which I have long had at heart, and in the fulfilment of an object which I have in common with you, but with this difference, that you are able to satisfy your aspirations for the good of mankind, and I have hitherto only been able to cherish the hope of being useful. Pescia is blessed with a fine climate, and is rich and flourishing, both by its agriculture and commerce, whilst the inhabitants enjoy competence, and are industrious and cheerful; but these advantages are not turned to the account they might be, because to all the advantages of life is not added the education of the heart and intellect. You may see a number of spirited lads, and with the best dispositions, hanging about the streets, sharpening their wits, of which they have a superabundance, by petty rogueries, thefts, or idle jests, polluting their youth, and corrupting their minds, at an age when they are most open to impressions.

"Since residing here, and watching these neglected youths, who show a singular aptitude for gymnastic exercises whilst at play, and for mimicry, but especially for music, I have come to the conviction (and the wisest here agree with me) that these poor lads, who if abandoned to themselves will grow up vagabonds and ignorant, might be rendered capable of better things if any one would take them in hand. I have been still further confirmed in my anticipation of a good result, by observing that when grown to manhood they easily turn to labour and to trade; for though the country is very populous there are not as many hands as are wanted.

"Much has been talked about schools and charitable institutions; but the fact is, that we are without resources for these objects, and those who have children are less embarrassed how to feed than how to educate them. All here are desirous of having some institution which will remove their children from idleness and vice, whilst leaving the parents leisure to attend to their affairs, with the assurance that they will not see their child return home with bodily injury, or corrupted in his mind.

"This wish is not, however, expressed as openly and as generally as it is felt, because, as usual, those who rule the country, whether magistrates or public opinion, are alike averse to, or ignorant of, all that is either useful or praiseworthy. Some who would be willing to help are prevented by their own affairs or by business, or are deterred by the fear of opposition which they must necessarily have to encounter; others are not listened to, or, if listened to, are suspected as innovators. Nevertheless, we should succeed if we had one strong will to direct all the various suggestions made by the community towards one aim. Some one person is wanting to concentrate and give an impulse to the popular will; but if once started in the right road I do not think it could be stopped.

"I therefore propose myself, to unite these scattered elements, and to endeavour, in some way or other, to satisfy the demands of the age and our greatest necessities.

F

"In order to give as little opening to suspicion as
possible (for unluckily a school now-a-days is regarded as
an attempt at regicide), I must begin by a girls' school ;
for if female education has everywhere proved a benefit,
it will prove doubly so here, where many of the daughters
of the first families are condemned to listen to nothing
but fairy tales, and to the gossip of servants and go-
vernesses ; I say it will prove a double benefit, because
we may the more speedily arrive at the end we have
in view, by giving the wealthy an interest in our success.

"We may afterwards occupy ourselves with the boys,
and introduce other useful things ; and first of all a
Savings Bank, in establishing which (to our shame be it
spoken) we are among the last in Tuscany.

"I ask you, my dear Piero, to be so good as to instruct
me how I ought to set about these matters, and how I
ought to act in order to make my way with the country
and with the Government.   As to the country, I am of
opinion that we ought to try and arrange matters so
as to obtain the support of the most influential men
before giving an indication of what we are about ; likewise to interest women in the subject, as has been tried
everywhere else with such advantage ; then strengthen
our hands abroad, and finally make the venture.   Without your co-operation, however, and that of your colleagues, it is impossible for us to come forward, new as
we are in all these matters ; nor can the best will in the
world lead to anything without experience.   It is ab-

solutely necessary for me to ascertain what might be the expense of establishing an infant school, that I may see how much would be required to provide all the means.

" I hope that you will think of us, and communicate your views to me, as I am in the greatest need of them ; for I am impatient to put my hand to this work, to which I am moved by the sad experience of the evil of a bad education, by the desire to serve my country, and the wish to do something which will be as satisfactory to our community as to my own heart."

Giusti added to this letter the following short essay on female education :—

" When the object in view is an institution whose success depends less on the light of the intellect than on the goodness of the heart, it is necessary to call to our aid those beings who render existence dear, by the affectionate and tender solicitude they throw into everything which concerns those they love.

" Women caress us as children, cherish us and prepare us for the pleasures and sorrows of life, and when we depart, they receive our last sighs. Though perhaps incapable of entering into public affairs, because nature has formed them averse to violence and tumult, few can equal them in the cares of domestic life, and none in gentle kindness, and in the entire resignation of the heart to pity, and in sympathy in sorrow. When God drew man's companion from the side where his affections

lie, He showed His intention to assign the dominion
of the heart to that gentle being.   Therefore, whilst
we listen with silent and respectful love to the
paternal counsels, we none of us, from childhood, can
resist the warm impulse of affection which leads us
back, instantaneously and full of confidence, to the
bosom of our mothers.   It is this influence which in
youth chases us from vain pleasures, from idle and
corrupt amusements, and teaches us the disinterested-
ness, the silent goodness, the cherished illusions, and
the blessed dreams of love ; it is woman who, in the
days we are permitted to live, makes us rejoice in a
faithful companion, makes us rich with a thousand
unspeakable joys, and gives us the sweet happiness of
children.

"But if an office of so much love is expected from
woman, upon man is imposed the duty of being her
guide and guardian in this short and dubious road ;
and it is to man, therefore, that we may impute her
wanderings, and the dangers and evils to which she is
exposed.   We see this gentle and angelic being converted into an object of pain and of disgust, when,
ruined by a bad education, she is sent into the world
to share the good and the evil of life, and either left
wholly to herself, or harassed by perpetual watching.
It appears to me, that excess in the gratification of all
their inclinations, as well as excess of severity, are the
poisons which destroy the natural kindness and the

docile and tractable character of women. I am anxious to remind you of the origin and the consequence of these two worst methods of education. . . ."

This essay on female education was left incomplete. Giusti's affection for his own mother, from which his respect and tenderness towards women appears to have been derived, is expressed in a beautiful and touching little poem he wrote in 1839, on a mother's feelings whilst watching by the cradle of her sleeping infant, and which is concluded in these words :—

> Oh! se per nuovo obietto
> Un dì t' affanna giovenil desio,
> Ti risovvenga del materno affetto!
> Nessun mai t'amerà dell' amor mio.
>
> E tu nel tuo dolor solo e penoso
> Ricercherai la madre, e in queste braccia
> Asconderai la faccia ;
> Nel sen che mai non cangia avrai riposo.[1]

---

[1] Oh! should thy heart for charms unseen before,
From youthful passion writhe in anguish sore ;
Think of thy mother's tears, and cease to pine,
For none will love with love to equal mine.

And if alone, and weary of thy grief,
Thou seek'st thy mother's arms, to ask relief ;
Then hide thy weeping face, and midst thy woes
Find, on that breast unchangeable, repose.

CHAPTER VI.

IN 1837, 1838, and 1839 Giusti produced several poems; the first of any note was "San Giovanni; or, An Address to the Coin of Florence." In the year 1251, the Florentines, having driven the Imperial party from the surrounding cities and country, as well as from Florence, celebrated their victories and inaugurated the recovery of their freedom by the introduction of a new coin, the Florin, of pure gold, and weighing the eighth of an ounce. It was divided by twenty soldi, and bore on one side the effigy of the Lily, on the other that of St. John the Baptist, who had succeeded Mars as the patron of the city.[1] The coin itself soon afterwards was called by the name of the saint, as we find in Dante's allusions to its forgery by Adam of Brescia, for the lords of Romena:

> Ivi è Romena; là dov' io falsai
> La lega suggellata del Battista.
>> *Inferno*, Canto. xxx. l. 73.

---

[1] See I Primi Tempi della Libertà Fiorentina, Narrati da Atto Vannucci.

There is Romena, where I falsified
The metal with the Baptist's form imprest.

CARY's *Trans.*

And, again, at Canto xiii. line 143, in allusion to
the Christian patron—

Io fui della Città che nel Battista
Cangiò 'l primo padrone.

In that city I dwelt
Who, for the Baptist, her first patron changed.

In the Grand-Ducal period the ruspone, a gold coin
equivalent to three florins, or nearly seventeen francs,
preserved the effigy of the saint on both sides.

Giusti's poem was intended as a satire on the venal-
ity and corruption of the times, which made money the
door through which alone access could be had to wealth
and power. The verses conclude thus :—

Ah! predicare la Bibbia o l'Alcorano
San Giovanni mio caro, è tempo perso,
Mostrateci la borsa, e l' universo
Sarà Cristiano.

To preach the Bible or the Alcoran
Is losing time : hold up to us the purse,
And, San Giovanni, then the universe
Will become Christian.

In 1838 followed the *Brindisi*, "the Toast," and the
Apologia del Lotto, "Apology for the Lottery." With

the first Giusti expressed himself better satisfied than with any of his previous compositions ; but with regard to the second, he afterwards wished that he had written it later in life.

The Lottery, which helped to demoralize the people, was sanctioned and encouraged by the Government, because an advantage to the exchequer. Idleness and prodigality, the result of gambling habits, were prevalent throughout Tuscany, and the source of all this evil was an appropriate subject for the pen of the satirist. In a poem entitled *Il Sortilegio*, "the Sorcery," written some years afterwards, Giusti again alludes to the misery occasioned by this gambling, when describing the ruin it brought on a happy peasantry :—

> Ecco il lotto a ficcarsi tra loro
> Il lotto, gioco Imperiale e Reale
> E quella pace e quel viver onesto
> Subito in fumo andar con tutto il resto.

> Here comes the Lottery to dwell among them,
> The Lottery, Imperial Royal game ;
> The peace they once enjoyed, their honest gain,
> All with their substance vanishing in smoke.

His last poem of this year was the *Incoronazione*, "the Coronation," written on the occasion of the coronation of the Emperor Ferdinand II. The attack here made upon established authorities was bolder than any of his previous satires, and Giusti considered this poem to be one of his most successful compositions. "These verses," he writes to a friend, "rise somewhat above the others, and are a kind of satire, which invades the region of lyric verse. To one who does not reflect that on that occasion the persons present, whether as actors or as spectators, were open to ridicule, and the fact itself serious, they may appear of two opposite complexions; but a poet could neither treat the persons seriously, nor the event in a burlesque manner." In this poem, Giusti reproaches the Italian Princes as the authors of the national degradation, by acting as the vassals of the German Emperor, bowing before him, and acknowledging his supremacy; among all the sovereigns of the petty States of Italy, Carlo Alberto alone refused to do homage to Ferdinand. Whilst describing, in turn, each of the Italian Princes, who were gathered round the new Emperor, Giusti thus paints the Tuscan Grand Duke, Leopold II. :—

Il Toscano Morfeo vien lemme lemme
Di Papaveri cinto e di lattuga,
Che per la smania d' eternarsi asciuga
    Tasche e maremme.

Co' tribunali, e co' casti annaspa;
E benchè snervi i popoli col sonno
Quando si sogne l'imitare il nonno
    Qualcosa raspa.

The Tuscan Morpheus softly steals along
With poppies and with lettuce garlands crowned,
Eager for immortality he drains
        Our pockets and the marshes.[1]

In law statistics' tangled mazes lost,
He enervates his people, lulled asleep;
But when he dreams of his great grandsire's deeds
        He dabbles in reforms.

The lines addressed to the Pope may remind the reader of the grandeur and the severity of Dante, as he exhorts him:—

O destinato a mantener vivace
Dell' Albero di Cristo il santo stelo,
La ricca povertà dell' Evangelo
        Riprendi in pace.

Strazii altri il corpo; non voler tu l' alma
Calcarci a terra col tuo doppio giogo;
Se muor la speme che al di là del rogo
        S' affisa in calma,

---

[1] In the year 1769 Leopold the First undertook the drainage of the Maremma, or marshy district of Tuscany; but owing to insufficient means he was unable to accomplish all that he desired. The work was afterwards resumed by his grandson, Leopold the Second, but proved a failure. The first Leopold, who conceived this great project, divided the districts into departments, with tribunals for the administration of justice, encouraged colonization, invited foreigners to settle there, and abolished oppressive duties upon the cattle sent to graze a part of the year. But this was only one of many acts which entitle him alone, among all the Grand Dukes of Tuscany, to the gratitude of his fellow-creatures.

Vedi sgomento ruinare al fondo
D'ogni miseria l' uom che più non crede ;
Ahi ! vedi in traccia di novella fede
  Smarrirsi il mondo.

Tu sotto l' ombra di modesti panni
I dubitanti miseri raccogli ;
Prima e te stesso la maschera togli
  Quindi ai tiranni.

Che se pur badi a vender l' anatêma
E il labbro accosti al vaso dei potenti
Ben altra voce all' affollate genti :
  " Quel diadema,

" Non è, non è (dirà) de santi chiodi,
Come diffuse popolar delirio :
Cristo l' armi non dà pel suo martirio
  Per tesser frodi.

" Del vomere non è per cui risuona
Alta la fama degli antichi padri ;
E settentrional spada di ladri
  Tôrta in corona.

" O Latin seme, a chi stai genuflesso ?
Quei che ti schiaccia è di color l' erede ;
E la catena che ti suona al piede
  Del ferro istesso.

" Or dia, poichè accorrete in tanta schiera
Piombate addosso al mercenario sgherro
Sugli occhi all' oppressor baleni un ferro.
  D' altra miniera.

GIUSEPPE GIUSTI.

" Della miniera che vi diè le spade
   Quando nell' ira mieteste a Legnano
   Barbare torme, come falce al piano
     Campo di biade."

Thou, who art destined to maintain in life
The holy stem of Christ's most sacred tree,
The wealth in poverty the Gospel taught,
     In peace resume.

Let others wound the body; do not thou
Crush with thy double yoke the human soul;
If the hope dies, which there, beyond the grave,
     Is calmly fixed,

Behold desponding, sinking to the depths
Of misery, he who believes in nought;
And ah! behold him seeking some new faith
     Wandering the world around.

Beneath the shadow of thy modest garb
Gather th' unhappy doubters to thyself;
Tear the dissembler's mask from thine own face
     And then unmask all tyrants.

If thou, content to sell Anathemas,
Sip of the self-same cup where monarchs drink,
The multitude shall hear another voice;
     " That crown

" Is not, is not," 't will say, " of sacred nails,[1]
  As legends wild have told, and been believed ;
  Christ does not give His tools of martyrdom
      To work deceit.

" Nor is it of the ploughshares made which once
  Exalted high our forefathers' great names,[2]
  But of the northern sword of robber-chiefs
      Who bent it in a crown.

" Oh ! Latin race, to whom do ye then kneel ?
  He is the heir of those who crushed your sires,
  And the chain now which clanks around your feet
      Is forged of the same metal.

" Forward, ye hosts, who gather there in haste,
  Fall on the mercenary robber crew,
  And in the tyrant's eyes let a sword flash
      Made from another mine ;

" The mine that furnished metal for the swords
  When at Legnano, filled with sacred ire,
  Ye mowed the barbarous hordes, as on the plain
      The sickle cuts the corn."

In 1839, Giusti produced *La Vestizione,* " the Investiture," in which he reproved the ambition of certain men, who, without any just claim to honour, seek and

---

[1] The iron crown of the Lombards, which the Emperor received at Milan, is supposed to have been made from the nails by which the Saviour was fastened to the Cross.

[2] An allusion to Cincinnatus, and to the simplicity of early manners.

obtain titles by mean acts; nor does he spare the prodigal and idle noble, who, by the neglect of duties
incumbent on his position in society, justly forfeits
the respect as well as the wealth which he derives
solely from the merits of a remote ancestor, and who
would yet deny to plebeians that which his own equally
plebeian forefather had earned by commerce and industry.   Though this satire is directed chiefly against
the manners or morals prevalent in Tuscany, the poet
intended to attack the same vices, under whatsoever
form, infecting society in every quarter of the globe.
In the character of a base sycophant here represented,
he was supposed to have alluded to a certain personage well known to his townsmen; but ill-natured
allusions to the peculiarities of private individuals
was so adverse to Giusti's nature and principles, that
his anger was roused whenever the idea was suggested
to him.

In a letter which he wrote about this time, to Carlo
Bastianelli, a merchant at Leghorn, he speaks with
pride and gratification of his compositions, which were
now circulating all over Tuscany and even passing
beyond the frontiers.   He adds:—" I will not allude
to the praises of friends and *dillettanti*, and I leave
newspaper critics to puff me up for the public, but I
will only mention to you, that Carmignani, Niccolini,
Azeglio, Manzoni, and Grossi either have encouraged me
themselves, or sent others to encourage me, and among

these, Mayer.[1] Requests reach me from all sides for my satirical compositions, and, in spite of my better judgment, I give them away, and then repent having done so.   Is not this enough to turn my head? . . . I do not write well, but I know, or think I know, what writing ought to be, from always having had the best books in my hands.   As nature has decreed that I should be slow in believing myself to be somebody, I am on my guard against being persuaded or tempted to think so by the flattery of others.   Nevertheless, I confess that the praises of men such as these, if they have not made me proud, have given me courage, and almost been a compensation for many a mortification to which my own inexperience and the malice of others have subjected me.   If my courage does not fail me, I hope not to live in vain.   In my writings I shall always bear in mind the aim of benefiting my country, and, without imagining, as many have imagined for themselves, that I have been sent by Providence, I will endeavour with my light satire to spread wholesome and strengthening maxims. . . ."

Such compositions could not have escaped curtailment at the hands of the censor, if their author had

[1] *Enrico Mayer* was of Swiss birth ; but he had become wholly Italian.   His contributions to popular education in Tuscany have entitled him to the esteem and gratitude of his adopted country.   He made a journey to England to study the popular schools, and communicated the information he had received in articles in the "Guida dell' Educatore."

attempted to publish them; they were accordingly only circulated in manuscript; but as every fresh poem appeared, it was greedily seized upon, copied, and read, till it was known throughout the whole country. Lawyers' and bankers' clerks, students at the school or university, laid aside every other occupation to make copies of Giusti's poetry, and thus by producing an edition in manuscript they contrived to evade a tyrannical institution.

In the midst of his successful career, Giusti was not unmindful of others struggling in the same path; and in the following letter to a young author he encourages him, whilst offering wise advice to avoid the affectation common to embryo poets:—

"MY DEAR SIR,

"The verses you have addressed to —— have made me desire your acquaintance. They show much genius, and, what I esteem more highly, a refined and gentle nature. If you do not allow yourself to be carried away by praise, you will occupy a very eminent position among the writers of the present day. But I warn you, with the Latin satirist, to beware of the hostile array of friends who pass their encomiums on mediocrity, incapable of rising by itself; they only fasten on those who are worth something better, in order to be allowed at least to share their renown; in a word, they are 'the

flies which plough the soil.'[1]   They will laud your verses
to the skies, and they have reason to praise them, because they are good ; if it be true what has been told me
of you, they are above what might have been expected
at your age ; but these friends will not say to you what
I say, who, although at a distance and unknown to you,
am as anxious as any one for your reputation.   I therefore beg you will take my observations in good part,
and, if they appear to you worthy of notice, profit
by them.

"You are at an age when the exercise of your
powers give a value to life.   Everything ought to smile
around you, as there is nothing in your circumstances
to disturb the happiness which, though fleeting, belongs alone to youth.   Why, then, my dear friend,
affect a misery you cannot feel?   Why tinge with the
colours of sadness the most delicate and the sweetest
images which spring from your imagination?   This
mania for woe prevails too much in our country.
The echoes of Italy, as a Frenchman would say, only
repeat one long wearisome *Jeremiad*, from the Alps
to the Lilybean Sea.   The habit of believing ourselves
unhappy leads us to accuse the order of nature of
injustice, makes us think ourselves solitary upon the

[1] Giusti here alludes to a fable of Pignotti's, in which a fly, settling
alternately on the oxen and on the plough, claims the merit of having
made the furrows in the land.   The fable with its moral resembles
that of the fly on the cart-wheel, with which we are more familiar.
See PIGNOTTI, Favola xiii. *La Mosca e il Moscherino.*

earth, and ends by throwing us into a state of apathy, degrading to a man ; it poisons his sweetest affections, his noblest faculties, and, in short, makes a sceptic of him. Everything has its reward, and you have the best, in your love of study. In this you will find an inexhaustible source of consolation, whenever either love or any other passion disturbs your soul. Every word and every sentence learnt from the rules of your art, and unfelt before, will awaken your mental vision, will sound delightful to your heart, and will seem to reveal the secret history of your life. You will then contract that gentle melancholy which cannot be assumed. . . . I do not therefore exhort you to fly from the affections, but to be a man. Beasts howl, men mourn.

"Do not suppose that moderation is a sign of any want of feeling. Whoever had fiercer passions than Dante ? But read his poetry ; examine every part where he speaks of love, and you will find intensity, and yet calmness.

"Petrarch is accused of having been violent, or, at any rate, exaggerated, in his expression of the passion. But whoever makes this observation has not the soul to comprehend him. Play the harp to the man who has no ear for music, and he will yawn over it ; rattle the tongs and the frying-pan, and he will delight in the noise. . . ."

In a letter to Silvio Giannini, a distinguished Florentine lawyer, Giusti insists on style in writing corresponding with the subject :—

" MY VERY DEAR SIGNOR GIANNINI,

"I was agreeably surprised by finding a friend of mine in the translator of the 'Letters of Panagiota Suzzo,' and in the author of the lyric scene. I made the acquaintance of this distinguished young man in Florence, when he came from Naples to publish a historical work. It appears to me that Greek literature may have considerable influence in rousing the inhabitants of the Ionian Islands, to whom every word will recall a fact, a hope, a desire ; but Italians, although they feel the same desire for liberty as the Greeks, have no general or recent event in their history to remember, and would therefore remain cold, whilst reading this poetic prose. When a high-flown style does not meet with a corresponding state of mind in those to whom it is addressed, the imagination and the heart are silent, and such a style has then a more freezing and pedantic effect than mere rhetoric and grammar. I wish, once for all, that these declamations and expressions of despondency would cease. At thirty years of age, any one who has not been hermetically sealed in an atmosphere of blessed hallucinations must feel only too well that he has lost the illusions of his youth ; but it appears to me an absurd contradiction to pretend that the world is advancing, and at the same time to despair of what has been done and what has yet to be done. Few of us Italians (I am sorry to say) know the meaning of political passions. Many of us, either from a desire to follow the fashion, or from ambition, or idleness, or to court popularity, talk of country, but who knows what kind of an idea they attach to the word? The variety of interpretations it has received proves that few or none comprehend its true meaning. To me it is as a god; it is felt and not understood. The Greeks heard it, and sacrificed to their idol; they may therefore now read and respond. We can only read by the intellect, and the intellect is too severe a judge. I may be wrong, but it appears to me that we, in these days, must make up our treasure out of family affections; first educate, then instruct; become good fathers before we become good citizens. Let us not put the cart before the horse, or, whilst we are composing more or less beautiful sonnets on Italy, Italy herself will for ever remain patched, like a harlequin's dress.

" Poetry tacked on to prose (be it said between ourselves) walks upon stilts; and it is easy to perceive that the author of this work has not had much practice in versification. The word *cimiterio* (cemetery), given as the title, conveys a sad and funereal idea to the reader, and prepares him for something grave and solemn. But the metre chosen by the author does not harmonize with this idea, as it summons us to meet death in a light versification.   All analogy between the metre and the subject is ignored and despised; but wherever this rule is despised and ignored it will be felt.   We may play lively airs on any instrument, and on all chords, but to accompany an elegy on the jews-harp and kettledrum is only fit for a Carnival jest.   I am sorry that my friend should have followed the stream when writing on these subjects.   We have enough of rhyming hypochondriasm reaching us from beyond the Alps, and if the gentlemen at the head of our finances would put a duty on these importations, the treasury would be better filled, and we less skinned. I do not say, that because I am perhaps myself born a buffoon, we ought all to imitate Punch; but this playing with dead men's bones, like Shakespeare in his tragedy, appears to me an exotic and false taste, particularly in one who has been reared under the sun of Southern Italy. . . ."

The following letter, written shortly afterwards, is addressed to Matteo Trenta, a priest of Lucca :—

"Florence, 13th August, 1840.

" My very dear Signor Matteo,

". . . I came here for eight or ten days, and still remain, less from choice than necessity.   I long to return home, and I am always on the wing, ready, when the time

comes, to take flight.   You will be surprised to hear
that I prefer the Valdinievole to Florence ; but if you
had lived here seven years, as I have, you would alter
your opinion.   I am now quite at home here, but my
health is not good, and then the number of my
acquaintance obliges me to pay numerous visits, and to
submit to certain conventionalities which I cannot
endure.   For a young man who knows how to choose
his associates, this place, where literary men abound, as
well as artists, *et reliquiæ,* of every kind and country,
has a great advantage ; and it is true that going from
Florence to Pescia one finds oneself somewhat isolated,
and out of place ; but, as the proverb says, 'In Rome
do as they do in Rome,' and I am studying to prove
it right.

"The true portrait of Dante, painted by Giotto,
about 1298, in the Chapel of the Podesta, in the Via
Palagio, has been discovered.   These frescoes had been
covered with whitewash by the native Vandals, and for
many centuries the miracle of Giotto and the revered
features of our ancestors have remained buried under
the whitewasher's brush.   Thus the fame and the name
of good men is sometimes darkened by a shade cast on
them by slander or calumny.   The crust of whitewash
has been removed with the greatest perseverance and
skill, little by little, and after various attempts the
form of Dante in the freshness of youth (for when he
was painted he was thirty-two or thirty-three years of

age) has appeared, for the wonder and veneration of his late and degenerate posterity.   Giorgio Vasari knew that the painting existed, but the search has only now been made ; better late than never.   It was a real joy to all present to find that the portraits we possess of Dante are true, and that in his case, at least, we have not been worshipping a false idol.   In the same painting the likenesses of Brunetto Latino and of Corso Donati must exist ; but I fear among the number of figures here represented we shall never arrive, with any certainty, at fixing on theirs.

" Mayer has been some days in Leghorn, having escaped from the prisons of Pope Gregory.   He remains there for the present, to comfort his mother, and he does right ; he will afterwards come here, to rejoice his friends.   You need not ask if I rejoiced in his liberation, and the more so, that I was afraid lest the heat of Rome, itself unhealthy, and of Castel Sant' Angelo, which is extremely unhealthy, might do him a bodily injury ; besides, the mouse had got among the cats."

The history of the discovery of Dante's portrait, to which Giusti alludes, is as follows :——Mr. Kirkup, an English gentleman residing in Florence, happened to read in some old writers that a portrait of the poet existed on a wall of the Church of Ste. Croce. On inquiry he found the wall had been destroyed ; and, when mentioning his disappointment to an Italian friend, Signor Bezzi, he added, that he did not, however, resign all hope of discovering an original likeness of Dante, since another portrait was said to exist in the Chapel of the Bargello [1] in Florence. Mr. Kirkup proposed that they should unite in an endeavour to get the whitewash covering the walls removed, to which Signor Bezzi assented ; and he prevailed on Mr. Wilde, an American, to join them. These three gentlemen subscribed in equal shares the sum of 240 scudi, or about fifty pounds, and engaged an artist, Signor Marini, to perform the delicate operation. Signor Bezzi, meantime, being the lawyer of the party, undertook to draw up the petition to the Government for leave to act. The petition was granted, and Marini set to work. The old chapel was at that time divided into two compartments, and had become a receptacle for all kinds of rubbish, which had in the first instance to be cleared away. Signor Marini, though highly recommended to his employers, proved incapable of the task, which he commenced by making two holes in the wall, each as large as a man's head, for the insertion of beams for the support of his

[1] The Bargello was built by Jacopo de' Lapi, father of the more celebrated Arnolfo de' Lapi, in the twelfth century, for the official residence of the chief magistrates of the city. After the fall of the Republic this palace was inhabited by the Bargello, or chief officer of police, and was subsequently converted into a prison. Since 1860 it is in the course of preparation for a museum of Florentine antiquities.

scaffolding; it was only after a sharp remonstrance on the part of Mr. Kirkup that he consented to place his scaffold on tressels, and relieved the antiquarians from their alarm.   Signor Marini worked for some weeks without discovering anything of consequence, and the Government then interposed, and stopped further operations.   Some time later he was allowed to resume his work, but this time he was paid by the Government. Signor Bezzi and Mr. Wilde had left Florence, when one morning the Marchese Feroni (the present Director of the Galleries of Fine Arts, in Tuscany) called on Mr. Kirkup to inform him that several portraits, painted in fresco, had been discovered on the walls of the Chapel of the Bargello; and immediately afterwards the head of Dante, described by Vasari as the work of Giotto, once more saw the light of day.   Unfortunately, the eye had been destroyed by a nail clumsily torn out, instead of having been carefully extracted, and with which, therefore, a large piece of the plaster had come away.   The paintings were left in this condition for a year, when, the Grand Duke giving permission for a scientific meeting to be held in Florence, it was thought advisable to restore the fresco, before presenting it to the eyes of so many learned connoisseurs.   The hole was accordingly filled up, and a fresh eye painted by Marini, under the direction of the Cavaliere Nerli, the Minister of Public Works.   Not contented with painting the eye according to his own idea, the artist

repainted the whole face and dress. Dante had been
represented by Giotto in the colours described in the
Purgatorio as those of Beatrice :

> Sovra candido vel cinta d' oliva
> Donna m' apparve, sotto verde manto
> Vestita di color di fiamma viva.
>
> *Pur.* Canto xxx. v. 31.

> In white veil, with olive wreathed,
> A virgin in my view appeared ; beneath,
> Green mantle robed in hue of living flame.

But these were the colours which had been adopted
by the Revolutionary party ; and green, red, and white
were accordingly transformed into chocolate, red, and
white, whilst the hood covering Dante's head was
converted into a sort of turban.

But meantime, the discovery of the portrait of the
greatest of Italian poets by one of the greatest of
Italian painters was hailed as a joyful event by all true
Florentines. The name of Dante, associated with days
of Republican liberty (dearer, with all its turmoils, than
the lethargic lullaby of a paternal government), had,
as we have seen, been always held sacred by Giusti ; he
could not but be inspired by a subject which gave him
so much pleasure. In verses addressed to his favourite
poet, he introduced various lines from the Divina
Commedia ; and the comparison to which the reader

is here invited only tends to raise his wonder and admiration at the genius which could dare to tread beside his great progenitor, without giving any sign of lagging or weakness. Giusti's lines are full of impassioned eloquence, whilst deploring his country's misfortunes, her wrongs, and her errors, and, though a kindred spirit, he proves himself no servile imitator of his idol. This is not the first time that in his graver verses he reminds the reader of Dante, by a deep and earnest feeling of patriotism, by a clear insight into the faults of his nation, as well as by the unsparing severity with which he reprobates that which he desires to mend. As far as a comparison can be drawn between a great epic poet and one who only aspired to the lyric muse, the parallel may be extended to their versification, in which both excel in conciseness of language and fulness of thought conveyed in short and pithy lines ; but it ceases when we place the bitter irony of a mortified and disappointed spirit, so prevalent amidst the noble sentiments of the elder poet, beside the genial good humour which pervades Giusti's satires, except when directed against sycophants and tyrants, for whom he can hardly find terms sufficiently strong to express his unmitigated disgust.

Addressing Dante as Master and Lord, he thus describes the degenerate state of Italy :

> L' antica gloria è spenta
> E le terre d' Italia tutte piene

Son di tiranni;[1] e un martire doventa
Ogni[2] villan che parteggiando viene.
Pasciuto in vita di rimorsi e d'onta,
Dai gioghi di Piemonte,
E per l'antiche e per le nuove offense
Caina attende chi vita ci spense[3]

* * * *

La mala signoria che tutti accora
Vedi come divora
E la Lombarda e la Veneta gente;
E Modena con Parma n' è dolente.[4]

Spent is our ancient glory; our cities
All are filled by tyrants, and each factious
Villager converted to a martyr.
Our only nourishment remorse and shame,
From the high range of Piedmont, stretching south;
But for our ancient and our recent wrongs
Caina awaits the soul who spilt our life.

* * * *

The evil rulers who grieve every heart,
Behold, devour the substance of the land;
Lombard, Venetian, Modenese, alike
With those of Parma, groan beneath the yoke.

Giusti proceeds to describe the slow and vacillating nature of the Government ruling Tuscany:

[1] Il Purgatorio, Canto VI. linea 126.
[2] Il Purgatorio, Canto VI. linea 128.
[3] L' Inferno, Canto V. linea 108.
[4] Il Paradiso, Canto VI. linea 75.

Volge e rinnuova membre [1]
Fiorenza, e *larve di virtù profila*
Mai colorando ; chè a mezzo novembre
Non giunge quello che Ottobre fila.[2]

Perhaps nothing could paint a lazy and superficial virtue better than these untranslatable lines, addressed to a nation of art and artists, the word *larve* signifying mask and phantom, or rather the image of the dead, as we frequently find it represented, rising from the earth in the hands of Mercury, as on ancient gems, or adorning the corners of monuments. Florence is therefore thus described occupied with tracing the phantom of virtue, but never filling it up, never completing it, or giving it life and reality.

After a glance at the condition of Europe, and an allusion to the government of Louis Philippe, whose betrayal of the Italian cause is ever recurring to the memory of Italian patriots, he continues :

Ma lenta della Senna
Turba con rete le volubile acque
La Volpe che mal regna e che mal nacque.
E palpitando tiene
L' occhio per mille frodi esercitato
All' opposito scoglio di Pirene
Delle libere fiamme inghirlandato

---

[1] Il Purgatorio, Canto VI. linea 149.
[2] Il Purgatorio, Canto VI. linea 145.

Temendo sempre alle propinque ville
Non volìn le faville
Di spenta libertà sopra i vestigi :
E d' uno stesso incendio arda Parigi.

Troubling the fickle waters of the Seine,
He slowly drags his nets in search of prey,
The fox who evil reigns as evil born ;
And, with an eye, practised in many frauds,
Fixed on the distant Pyrenean heights
Encircled by the flames of liberty,
With beating heart he watches anxiously ;
Trembling lest sparks perchance should fly across,
And fire the neighbouring cities, kindling there
The smouldering ashes of spent liberty,
And, midst the conflagration, Paris burn. . . .

In conclusion, the poet represents the soul of Dante
reading the future of his country :

Sai che per via d' affanni e di ruine
Nostre terre Latine
Rinnoverà come piante novelle
L' amor che muove il sole e l' altre stelle.[1]

Thou knowest that through suffering and decay
Our Latin cities will renew their lives,
Like plants spring up again, moved by that Love
Which guides the sun and planets in their course.

---

[1] Paradiso, Canto XXXIII. last line.

The verses from Giusti's pen which this year excited most attention were *Il Brindisi di Girella*, "The Toast of the Weathercock," *dedicato al Sig. di Talleyrand, buon' anima sua*. In a fragment of what was intended for a preface to an edition of his works, the poet thus speaks of this composition, which he classes with two others, *Gli Umanitari*, "The Humanitarians," and *Il Re Travicello*, "King Log." "Allowing for the blindness of paternal affection, the author believes that these are among the best of his productions, and that in these few lines he has approached nearest to the expression of his ideas. Our cosmopolitan spirit, the facility with which we change banners, and our submitting to be the grumbling yet weak subjects of harsh yet incapable sovereigns, appear to me our deepest wounds, and that these three satires have probed them to the bottom, calmly and fearlessly, like a good surgeon. To affect to be citizens of the world, without being at home in our own house ; to aim at a reputation for wisdom and prudence whilst changing our livery with every new master ; to cry out against tyranny without resenting oppression, nor using the opportunity when the tyrant sleeps,—are follies which deserve a shake of the head and a smile of compassion."

The burden of the Brindisi is always *Viva le maschere !* long live the masks, or shams, wherever found, juntas, clubs, princes, churches, Loretto, and the

French Republic! Girella turns with each and all,
whoever happens to be with the wind, and, having
witnessed the fall of every man and of every system,
congratulates himself and his fellows in these concluding lines :

> Noi valent' uomini
> Siam sempre ritti
> Mangiando i frutti
> Del mal di tutti.

CHAPTER VII.

A SECOND EXCURSION INTO THE MOUNTAINS.

To Pietro ——.

" MY DEAR PIETRO,

"We have just made an excursion on foot, in the mountains in the neighbourhood of Pistoia. We left Pescia at four in the morning, and ascended the river, sometimes by carriage-roads bordered with houses and olives, and sometimes by solitary goat-paths, and arrived at a certain village, called Calamecca, a name which has something Saracenic in it, and Heaven knows by whom it was given or whence derived. At this spot our mountains of Pescia and Lucca may be said to end, and those of Pistoia to begin, which are well known, and deservedly held sacred in history. The first, however, do not in any respect differ from the last, except in name and fame. Imagine a continuous chain of hills and valleys, interspersed here and there with little villages, and clothed with chestnut-trees and thick woods, interrupted by beautiful plantations of the olive and vine, carried up here from the

H

lowest part of the Apennines by the persevering industry of the inhabitants, and almost in defiance of the
climate.   There are besides, everywhere, little rivulets
of the purest water and enormous masses of rock—
enough to drive a landscape-painter wild, or to make a
poet bleat forth an idyl, even in these days when such
kind of poetry has gone out of fashion.   It is said that
this is the very road taken by poor Ferruccio,[1] when

[1] Francesco Ferruccio, a Florentine gentleman, and a soldier of
fortune, of the sixteenth century, who soon rose to be one of the
greatest captains of the age.   When Florence was in 1530 closely
besieged by the Imperial troops, and made her last struggle for
the maintenance of the Republic, Ferruccio was engaged in the service of his native city.   He contrived to throw in provisions and
evade the watchfulness of the Prince of Oranges, who commanded
the enemy's troops.   At length the stronghold from whence he had
made his sallies was taken, and when a messenger arrived from
Florence, confiding to him dictatorial power, in the hope that he might
yet save their city, he lay wounded and ill with fever.   He, nevertheless, placed himself at the head of his little army, and made for the
mountains, in the hope of attacking Oranges in the rear.   At Pescia
he was refused a passage, but proceeded by the other road mentioned
by Giusti.   Ferruccio reached Calamecca, where a message from the
Florentine Government assured him that their general, Malatesta, was
prepared for another effort to save the city.   On the 2d August Ferruccio gave battle to Oranges on the Colle di Prunetta, near that part
called the Croce dei Lari, above the fortress of San Marcello.   Oranges
encamped at Gavinana.   A duel occurred between the two commanders,
in which Oranges accidentally fell to the ground, and might have been
taken prisoner had not timely succour arrived.   But a few minutes
later, in the midst of the fray which followed, Oranges was shot dead
by one of his own men, instigated to the deed by Pope Clement, to
prevent his marrying his niece Catherine de Medici, which Oranges
had intended doing as soon as he gained possession of Florence.   After

our ancestors of Pescia would not allow him to pass. God reward them as they deserve!

"The churches, like the houses, are ancient in form, simple, modest, and with a solemn aspect externally; within, almost all are in a dilapidated condition, patched up with plaster or with part of the cornice from some neighbouring temple. The bell-towers are sometimes very beautiful, and are the remains of fortresses and towers; and there are everywhere fountains, plenty of water, a washing-trough, and a horse-trough. These villages, whether seen from below or from above, look like houses piled up one above the other, as if in these

the death of Oranges, the Imperialists were completely routed, and Ferruccio, bleeding and still suffering from fever, retired with his soldiers into Gavinana. Attacked there by a still larger body of Imperialists, he was overwhelmed by superior numbers, and slain by a Spaniard, Maramaldo, who plunged his dagger to the hilt into the body of the wounded dying Ferruccio: and thus ended the last hope of the Republic of Florence.—*Marietta de' Ricci*, by ADEMOLLO, 6 vol.

Giannotti, who, after a brief interval, was the successor of Macchiavelli, as Secretary of the Florentine Government, was the contemporary and personal friend of Ferruccio, and has left a short account of him. As a youth, Ferruccio was brought up to trade, "*come fanno la maggior parte de' nostri, così nobili come ignobili;*" but, having no taste for it, he gave it up, and took to a country life in the Casentino, where his property lay; but, urged by Giannotti, he came to Florence in 1527, where he was employed in the commissariat department of the army, and soon rose to a chief command. He encountered the forces of the Prince of Oranges at Gavinana, in the mountainous district of Pistoia, was taken prisoner, and brought before Fabrizio Maramaldo (who succeeded to the command when Oranges was killed in the action), who, after insulting him by a blow in the face, ordered him to be put to death.—*Donato Giannotti*, Opere I. 43.

solitudes men drew the bond of human brotherhood closer, or that they herded together like sheep, to keep out the cold. The inhabitants are healthy, tall, and slender-built, lively, and crafty, but ready to serve you, except those few who have ruined soul and body down below in the Tuscan and Roman marshes.

"They winter in the plain, and migrate in herds with the cattle, leaving the old men, women, and children up here. Some are employed cutting brambles and wood for the manufacture of charcoal and potash, some spread nets for birds; and the quantity of woodcocks, blackbirds, and thrushes for roasting, which gourmands devour at the dinners of the great, are the fruit of the labours of these poor people, who toil for three or four months, in the midst of winter, to carry home twenty francesconi. They return to their mountains in May, with replenished purses, diminished health, and often infected with vice, which, up here, in these places remote from the sink of corruption, strike you the more because it is least expected—like virtue in great cities. There is a great difference between those who have always remained at home and those who descend to the plain to seek their fortunes. We observed this in two guides we took on our return—one, born and grown to manhood and old age in these mountains; the other, having worked on various estates and for different persons, and, among others, for Bourmont, the conqueror of Algiers. The first related to us eagerly the whole story of Ferruccio, and told us with implicit faith of miracles which had happened in various places ; the other told us stories of robberies, and of the secret quarrels and suspicious dealings in the Bourmont family. What contrasts! Ferruccio and Bourmont, like a brace of fowls in the market—one good, the other bad. But though these mountaineers who wander from their homes are corrupted by their intercourse with us, they never approach within a thousand miles of the polish of the plain.

" From Calamecca we ascended to a place called *La Macchia dell' Antonini ;* from thence we came upon the new road lately laid down between Pescia and Mammiano ; and after three hours' walking, we reached the summit, to the paper-mill of Cini, which we wished to see before ascending to San Marcello. You must know that the Cini were the first to introduce machinery for making paper to any length into Italy ; but you can form no idea of it without seeing it. We arrived tired and hungry ; and, to crown all, the machinery was not at that moment at work. But the overseer of the paper-mill, a worthy Modenese, had the courtesy to set it going. Wearied, and with craving appetites, we felt annoyed at being detained from rest or refreshment, and wished to be excused ; but the cylinders having been cleaned, and all prepared, the machinery began to move, and such a sight as it proved was enough to cure us of our fatigue.

"San Marcello is the chief place in the mountains around Pistoia. It is a town of a few hundred inhabitants, and has an appearance of prosperity. The hospitality of the family of the Cini makes it still more agreeable ; and if I refrain from commenting upon this, it is only because, having experienced it several times, I cannot say enough in its praise. I must add, there is here, likewise, a machine for the manufacture of felt cloth ; and the younger of the two brothers Cini, who is between twenty and thirty years of age, is the architect, chemist, and director of all these works.[1]

"All through this tract of country you meet with the names of towns, valleys, and little streams, which afford

---

[1] The Cini have introduced in this mountain district, besides the manufactures of cloth and of paper, many useful institutions, such as a savings bank, &c. The wages are no longer paid on Saturdays, or to the men, but to the women of the family, and on market-day, at an hour when the men are engaged at the works ; that the money may be used for family expenses, and because women are supposed to be the better economists. The Marchese d'Azeglio describes this part of the country in his novel of Niccolo de' Lapi, as delighting the traveller, by the amenity of the place, its peaceful charms, prosperity, and the courtesy of the inhabitants. "Time, which ruins so many things, improves some, and has here exhausted all the former fury of party warfare, and even cancelled its memories. Hands accustomed to agricultural labour are used for the manufacture of paper, established by a family whose name recalls one of the first in Italian letters ; a family who employ their wealth in the most noble manner, because most generally useful. This branch of industry, besides various trades, renders the people industrious, and affords them a competence ; they are therefore happy and contented."

ground for the belief that the district was the site of ancient Roman colonies or stations. For example : Rio Flaminio, Vellano, Pupiglio, Pitoglio, Gavinana, Val Papiana, &c.; a certain Captain Cini, of the mountain, a most diligent antiquarian, insists that these names are all of Roman origin. Besides these monuments of ancient history, there are some of modern origin, and several fanciful and absurd traditions, belonging to a much later period. . . .

" We left San Marcello at three in the morning, to ascend to Lake Scaffaiolo, which is situated on the summit of the mountains dividing Tuscany from the Bolognese territory and that of Modena. We wished to reach the top by daybreak, to see the sun rise in all his majesty, from the Adriatic. We ascended nine or ten miles, meeting first with chestnuts, and next beeches, as the chestnut will not grow above a certain level. After passing the beeches, and reaching the highest part of the mountain, you do not meet with a stem or plant of any kind, but extensive grass-slopes everywhere, broken here and there by deep hollows in the ground, caused by water, besides fragments of projecting rock. From June until the end of September these summits are covered with flocks of sheep and with horses, kept here for pasture by the owners of the land upon the mountains and in the plain. They are quite deserted at this season ; and these meadows, which yield like a cushion to the feet, are composed of close yellow grass, dried

up by the hoar-frost, and remind one of a hair mat, as
much by the feel as by their colour. We had not yet
reached the highest point, called the Corno alle Scale,
when so thick a fog came on that we could hardly see
before us ; and all the time it lasted the lines of our
divine poet rang in my head :

> ‘ Ricorditi lettor, se mai nell’ Alpe
>   Ti-colse nebbia, per la qual vedessi
>   Non altrimenti che per pelle talpe.’
> > *Purgatorio*, Canto xvii.

> ‘ Call to remembrance, reader, if thou e’er
>   Hast on an Alpine height been ta’en by cloud,
>   Through which thou saw’st no better than the mole
>   Doth through opacous membrane.’
> > CAREY’S *Trans.*

"Farewell to our hope of seeing the sun rise; farewell
to the beautiful view of the Bolognese and Modenese
plains on one side, and of Tuscany on the other ; yet to
find ourselves at that height, seeing nothing beyond a
few feet before and around us, without a sound of man
or beast, surrounded by an ocean of fog, like a family
escaped from the flood, produced a feeling of solitary
pride in the midst of darkness, which was sufficient
compensation for our disappointment. The fog thickened, cleared, and thickened again several times, and
at length dispersed, but never enough to allow of our

seeing any great extent of country; and whenever it became more dense, we observed, rising from the sides of the hills which surround the valleys, thin white threads of vapour, ascending slowly like thick smoke in a still atmosphere, and which, as they spread out, assumed an ashen colour. As we approached the Corno alle Scale, we heard a voice, and our guide remarked that there must be smugglers about. But, instead of smugglers, it turned out to be a native of Modena, who was collecting a kind of fungus which grows on the bark of the beech, and of which tinder is made. I inquired if the profit upon tinder had not been reduced to little or nothing since the invention of lucifer matches; to which he replied, in the accent of his district, 'Certainly; but lucifer matches are prohibited with us, and so we are able to live.' Observe, that this prohibition is likewise in force in the kingdom of Naples, and in Piedmont, and was occasioned by some fires having taken place from the carelessness of those who used them; just as if the same might not have occurred with tinder or with brimstone matches. Candlesticks will next be prohibited, and we shall be sent to bed in the dark, like fowls to roost. One of our party remarked: 'They are prohibited because the Government takes umbrage at everything that will cause a blaze.' This may be; but if they see the type of a revolution even in a lucifer match, they must be in a deplorably weak condition. You and I at any rate can only discover in it the type of that kind of patriotism which sometimes flares up in the liberal of a *caffè,* or is heard in the noisy declamation of the cíompi [1] and sans-culottes.

'The Corno alle Scale is the highest mountain in Italy after the Monte Bianco and the Cimone di Fanano. It is said to have been crossed by Hannibal ; but in these days everybody declares he passed their door, and according to some historians great men are ubiquitous.

"The Lago Scaffaiolo lies lower than the Corno alle Scale, and is in a basin, formed either by a volcano or some other means. It has a circumference of about five hundred and fifty feet, and seems to be fed from underground springs ; as the streams which fall into it, considering the size of the basin, cannot be sufficient to restore what it loses by evaporation. It appears very deep, for on throwing a stone into it there followed a hollow sound, a sure criterion of great depth. Although not unusual in high mountains, it is a singular effect seeing a lake at that elevation ; but the most singular part of the phenomenon is, that there is not a fish, nor aquatic bird, nor a sign of vegetation, not even a blade of grass, near it. Perhaps grass may not grow in that climate or soil ; and the ice, and the absence of

---

[1] The *Ciompi,* wool-carders ; another name also for clowns. Giusti alludes to a celebrated popular revolution which took place in Florence in 1378.

vegetation and of insects, would leave nothing upon which fishes could feed, nor aquatic birds, if their wings ever carried them so high. We found an immense heap of stones on one side of the lake, covered with names and marks, some old and worn away, and some recent, cut with the points of knives or nails. Every vestige of human life touches the heart amidst these solitudes; and it is only now that I can laugh, as I recollect having read among the names, Count So-and-so, the Marquis So-and-so; as if time would respect these titles. It were better to bear the remembrance of such spots engraved in your memory than, whilst forgetting them as soon as seen, leave your name behind you. But it is everywhere the same: there is not a wall, nor a stone, nor anything celebrated, which is safe from this worthless record, as the most insignificant persons are most lavish of their names, like the weak members of a firm. At the Great St. Bernard, at Petrarch's house in Arquà, and in many other places, a great book is kept, in which all that pass that way may write something. This custom (which has produced for us a sweet sonnet of Ariosto) has now become contagious, and there is not a villa or a table which has not its album. May God preserve us from album persecutions, which can now count more martyrs than that of Diocletian! If, among so many sufferers, any one would take the trouble to select the cream, that found to be worth reading would be at an average of one in ten thousand,

and in a calculating mercantile age like ours we ought
to be a little more economical in paper.

"From the Lago Scaffaiolo to Cutigliano is a descent
of five miles, which, you may imagine, did not afford
much enjoyment to our knees. Cutigliano is a village
situated on the Lima, and at a short distance from the
road to Abetone, opened between Pistoia and Modena
by the Grand Duke Leopold I., a worthy soul long ago
passed away from this earth ; and rendered almost useless by Duke Francis of Modena, a bad soul, who, by
the grace of God, is alive and flourishing. The village
is a pleasant spot, agreeably situated, supplied with all
it can want, and, among the rest, with beautiful undulating hills, mere trifles to a half-sorefoot traveller, who,
when he has come down that interminable descent,
thinks nothing of them. . . .

"On Wednesday, we proceeded to Abetone, thirteen
miles distant from San Marcello, thirty-two from Pistoia, and fifty-two from Florence. Halfway the traveller
reaches the celebrated bridge of Sestaione, uniting two
hills, a wonderful work of Ximenes. It is said that the
road was to have taken a different direction, which
would have been more convenient, but that Ximenes
had it cut here for the sake of a mountain girl, called
Regina, who belonged to these parts, for which reason
the place has always since been called Le Regine.[1]

---

[1] The idea of a road over the romantic mountain of Pistoia was entertained as early as 1225, without any practical results until 1698, when

" But here we reached the most important part of our journey. Early the next morning we left San Marcello to return home, and stopped at Gavinana. At this name every good Italian starts, and feels a sensation of pain in his heart, as well as reverence for the tomb of Italian liberty. Thanks to the author of the *Assedio di Firenze* [1] (Siege of Florence) and to Massimo d' Azeglio, that village, and all that happened there and in its vicinity, are not only known to the learned few, but to all, and by all. However, if these two authors even had not made the story of Francesco Ferruccio and of his deeds famous by their writings, he who might chance to visit this country in entire ignorance of the story would always find its tradition and fame cherished and respected by the people. It is delightful to hear these poor mountaineers say, 'Here the soldiers of Oranges reposed ; here Ferruccio was conquered ; this is called the *selvareggi*, because that was Francesco Ferruccio's cry when leading on his soldiers ; here they entered the village ; down there

the plan was resumed, but soon discontinued, on account of the wars of that period : again, in 1732, this scheme became an object with both states (Tuscany and Modena), and a bridle-road was opened, which Leopold improved in 1766, and finally completed, by the helps of his engineers, the Abate Leonardo Ximenes, and Anastasio Anastagi, with a noble bridge uniting the lofty wooded banks of the river Sestajone, exhibiting a pleasing spectacle of human art, taming and subduing, as it were, some of the wildest beauties of nature.—NAPIER's *Florentine History*, vol. vi. p. 127, 128.

[1] Guèrazzi.

Oranges fell ; from that spot came the arrow which wounded Francesco Ferruccio ; on this terrace he was slain, and when they were about to wound him again, he exclaimed, " It is a noble thing, indeed, to kill a dead man ;" in this ditch ran his blood ; if we were to dig here we should find heaps of bones, as we found when digging to make the portico to the church.' We stepped into the house where they preserve some arms of that time, and taking some of the pikes in my hand, I said to the servant girl, ' If any such are found, I should be glad to buy them ;' she answered me nearly as the author of the ' Siege of Florence, was answered:[1] ' You do not suppose my master would give away one of them, not even if. . . .' leaving unsaid what said so much. With a certain feeling of horror we ascended the terrace where Mara-

---

[1] F. D. Guèrazzi, who thus describes his visit to the same scene :— " When visiting the village of Gavinana, I asked if any ancient arms were still in existence. They answered me in the affirmative, and led me to a cottage near where Ferruccio was slain. The proprietor conducted us to a room on the ground-floor, where weapons of all kinds were preserved. I took one in my hand, and offered him the value of a gold Napoleon for it. The mountaineer refused, saying it was not worth as much ; but I, thinking he refused because I offered too little, doubled it, but was again refused. . . . Finding, from my perseverance, that I did not comprehend the reason of his refusal, he addressed me, not without pride, in these words :—' These weapons were bequeathed by my grandfather to my father, and I must leave them to my sons.' There are two shops in Florence where a dealer in second-hand articles has curious weapons for sale, for the great families of the country."— *Assedio di Firenze*, vol. iv. note, p. 173.

maldo slew Ferruccio, and we felt grateful to Massimo d'Azeglio when we read the inscription which he has caused to be placed on one of the external walls of the church. The most remarkable objects within the church are two large reliefs by Luca della Robbia, which, although a little injured, are such as to ... but of what else can I speak, after having spoken of Ferruccio? It is twenty-eight miles from Gavinana to Pescia, and these sacred memories accompanied us all the way, and slept with us on our pillows at home."

CHAPTER VIII.

IN the continuation of the letter given in the preceding chapter, Giusti gives a lively description of a rustic ball to which he was invited in the little town of Pescia; a curious and amusing picture of country life and manners in Italy.

". . . As you are one of those who, when I return to Florence, after an absence of three or four months, ask me, 'What the devil were you about in Pescia?' I must tell you that yesterday we were at a rustic ball at the villa of a certain notary. Although invited without ceremony, and coming in our velveteen coats and walking-shoes, we were ushered into a superb room (a temporary wooden building), and we were made to pass through the garden, which is in a very early stage, and was full of clients, who, after having provided so many years for the Doctor's maw, have just discovered that the gentleman had a nose which likewise expected to be provided for. From the garden we entered the ground-floor of the house, and from that descended two or three steps lower, into the great ball-room, which is, in reality, the

entrance-hall, the door opening on the side opposite
the garden: you perceive how practice in law accustoms
a man to crooked ways and loopholes for escape. By
thus having made us enter the house at the wrong end,
and begin with the tail, the master contrives to im-
press you with due respect for himself, and to acquaint
you with the fact that he possesses a garden, besides
mystifying you as to the fact of his having been obliged
to give the ball on his ground-floor. Above the door
leading to the ball-room the orchestra was placed, but
so low that it blocked up one-third of the entrance ;
if it had been higher, the musicians would have
knocked their heads against the beam. A servant
was placed there as a sentinel, whose dress and face
were somewhat rustic, but his manners most courteous,
and, perhaps, even a little too courtier-like. Do not
suppose he was placed there to announce the visitors :
not at all ; he was there to call out, ' Beware of your
heads, gentlemen ; gentlemen, stoop your heads ; take
care how you pass, gentlemen ;' and sometimes enliven-
ing the warning, by, ' Gentlemen, the roof is low ; pray,
do not knock it down ;' and on the arrival of one of his
own acquaintance, ' Hallo! you ; stoop your pate, or
with one thrust you will bring down all the musicians ;
girls, look to your pumpkins (head dresses), that you do
not lose your caps.' Meantime, the master of the
house tripped forward, all delight, with a great cravat
put on in the last French fashion, and with a coat

I

fit for a government official ; but so happy, so polite, and with such frank cordiality, shaking all and each of us with both hands, and capering about. Accustomed as I am to that ease and those smiles which belong to and are riveted on certain infallible lips, and to conventional manners,— I was actually so dull, as at that moment to prefer this unpolished, chattering, awkward welcome to town etiquette. ' Here we are,' he shouted, ' quite at our ease, *sanfasson ;* a couple of fiddles, a few roasted chestnuts, a cup of wine, and, for the rest, you must accept a hearty welcome.' Then leading us to the ball-room—' Well, boys, have I not succeeded, eh ? I know what's what.—I was once young too. . . .' Just then, a peasant lad approached us : ' Where are your sisters ?' (shouted the host) ' you rascal ; why did you not bring your sisters ?'—' What could I do ? they have to get up early to-morrow morning. . . .' 'Get up early ? What does that signify ? Catch the moment as it flies. You lazy fellow—stay you here, and I will manage it.' To put on his hat, run out, and disappear, was the work of an instant. We, who were left behind, took the opportunity to pay our respects to the mistress, who we had not perceived whilst we were engaged with the doctor. She looked like a Corsican priest in a cap, and the cap like a great basket of endive. When she saw us, she rose from her seat. ' Welcome, gentlemen,' she said, fidgeting with her hands, as if she did not know what to do with them. ' I hope you are all well,—the girls will have dancing enough, and we—' 'Pray sit down, madam; you will do us a favour by remaining seated.'—As you please; but I have so much sitting; I must stand a little to rest myself: here, a little wine and lemonade; the wine is ready, and the lemons will soon be gathered. Betta, take the gentlemen over there.' Here I was guilty of a second sacrilegious thought by maintaining that in point of courtesy, and with all respect for Galateo,[1] that salad-head might rival the coiffures of fashion. Meantime the room was filled, the adjoining rooms were likewise filled, the partners were arranging themselves for the dance, the chatter of the women increased, and the orchestra, with a long scrape of the bow, prepare to fiddle away till midnight. The ball, however, could not begin because they waited for the doctor. Whilst waiting we took a survey of the ball-room, the cards, and the refreshments. The room might accommodate six quadrilles, and there were people enough for twenty, neither more nor less crowded than in fashionable balls. The floor was of clean bricks, and ranged round the walls were benches and chairs; there were screens of green silk fastened before groups of three wax candles placed at intervals; the screens protecting the eyes from too strong a light, in place of looking-

---

[1] A work by the Milanese Melchior Gioja, which, as a rule for good manners, is cited in Italy as Lord Chesterfield with us.

glasses to add to their brilliancy. The orchestra was made up of tables kept steady by wooden poles bound together with ropes, like a whitewasher's scaffolding; the philharmonic professors kept up a perpetual dialogue with the impatient crowd below. At the upper end of the room was a wooden clock with a pendulum, and the hands put back to let the mammas know at two in the morning it is not yet midnight; and thus even the clock is condemned by the notary to bear false witness. In the room to the right were three tables for cards. The curate, the judge, the doctor, and the blacksmith played one game; the tailor, an attorney, a student, the bell-ringer, the apothecary, the under-townclerk, and a dealer in oil played another; at the third table were placed a stone-cutter, a stocking-weaver, a mason, the standard-bearer, and the fishmonger. What disputes! What jabbering and accusations at two of the tables, whilst silence reigns, with rapping of the knuckles, at the third; but the game finished, squabbling and invectives from the silent set, enough to deafen one; the rules of the games allow talking in the two first, but enjoin silence in the third. —You should see the cheating that goes on; the doubts as to what the rules are, always renewed upon fresh accusations, as in the Convention, and every now and then an appeal to the lookers-on.

"The refreshment room is the kitchen. In one corner Betta is busy plucking fowls; in another, women, with their heads bent over a pot, are stirring something. At the fire stands a peasant, without his shirt, and such an apron! as large as a motuproprio,[1] is superintending the roasted chestnuts. The apron is indeed somewhat stained with blood, but this does not spoil the simile. A great rack against the wall, full of pots, pans, and dishes, is decorated with laurels. There are also suspended from the wall an array of kettles, muskets, saws, frying-pans, hedging-bills, cowskin shoes, ladles, swords, and halberds ; and below all, the Calendar is fixed, with a sonnet on the feast of the tutelar saint, and beside it, a picture of St. Anthony and his companions. In the middle of the kitchen a great table is prepared, and on it are bottles, flasks, decanters, cheeses, plates of *brigidini* (a sort of wafer), a great cloth of polenda,[2] the cheese-grater, and a hat. Meantime, whether from a draught at some opening, or that the great fire caused a current of air, the smaller feathers flew about here and there, upon plates, into cups, in the fire, and in the frying-pan where the chestnuts were roasting, which the master of the chestnuts resented by calling out to the servant girl,—

" ' In all this time that you have been plucking fowls, how is it you have not yet learned the right way ? '

" ' Who is meddling with you ? ' she instantly rejoined.

---

[1] *Motuproprio*, or mandate, signifies an autograph expression of sovereign will, countersigned by the Secretary of State.

[2] Polenda, a dish of maize-flour, the common food of the peasantry in Northern Italy.

"'Who is meddling with me? Why you, who send all the feathers flying about the room.'

"'Stuff! What should I send them to you for? You want something to grumble at: but you had better look after your chestnuts, that they are not, as usual, over-roasted.'

"'Mind yourself, you hussy! There, again, more feathers! Get yourself farther off with your basket, you gaby. Don't you smell them burning in the pan?—they catch at everything.'

"Just then arose a great hubbub; but as we were listening to this dialogue, we did not notice it. It was the doctor, returning with his victims; he entered the kitchen driving before him three figures, all out of breath.

"'Be quiet, now! What is the matter? What is the use of scolding? Courage, girls, take something. Betta, mind what you are about: you are covering everything with feathers.'

"'There, I told you so,' said the chestnut-roaster, with an air of victory.

"'Very well, sir,' exclaimed the girl, in a rage, 'there are the fowls, and he who likes to pluck them, may.'

"'I will pluck them,' said the Notary, 'Excuse me, gentlemen; I am so bothered with these people. Come, girls, drink, eat; there's enough for all. I cannot be both Martha and Magdalene.'

"Then, taking a thrush from the hands of Betta, he

seated himself in an instant, with the basket between his legs. The five or six birds remaining were plucked in a few minutes; and any one who did not know that he was the Notary would have supposed that he had done nothing all his life but pluck fowls. It is as well to know how to do everything.

"The music had begun. The scrape of the violins, however, would not have been heard in the kitchen (I ought to have said the refreshment room), had not a clarionet announced the opening of the ball; which in its shrill high notes reminded us of a bagpipe, and in its bass of the quacking of a duck. We, meantime, had made acquaintance, or rather had struck up an intimate friendship, with the last comers—we had obtained their confidence, and pledged ourselves to dance together the whole evening; and all this in the time the doctor took to pluck the fowls. But I, who am accustomed to go through the ceremony of introduction before asking a lady to dance, and am more attached to the usages of good society, and consequently more backward than my companions, should have been left in the lurch, had not one of the girls—seeing that the other two had already got partners, and afraid of being left sitting, by the fate which sometimes allows the most ill-favoured to be first chosen—said to me, nudging my elbow—

"'Are we to stop here, looking on?'

"I was immediately recalled to my duty, and offered

her my arm. We began with a lively, rustic dance, now banished from the city, but kept up in the country. After a quarter of an hour I was put into a quadrille. The barber, as master of the ceremonies, was dressed in his best, with a great beard and crop of hair, his jaws encased in two enormous whiskers, which were cut below his ears and projected forwards like two knives; or, for lack of a better comparison, like a pair of elephant's tusks, which one felt afraid of approaching too nearly, lest they should poke one's eye out. To show off his learning to us he gave the word of command for all the figures in French —plague take the varnish: *inavancatre, dimiscene, ballanzé, cudescià, grascene, scendidame, isciassé.* The peasants, who did not understand a word, and kept turning in their places, confused, and shoving up against one another, exclaimed, 'What does he mean by his *isciassé?* Let us dance in our own fashion; these gentlemen know that we are ignorant people.'

"At this, the inclination we had to laugh gave place to a more charitable feeling. Poor people, how modest and truly well bred they are in their simplicity! I am certain that the Parisian just arrived in our city, and seeing himself aped by us, must laugh in his heart as much as we could laugh at the barber. But which of us would have the courage to say to his country-man, who he sees made up after a French model,

'Come, come, we are all born in the Boot; let us live as in Italy; and let him who does not like it, make off?' But the scene beyond all was the waltz. The dance began by a woman and man, in a couple, advancing at a walk for a good bit, marking the time by motions of their head and body; then one after another catching the step, and at last making a long run, and holding one another round the waist with both hands, they began twirling and performing arabesques on the floor. But most of them, before they could catch the step, required to stop five or six times, and were knocked here, and knocked there, by couples who had started fairly; and then followed a zigzagging all over the room, and the most delightful confusion. At a quarter before eleven, when, according to country hours, the festivity was about to end, three villagers entered, two men in frock coats, and a lady dressed in a most exquisite *negligé.* We will pass over the bows and courtesies, the state of excitement of the doctor, and the embarrassment of the doctoress, in their endeavours to make room for them and to persuade them to sit down. I shall only give you the remarks which were heard on all sides:

" 'How! at this hour?'

" 'Look at the fools! dressed in morning coats. Look at their thin arms and figures!'

" And the girls added, 'How many petticoats do you think she has on?'

" In short, an exotic plant has as little *succès* up in the mountains, as an honest countryman would have who intruded himself in the *salons* of the capital. *Habent sua fata libelli*, &c.

" Between the dances, the peasant who saved our heads from the cross-beam supporting the orchestra, went round the room with a dish and a pair of scissors (the same which served to clean the fish and cut out the doctor's shirts), and, making the women seated under the candlesticks, rise, mounted on the chairs and snuffed the candles, leaving the marks of his shoe-nails on the straw bottoms; when he had finished his round, he stopped to converse, whilst perfuming the whole room with candle-snuff. He then returned, with a tub of chestnuts in one hand and brigidini (wafers) in the other, the doctor following close behind, with cups to pour out the wine. Among the party there was an old peasant woman belonging to the house, wearing a man's hat, like a bushel, on her head. One of us asked her in jest, ' Do not you dance, mistress ?' ' That I could, once,' she answered; ' in my time I was in request, and I did as well as any of them.' ' Well, but you are still young.' ' Why, I am past eighty.' You must have observed that after a certain age, years diminish; that after passing a line the past is past, and if before that period of life people who are forty-eight call themselves thirty, after it, people who are sixty call themselves ninety, and the ambition for a youthful complexion is succeeded by the ambition for wrinkles. The doctor now made a third in the group, exclaiming, 'Our granny here! Shivering, eh? We'll give you a dance, and let them see how you can perform.' To this all shouted 'Yes, yes—make her dance, make her dance, but with you, doctor—you must dance too, doctor.'—'Mosca, Mosca (the name of the leader of the band), play away.'—And the old woman was dragged into the midst of them, amid shouts and clapping of hands; she bobs her old head and begins to bridle her neck and jump about like a little cock; and having caught the time, up she gets on her tiptoes with her hands to her sides, till she looked like a spindle with handles. The doctor followed his partner with awkward gestures, throwing his legs about till they might have been taken for a pair of empty trousers when shaken. The laughter and shouts which resounded on all sides made a perfectly bacchanalian scene. Meantime a violent storm had arisen, with thunder, lightning, and torrents of rain. The hour which ought to have ended the ball was past, but our hosts had not the hearts to bid us be gone. They yawned, they stretched, they looked out of the window, and every now and then they opened the door and exclaimed, 'It seems as if it would clear.'—They asked what hour it was; and God knows they repented having been persuaded to put back the clock in the hall."

CHAPTER IX.

IN December, 1840, Giusti wrote a letter of advice to a boy entering school, which is not only interesting because it presents a faithful picture of the mind of the writer, and of the principles by which he was himself guided throughout his life, but because it is in these days read in the schools of Italy as a lesson to youth.

To Giovannino Piacentini.

"7th December, 1840.

" MY DEAR GIOVANNINO,

" I was sorry to have missed seeing you before you left for Lucca. I was anxious to say some things to you which it is desirable should be told a boy of your disposition when about to enter school ; I will therefore now write what I was unable to say, and I hope you will value the words of one to whom you have always shown affection. Remember that I do not presume to put myself in the place of your relations, or of those whose duty it is to watch over you where you now are, but I only wish to join them in encouraging you always to follow the path of virtue and truth.

" Before all, you ought to be aware of the blessings you already possess, that you may duly appreciate them and be grateful to God who has bestowed them on you, and likewise that you may be enabled to make a right use of them. You are a good boy; your mind has been awakened and well directed ; you are favoured by ortune and do not require to earn your livelihood by your brains. Besides these inestimable blessings, you have one still more inestimable, which is, that you belong to a family by whom you are sincerely beloved, and who will do all in their power for you. When you have attained my years, that is when you have learnt by experience in how few you can confide, you will know the reality of this blessing. I shall not therefore now address you on the subject, nor dwell upon that other advantage you possess, of being born in a good position in life—an advantage you should value, but not found your happiness upon. . . .

" Most people would begin by recommending to you application in study ; but I begin by recommending to you the practice of virtue. Learning is often a vain ornament, of little use in the business of life, and generally reserved for show on gala days, like tapestry and silver plate ; but virtue is of the first necessity, required every day, every moment. Believe me, the world would go on very well without learned men, but without good men everything would be in confusion.[1]

"You may hitherto, my boy, have naturally supposed that the companions with whom you have been educated would be the companions of your life ; but when we become free to choose for ourselves, we make new friends and many, perhaps too many, acquaintances, who go under the name of friends ; the truest, however, those who are nearest and dearest to our hearts, are always the friends formed in early youth, among our fellow-students. Young men who have a common desire for knowledge, such as you ought to have where you are now placed, are more disposed to form real friendships than those who only meet to satisfy a craving after pleasure : the sacred love of science unites the minds of men in an indissoluble tie with all who share in the same passion. Besides, from this period of life, and as long as you live, you will find yourself associated with men of all kinds and of all ages, and thus you learn to know them and to know yourself, whereas, at home, you always associated with your equals. But

---

[1] The estimation for learning in Italy is expressed by Maxime Du Camp, in a note to an article, "Naples sous le Roi Victor Emanuel," in the *Revue des deux Mondes*, published September, 1862, p. 6. "En Italie on *respecte* les gens de noblesse et les gens en place, mais on ne considère que les lettrés. En 1858, je visitais sur les bords de la Brenta une fort belle villa qui avait appertenu au général autrichen G —— homme de haute famille ; le *contadino* paysan qui me la montrait me dit, en parlant du général, c'était un grand seigneur mais sans littérature ' *senza lettere.*' "

beware of that absurd and hypocritical pedantry, which seizes on certain vain persons, who affect the old man before they have wrinkles or grey hairs.

" If your superiors in the college are satisfied with you, and show a preference towards you above your comrades, be grateful to them, but do not allow yourself to be carried away by vanity, nor use your advantages to set yourself up above your fellows. If you afterwards find that others are preferred before you, strive to do your duty and to deserve as much, but never envy any one. Envy, my dear boy, is the most hideous, the most self-tormenting of the passions, the basest which can contaminate the heart of man. The envious man feels himself low and mean compared with others ; and unable to shake off his meanness, he lives in perpetual strife and mortification with himself and with mankind. You have not and cannot have in you even the germs of this execrable vice, but the example of others might insinuate it into your heart. Guard yourself from it for your own sake, and for the sake of your nearest relations, and also for my sake.

" If you happen to fall into an error which may injure another, confess it frankly, even though no inquiry should have been made. You would not like to suffer for another's fault, then do not allow another to suffer for yours. Besides, he who confesses his faults has already begun to mend. This will cost you some effort at first, but your heart will afterwards experience that satisfaction which we all feel in allowing others to see us as we really are, and acting honestly.

" I will now give you some advice about your studies. Always treat your teacher with respect. Those who take pains to communicate knowledge to you, give you the key for the possession of an inestimable treasure, indeed, the only treasure a man may increase and guard jealously, with nothing to be ashamed of. Do not be discouraged in the study of the Latin language, which will be of the greatest service to you, and, if for no other purpose, for enabling you to comprehend your own better. When I was at college I was impatient at having to pore so many hours over Porretti's grammar ; now I am sorry I did not take more pains when it was required of me ; not because I have a mania to become a Latin scholar, but to use it as an aid in study and composition ; and I must confess, that later on in life it has given me double trouble to acquire enough to enable me even to read and understand a book in that language. Remember this is a study you must some time or other accomplish ; therefore, try and get over it as soon as you can ; you will thus please your relations, you will acquire one of many things you will have to remember, and you will possess a key which will open to you the history of a noble people, whose sons, although degenerate, still feel the greatness of their destiny.

" Meantime, do not neglect the study of the Italian language, which is your own, the most beautiful, the richest language in the world, superior in force, in dignity, and in sweetness to all modern languages, and which rivals the ancient. In this you will converse with your fellow-citizens ; in this you will transact business ; and in this you will follow up whatever profession you may please to adopt. It is not enough, therefore, to have it familiar on your lips, for unless you accompany the practice with the study of rhetoric, and learn to speak it correctly, it is like an instrument you have found in your house, but do not know how to handle.

" After preparing your lessons for school, you will have some time left for reading. I recommend you to begin, whilst your mind is plastic, with the Lives of Illustrious Men by Plutarch. The varied relation of so many glorious events, of so many noble and wonderful deeds, will charm and elevate you, and will inspire you more than ever with a love for virtue. I must, however, warn you, that when you enter the world you will not find men as they are described in that book. Not that such men cannot exist, or never did exist ; but when you are older you will know and discover for yourself the reason of this change. For the present, be satisfied with the worship of all that wears the appearance of virtue and greatness.

" I must ask your full attention to what I have next to say. Any one devoting himself to a life of study

K

must determine on pursuing one of three aims ; gain,
honour, or the satisfaction of his own mind. You do not
require to study for gain, and you may thank God, who
has preserved you from the danger of thus soiling your
mind and soul ; this aim, low in itself, generally ends by
debasing the heart and head of the man who makes it
his ulterior object, and converts the wholesome food of
science into poison.   I hope you will not allow yourself
to be too much allured by honour ; you are yet a child,
and cannot have learnt the bitter side of certain things
which outwardly bear a fair and pleasant aspect.
Honour is a dream, which has a powerful attraction for
all, but especially for the young ; but it is uncertain
and fallacious, like everything which depends on ourselves, erring and miserable creatures as we are.   You
have not yet had the opportunity of seeing, as I have,
honour refused to merit which did not know how to
stoop, and lavished on cowardly asses who were willing
to drag themselves in the mire, before the few in
authority, who they fear or bribe, or before the many,
who are always volatile and blind.   I do not propose
that you should fly to the other extreme, and despise
honour, because you see it grasped at by the mean
and unworthy, or to fly from it as from darkness.   Keep
your eye fixed on that which is good, and take delight
only in that ; all else is dirt, street-mire.   I can never
find sufficient words to warn you against seeking after
that which is not true honour, but its false image—I

mean the applause of every passing stranger or insignificant person, at the cost of your dignity and of your conscience. Socrates, the most learned of men, rather than flatter his fellow-citizens, who were of a very different stamp from the men of our days, chose to die; but his memory will never die.

" Study, then, rather for your own improvement, to train your character in the love of all that is refined and elevating, and to form for yourself a noble and delightful occupation, which may one day be of great service to yourself and to others. As you grow up to manhood, and enter into the world, you will know that life is not all as pleasant as you think it now. I am sorry to disturb your simple, confiding, affectionate nature ; but I cannot avoid telling you that you will not always find men as amiable and as disposed to help you. You will feel the need of advice, of consolation, of aid, and perhaps you will not be able to obtain them from your fellow-men. If you are not early accustomed to be sufficient for yourself, and to seek a refuge in your books, good and ingenuous as you are, you will live to be unhappy. I tell you this, because I have experienced it myself, and, young as I still am, and independent, I should often despond if I had not this solace, that I can shut myself up in my room, and forget present annoyances whilst meditating on books and on the recollections of men of the past. I do not mean by this to offer myself as an example, but as I know the affection and confidence you have in me, I think that by telling you my experience, you may the more easily be persuaded to follow my advice.

"The path now before you is all pleasantness, and strewn with flowers. Many dream that it is encumbered with thorns, but this is mere imagination; and if you become fond of study, you will see I am in the right.

"I have often embraced you when a child, charmed with your vivacity and innocence, and with the promise you gave of much future excellence of heart and head; but I hope, some years hence, to embrace you when a youth grown strong in study, and impressed with the necessity of pursuing the delightful, and, if delightful, easy career of knowledge. We shall meet again in the turmoil of the world; you, rejoicing in the full vigour and in all the hopes of youth, I, at a more serious time of life, verging on decline, sad, weary; perhaps disgusted. But it will always be my highest gratification to be able to offer you advice, and, perhaps, more useful and sounder advice than that which I now send you."

In the spring of 1841, Giusti was again in Pescia, where he had not spent that season for several years. One day, when watching a snail on a wall, which happened to fall in with the reflections passing in his mind, he composed one of his best-known lively little poems, of a moral rather than political character. He describes the occasion in the following letter :—

"MY DEAR ———, "Pescia, April.

"I came here to amuse myself for a week or a fort-night, and I am still here, without being able to say why, even to myself. It is six years since I spent a spring in the country, and I cannot tell you how much I am now enjoying it. We are in a valley bounded to the east, north, and west, by hills, more or less high, but all cultivated, so that there is not a foot of barren land to be seen. The town is situated in the midst of gardens, which here and there follow the course of the river by which it is divided. Fruit trees are scattered by thousands over the plain and hills, all in blossom, form-ing the most beautiful sight in the world. But I am not going to bore you with Arcadian descriptions, but confine myself to the fact that my health has improved and my mind has been restored to serenity. When we country people are transplanted beneath the shadow of the cupola of Brunelleschi, and when April arrives, and when, instead of a beautiful plain and range of hills facing the window, we see before us the front of a building, we feel suffocated, and are seized with that peculiar melancholy—that disease which the Swiss call *maladie du pays*, and the doctors, *nostalgia*.[1] Those who have tasted the amusements of the so-called great world cannot understand the pleasure of being confined within the limits of one's home, nor the refreshing

[1] Home-sickness.

influence of one's native air. Brought up as we have been to inhabit the same house from infancy, accustomed to the roads of the village and the country round, where we have walked with those dear to us, or in the company of our thoughts which speak to us of them, we feed on the food with which we have been nourished from childhood, and find in it our solace and comfort. The desire for a tranquil life, for the forgetfulness of all ills, and for peace, take possession of a man who is weary of the world, and who, after many years, returns to his home. Unhappy those who have no home! His native place is the longed-for haven of him who has crossed the tempestuous sea of life, and has escaped shipwreck. I have met with cosmopolitans who, from a foolish desire to make themselves citizens of the world, cannot rest at home in their own country. I like to think, that as plants vegetate better in one soil than in another, so we live and flourish better in the place in which we were born.

" Whilst making this and similar reflections during a walk in the country, I happened to stop by the way to watch a snail. By an association of ideas, I thought this little animal might become the living image of the thoughts which were crowding into my mind, and, reflecting on the vain arrogance of man and his undisciplined passions, on anger and on pride, I was ready to exclaim *Viva la chiocciola!* (Long live the snail!) Everything depends on seizing the suggestion of the moment. I took a fancy to the metre; and gathering together the ideas which had been floating in my mind, I strung the lines into a poem, and produced these light verses, the natural consequence of a liver refreshed by its native air, and of a head which every evening before ten o'clock lays itself to sleep upon the pillow of its home :—

" Viva la Chiocciola
Viva una bestia
Che unisce il merito
Alla modestia.
Essa all' astronomo
E all' architetto
Forse nell' animo
Destô il concetto
Del canocchiale
E delle scale
   Viva la Chiocciola,
   Caro Animale.

" Contenta ai comodi
Che Dio le fece,
Può dirsi il Diogene
Della sua spece.
Per prender aria
Non passa l' uscio :
Nelle abitudini
Del proprio guscio
Sta persuasa
E non intasa.
   Viva la Chiocciola,
   Bestia di casa.

" Di cibi estranei
  Acre prurito
  Svegli uno stomaco
  Senza appetito :
  Essa, sentendosi
  Bene in arnese,
  Ha gusto a rodere
  Del suo paese
  Tranquillamente
  L' erba nascente
     Viva la Chiocciola,
     Bestia astinente.

" Nessun procedere
  Sa colle buone,
  E più d' un asino
  Fa da leone :
  Essa al contrario,
  Bestia com' è
  Tira a proposito
  Le corna a se
  Non fa l' audace,
  Ma frigge e tace.
     Viva la Chiocciola,
     Bestia di pace.

" Natura, varia
  Ne' suoi portenti
  La privilegia
  Sopra i viventi,
  Perchè, (carnefici
  Sentite questa)

Le fa rinascere
Perfin la testa ;
Cosa mirabile
Ma indubitabile.
 Viva la Chiocciola,
 Bestia invidiabile.

" Gufi dottissimi
Che predicate
E al vostro simile
Nulla insegnate
E voi girovaghi
Ghiotti, scapati,
Padroni idrofobi,
Servi arrembati ;
Prego a cantare
L' intercalare.
 Viva la Chiocciola,
 Bestia esemplare."

There are neither Tuscan words in this little poem, nor allusions which require explanations, to apologize for an attempt at translation, which would only divest it of the fresh grace and gaiety of the metre, constituting a charm alike to the foreign reader and to him who delights in the musical sound of his native language.

CHAPTER X.

IN 1841 Giusti had produced a greater number of poems (since published) than any previous year. Besides The Chiocciola, he wrote, Lines to a Friend, On a Singer having a Cold, On the Humanitarians, To Girolamo Tommasi, The Ball, Memories of Pisa, and *La Terra dei Morti*, " The Land of the Dead," a reply to the insulting language of Lamartine, when speaking of modern Italy, and addressed to the Marchese Gino Capponi, concluding,

Veglia sul monumento
Perpetuo lume dal sole,
E fa da torcia a vento :
Le rose, le viole,
I pampani, gli olivi,
Son simboli di pianto :
O che bel camposanto
Di fare invidia ai vivi !
Cadaveri, alle corte
Lasciamoli cantare
E vediam questa morte
Dov' anderà a cascare.

Tra i salmi dell' Uffizio
C' è anco il Dies irae :
O che non ha a venire
Il giorno del Giudizio ?

Besides this, *Il Mementomo,* " The Monument ;" *Il Re Travicello,* " King Log ;" *La Scritta,* " The Contract of Marriage ;" *Avviso per un Settimo Congresso,* " Advertisement for a Seventh Scientific Meeting ;" and, lastly, *Gl' Immobili e i Semoviventi,* " The Stationary and those who are only Half Alive."

Early in the year 1843 Giusti was called to the sick-bed of his favourite uncle ; and he writes as follows to the Marchese Gino Capponi, from his birth-place, Monsummano :—

"Monsummano, 19 February, 1843.

" MY DEAR MARCHESE,

" I found my uncle in a deplorable condition, of which I had not formed the least idea, even after the indifferent accounts I received last Thursday. The sight of him, confined to his bed, was such a shock to me, that for some time I was so overcome I could not utter a word. Those who have watched him day by day cannot perceive how much he has fallen off ; but I, who have been two months without seeing him, felt my heart sink within me the instant I was taken up to him. He frets and complains, and cannot find rest in any posture ; he neither sleeps nor eats, and hears continual noises in his ears; his mouth and his stomach are in as bad a state as they can be; his strength is failing; and, what is worse, he has had several strokes of paralysis, more or less severe, at intervals, in the tongue and in the right hand. You will believe what a trial it is to see and to listen to him. My heart is torn, yet I am anxious to put every restraint on myself in his presence, that I may not annoy him with my grief. There is one peculiarity in his character, but not the less painful, that he has the habit of turning his own infirmities into ridicule. Everybody is amused, and thinks this a good sign; but it gives me double sorrow, as I know the invalid, whilst laughing at his sufferings, is struggling against the pain for which there is no remedy but smiles. Added to all this, we are here in a country unprovided with any physician of reputation, far away from the friends to whom he is most attached, and without a single individual who understands those delicate and disinterested attentions which are perhaps more efficacious than physic. You may, then, imagine what is the state of my poor uncle, and my state, who see him sinking before my eyes—I, who have always felt to him more like a son than a nephew. I will send for, or come and fetch, Bufalini;[1] but this is a delicate subject, which I can only gradually approach with him, for fear of increasing the malady, as he has such a dislike to new things and new faces. To keep

[1] An eminent Florentine physician.

him as quiet as I can, I have closed the door to many, and I find it will be necessary to exclude many more of this place who are indefatigable, tedious, noisy, and idle visitors. The women, who certainly are more in the habit of attending sick-beds than we men, and who administer those kind offices which are of such service, are, however, cursed with the desire of making up to themselves for the hardship of temporary silence, by relating, over and over again, every particular of his illness for the benefit of those present, as well as of the suffering patient. I sometimes join in the gossip, for we must take the flies with the honey. He has a stove in the room, and the servants and visitors together had contrived to heap on enough wood to make a fire fit for the infernal regions ; rather considering his habits when well, than what is desirable for him in illness. No one knew what ought to be done, and there was no one to give orders ; so the patient had the worst of it, as he is nailed to his bed, in the hands of Goths and Vandals : which proves that where a man has not attentive and well-trained servants, he is ill off unless waited on by his own relations. I shall remain here until I see him restored to health. I am the more glad to do this, as he expressed himself much pleased when he heard I had started to come to him, although he is constantly saying to me, ' Go and amuse yourself ; go to your mother ; you will find this very dull.' *You* will not suppose that I either feel it dull or have the least desire for amusement. God grant that he may recover! but these strokes of paralysis make me anxious."

A few weeks later, Giusti writes to Luigi Alberti, an advocate and man of literary tastes, the editor of an annual called *La Rosa di Maggio* :—

" Monsummano, 20 March, 1843.

" MY DEAR GIGI,

" In a few days we shall meet ; as, although my uncle is not much better than on my arrival here, he has so much resolution that he wishes to try if he may find those advantages in Florence which, until now, he has been unable to obtain here. Whilst he is ill I am not able to resume my usual habits, as I have resolved not to leave him a moment. . . . I have heard all about ——— ; but much as I should lament for his sake, if it be true what is believed by those who, in the affairs of this world, do not, and will not, look below the surface, I am equally pleased to find in you, who retain the pure and delicate sentiments of boyhood, that you do not allow yourself to be dissuaded from your belief by mere outward appearances, and that you honour your friend by a kinder interpretation of his conduct. My dear Gigi, leave evil-thinking to those who find in calumny a miserable relief from the uneasiness of their own consciences. The man of a generous heart dispenses his treasure with a liberal hand, and bestows it on all alike, knowing that he cannot be impoverished by such prodigality. Besides, we must remember that there are sometimes trials in the inmost sanctuary of family life which none know of; there are tears which would flow freely and openly, but which are checked as they rise at the remembrance of an offence known only to ourselves. Who can measure the gulf which a word, an act, sometimes suddenly opens between us and those most sacred to our hearts? And though reason or convenience may sometimes fill up this gulf, the heart is never again filled. We ourselves, my dear Gigi, are the only true judges and witnesses of our own thoughts, whilst these great mysteries are left in the darkness to which they are fated. It is only the foolish who are in a hurry to lift up every veil, and, even when they see nothing, boast they have always been able to see, for no other reason but that they may not be supposed to have made the attempt and failed. . . .

" You are quite right not to leave her who is your best half alone in her sorrow. Blessed is he who can say that he has dried a tear; more blessed he who can dry the tears from those eyes which have kindled the flame of love in his breast. I hardly know whether it is pride lurking beneath the folds of piety, but when called upon to assist the woman we had adored and served with trembling, and when a sudden but generous impulse of the heart prompts us to hasten to her succour, the pleasure we experience is so great that it compensates for a whole life of misery. Thank kind Nature who permits you to taste of this happiness so early, and in such sweet company.

"I am delighted to hear that my distinguished and most dear friend, Gino Capponi, discovered nothing exotic in the verses that I gave you for the *Rosa di Maggio*. I certainly did not find them in books or fashions rained upon us from abroad, but in my own heart, which is truly Italian, and which feels every now and then a longing to rise from this mire in which I also have imbrued my hands too deeply, when touching the chord of satire. . . ."

In May, Giusti writes to Giuseppe Vaselli, a distinguished literary man and poet, of Siena :—

"*Florence, 5 May, 1843.*

"MY DEAR BEPPE,

"I ought to thank you for your attentions to my mother, and I would have done so by word of mouth, if the unhappy state of my poor uncle had not obliged me to give up the journey to Rome and Naples. My mother, passed through Siena again twenty days later, but did not seek you out for fear of troubling you. I scolded her for it, telling her that she might have treated you like myself, and I added, if you had known of her having been there, you would have been vexed.

"I have now for more than two months been watching the slow but inevitable decline of a man whom I have looked upon as a second father, and who, in many respects, harmonized with my nature. If you can conceive the combination of great natural talents, a high sense of rectitude, frankness, experience of the world without injury to his heart, the utmost cordiality, a temper always firm, always even, and always full of gaiety, you have the image of my dearest uncle Giovacchino. God grant that as I have always lived friends with him, I may be enabled to resemble him! The loss of such a being cannot be compensated to me by anything on earth; yet I see that end approaching, and I have not the courage either to hope, or to cease to hope. He has up to this moment suffered the pains of hell; though now tranquil, alas! it is the tranquillity of the tomb. He is sleeping beside me, and I hear his heavy, slow, deep-drawn breath, and with what a heart, you may imagine, my dear Beppe. I no longer seem to live either for others or for myself, but only for him, and I do all I can to keep him as long as possible in life, at least to delay one more day losing him. If it is decreed that this dear head must bow beneath the Hand which strikes it down, never to rise again, I will hasten away to seek a refuge with you, when I have arranged his affairs; I had resolved upon this as soon as I heard the danger was imminent. I hope, I shall not be prevented, for in the solitude which I see

L

before me, I look around, and only see you. I never
yet was present at the solemn scene of a man departing
this life, and I must learn what death is from him for
whom I would give all the years I have hitherto lived
and all those which remain. . . ."

A few days later, on the 21st May, Giusti lost the
uncle to whom he was so much attached, and in the
next of his published letters, dated Pescia, the 23d June,
we find merely an allusion to this loss, and to his severe
affliction. In the summer of 1842 he met with a singular accident, which, owing to the nervous state of his
body, left an impression on his mind from which he
never wholly recovered. When walking in the Via de'
Banchi, in Florence, he was attacked by a furious cat,
and though he did not receive any bodily injury, the
start and terror produced such an effect, that he frequently alludes to this accident in subsequent letters,
and it appears to have shaken his whole system. Soon
afterwards, his physician discovered the germ of an
internal disease, which conducted him to an early grave,
and embittered the rest of his days. He sought relief
and abstraction for his mind in literary labours, but the
more necessary they became to his happiness, the less
capable his body was becoming to endure the strain of
composition. He alludes to his sufferings in a letter
to Professor Atto Vannucci, the present librarian of
the Magliabecchian Library, in Florence. Professor

Vannucci is an elegant writer and classical scholar, the author of several highly esteemed works, a good citizen and patriot; his simple, honourable, and dignified character, no less than his genius, has gained for him the respect he so well deserves.

" MY DEAR VANNUCCI,

" I am sorry to hear that your eyes continue to trouble you, and I hope that you will not make them worse, by overhaste to use them. Your long letter, which, as you will believe, gave me much pleasure, reminded me of the trouble it must have cost you to write it, and, though against my own interest, I therefore beg you to cut me short, and even not to send me a single line, if likely to injure you. You think that you have not been sufficiently diligent in study, as all think who really know anything; but I am convinced that you have sufficient range for your thoughts in what you have hitherto seen or read to be able to dispense awhile with books, at least until your sight has recovered its activity and strength. I lament to have a warning to set before you, in the friend who is dearest to my heart, but you see that Gino Capponi ended by destroying his sight, from having persevered in using his eyes at the very time when he ought to have given them rest. I am obliged myself, from another cause, to abstain from sitting too long at my writing-table; and if I had

L 2

yielded to my inclinations, I should by this time have been fit for nothing, because writing is as exhausting to the body as it is refreshing to the spirit. If the choice should lie between the two, let the body go; but if we may avoid ruin to health by the delay of a month, a year, or even two years, we must comply, in order to return to work with greater strength and safety. You will not want friends to read to you and to write to your dictation, and you ought to recur to them, and to spare yourself as much as you can. This is not only desirable for your own sake, but also for the sake of the cause of truth, and for the love you bear your fellow-creatures, as you are one of the few who are not afraid to profess both openly.

"You say truly that mental labour must be my greatest consolation; but if I take up a book I am obliged to put it down again immediately, from a sensation of weariness which seizes upon me. Writing is out of the question, and my imagination is almost dried up. If my happier days had lasted, I might have carried through many works which I have begun, or mentally composed, and afterwards laid aside. Besides the Proverbs,[1] I meant to have written some remarks on the rural manners of the mountains as well as of the plains, and to have inserted here and

---

[1] Giusti's work on Italian proverbs was published after his death, under the title, "Raccolta di Proverbi Toscani, con Illustrazioni cavata dai Manoscritti di Giuseppe Giusti, ed ora ampliata ed ordinata."

there traditions relating to them. I intended to have collected the notes I had taken on Dante, and to have published them in the form of letters to friends, in which, without writing them all over again, I might have brought together everything that has been said by the best authorities on the divine poem, and explained my own views on its internal signification. I have had many satires running in my head, or on hand, among which one entitled *L'Adunanza*, " The Meeting," in which I proposed to aim a blow at the various parties in literature ; and *Il Vivaio*, or " The Manufactory for Candidates," in which I intended to have exposed the way by which certain persons rise to office. . . . Among other compositions, I had written a kind of romance, and a novel, both founded on facts which I had myself witnessed, and in which I intended to have held up to the light some of the absurd and mean conduct exhibited in the last ten or twelve years. You see what a quantity of work I had in hand. But I felt myself capable of accomplishing all, and I revelled in the thought of the delicious hours I should enjoy in composition and writing. All these projects, these dreams and fair hopes, now lie buried in a corner of my mind, and if they occasionally try to waken up, pain drives them back again into shade and silence. When I compare myself now to the man I was a year ago, I am almost astonished to see how, before an entire break-up, one can thus gradually decay. Either I do

·not understand myself, or I am an altered man. Nothing remains entire of what I was, except my faith and attachment to certain principles. And to add to my suffering, life had just begun to be smooth before me. Certain family disagreements, certain vexations which I had brought on myself, had wholly disappeared, and now my health has all of a sudden abandoned me, and bound me hand and foot, heart and head.

" To survive so great a part of myself is a calamity which exceeds in bitterness all that can be endured or imagined, and I esteem that man happy who descends to the tomb in the full enjoyment of his faculties. At the first alarm, on feeling an insidious and terrible complaint insensibly creeping over me, I often said to myself: Oh, that my mind, at least, may be spared as long as I live. . . ."

Giusti endeavoured to find consolation for an affliction from which he inwardly shrank, in recalling the many blessings sent him by Providence ; and he expresses these sentiments in a letter to Marco Tabarrini, a young man of great talents, who distinguished himself later, in 1848, and again in 1859, when he was of much service to Baron Ricasoli, and he thus made amends for having accepted office under the Austrians, which, at the time Giusti writes, exposed him to the censure of his countrymen.

To Marco Tabarrini.

" DEAR MARCO,

"You are right. The story of Luca della Robbia is very touching.[1] Such strong, generous characters almost surpass our comprehensions, who are born in an age which has been paralysed, and is incapable of great crimes as of great virtues. These men hearkened to God ; we hardly listen to the lessons of the priest : manly ideas of morals and of religion were to them both a restraint and a spur ; in these days, all thought of retribution is cold within us, and with many even the fear of the devil. . . . To reply frankly to your question : I have met with men who would hardly soil their linen, which can be washed, and yet do not seem aware that they are themselves sunk in the deepest mire of abominable vices. On the other hand, I have met with men who, in the midst of filth, have kept their hands clean. To which would you desire to belong ? . . . I thank the Supreme Disposer of good and ill for three things. First of all, I thank Him for having given me at my birth a moderate fortune, to increase which I never

[1] In the life of Luca della Robbia, by Vasari, we find related that he was so resolved and so earnest to make himself perfect in his art, that he worked day and night, and that often when his feet were benumbed with cold he sat with them in a basket of shavings, rather than stir from his work, to warm them at the fire.

have done, and never will do, anything that is base ; next, for having made me feel, in time, the necessity of cultivating my mind, and of seeking a refuge within myself ; and lastly, for having preserved me from all charlatanism, and given me a free spirit, and a tongue ready to own and to ridicule my own failings and the follies of my early youth. Whenever I retrace the footsteps of the past, and severely scrutinise the recesses of my conscience, I find an infinite number of errors and defects which grieve me, and provoke self-condemnation ; but in the midst of this inward conflict the consoling thought arises, that I have known how to retrieve my errors, and I am thus more unhappy than desponding. . . ."

The serious thoughts which his state of health suggested to his mind are thus expressed by Giusti on the occasion of some misfortune which had befallen his friend, Giuseppe Vaselli :—

"MY DEAR BEPPE,

"I have long known of your affliction, and if I did not tell you so, it was because I would not touch the wound when it was fresh. . . .

". . . I believe that God sends the solemn lessons of adversity to those capable of feeling them most, because it is from sorrow, and only from sorrow, that great things are born ; and strong characters spring

from affliction, like flowers on the thorn. In prosperity
man is careless, improvident, barren. The finer qualities of the heart and of the intellect either do not
show themselves or do not exist in those who are
blessed by fortune ; a calamity sends out sparks as
steel does from flint. But *you* did not need this most
hard trial to be considered a good and honest man ;
yet misfortune has fallen upon you, and in the severest
form. . . . This life is, and always will be, a mystery.
I have myself nearly lost my head and my health by a
wretched mad cat, which attacked me in the streets of
Florence. Both my medical men and my own reason
assured me that I had not been injured. I could see
with my own eyes that the place was sound and healthy,
but my imagination continued to torment me for weeks
and months, and I experienced the truth of the old
saying : ' Minus afficit sensus fatigatio quam cogitatio,'
and I felt ill, very ill, in spite of all the excellent
reasonings of others and of myself. . . .

"I have spent October and part of November on
Monte Catini ; the day after to-morrow I shall return
to Pescia, and by no means willingly. If you ask me
why, I cannot give you any reason, except that I feel at
home up here, and that everywhere else I am like a
bird without a branch to rest on. To drive away low
spirits and the beginning of a liver complaint, I have
returned to horse exercise ; the horse knows as little as I
do where we are going, but we jog on in kindness to one

another, and we have hitherto returned home safe and
sound, and in love and harmony.   At one time I was a
good horseman, or at least tolerable, but I have not
been on horseback for ten or eleven years.   I make the
tour of these hills, I visit all the little villages, and lead
a wandering life, but not wholly without profit. . . ."

The popularity of Giusti's poetry, ever on the increase, raised up a host of imitators, who attempted to
pass off their feeble productions for his.   The frequent
appeals made to him to declare against such nefarious
proceedings at length produced the following lively
refutation, addressed to the Marchese Carlo Torrigiani,
a gentleman whose philanthropic labours made him an
appropriate channel of communication with all classes
in Florence :——

" *Warning for the Press and for the Pen acting
without the permission of those in Authority.*

"The author of the burlesques below-mentioned
begs from his heart to thank the collectors of his vaga-
bond rhymes ; but having scruples in decking himself
out with borrowed plumes (*penne*, plumes, or pens),
from a certain paternal jealousy, and also because he
does not wish that the worshippers of the Muses should
take him for a kind of Commissioner for the Foundling
Hospital, obliged to receive and support their bantlings,

declares, that the only children he claims as his own, up to July, 1843, are the following " :—

He then proceeds to give a list of thirty-six poems in circulation, and nine additional, which, though his own, he considers less worthy of acknowledgment ; and continues :—

" All the rest of the satires which circulate under the same name have been fastened on the author, either by the carelessness of those who have made the collection, or by the mean trick of certain persons who, wishing to bite and not having the courage to show their teeth, lurk concealed under another's hood, and bark at all who pass. The author, once for all, protests that he has never aimed at, nor ever will aim at, any particular person, or isolated fact, except in so far as these relate to the general interests, as in ' The Coronation,' ' The Scientific Meeting,' &c. He detests all personal satire, for three reasons : first, because it is an offence against social comfort ; secondly, because it limits the range of the art of composition ; thirdly, because few rogues and no absurd persons deserve even notoriety. May the public and the author in future understand one another."

Not only was Giusti's poetry accepted with delight by those who saw in him one of the best champions of their country's cause, and by others whom it was intended to elevate and improve, but it was read and feared by those who fell under its just castigation ; even Government officials tried by flattery to mitigate the severity of his pen. Giusti was, however, of far too generous a nature to dwell with pride or exultation on such petty triumphs, and his greatest glory was the approbation he received from men who were looked up to as honours to Italy—from Manzoni, Grossi, and his friend the Marchese Gino Capponi.[1]

[1] Giusti's name, as that of the "Anonymous Tuscan," was by this time bruited through Italy, with that kind of underhand mysterious celebrity which perhaps is the most flattering and emphatic of all the forms of fame. He was known as equal to the great writers of his nation, &c.—*British Quarterly Review*, p. 33, Feb. 1853.

CHAPTER XI.

IN February, 1844, the physicians having recommended a journey, Giusti visited Rome and Naples, accompanied by his mother, during which time he kept a journal, from which we give a few extracts :—

"I saw Siena again with the pleasure which one feels at beholding a longed-for friend. . . . As we approached Rome, and when still at some distance, I fancied I should see sarcophagi, or the ruins of ancient buildings; but imagination and desire in vain strove to discover them in a miserable hovel or wretched tavern. What a state of depopulation and abandonment! the ancient empress of the world is surrounded by a desert. Here and there we met with a tree, flourishing just enough to prove the land would yield to cultivation if the hand of man would lend itself for this purpose. The *vetturino* and my mother's maid, both accustomed to see not a rood of land left bare at home, kept exclaiming every instant, 'If we could only have this in Tuscany!'. . . Here we are, at last, in Rome. The elevation of the cupola of St. Peter is not graceful, like that

of Brunelleschi, which is, indeed, a true miracle of
art. From a distance, Rome appears scattered in all
directions. . . . St. Peter's is vast and rich, but there is
too much display of wealth. . . . In the modern buildings there is generally pomp and space, but true magnificence, grandeur, and the marvellous is confined to the
remains of antiquity. The Colosseum is something which
it is impossible to conceive. It were as well to visit it
last of all, because it diminishes the value of everything
else. Arches and columns may be seen everywhere,
but in the Colosseum you behold the Roman people.
The descriptions of this building, and of what was
enacted here, appear the mere dreams of antiquarians
and romance writers ; but once seen we believe even
more than we have been told. I left it so filled with
reflections, so deeply penetrated with the sight, that all
the rest appeared as nothing. I believe I remained
two hours without ascending to the top, and, for-
tunately, there was no one else there, for a swallow-
tailed coat would have disturbed me among the togas
and the visions in which I lived at that moment. I
seemed to behold an immense population, full of valour,
and armed with swords, crowding up those steps, and
thousands of faces, unlike ours, one above another,
looking down from those benches at the gladiators and
wild beasts : and I saw the wild beasts themselves
rushing out of those dens, and rivers of water gushing
forth from those subterranean conduits, and I heard the

applause and the groans ; the visions I had conjured up were too vivid for the grass growing amidst the ruins to dispel. . . . The pavement and the quantity of mud are what spoil Rome. A fine city ill paved or ill kept is like a room with fine furniture and a dirty floor, or paved with uneven bricks ; or it is like a person in rich and magnificent clothes, with shoes full of holes. . . ."

At Naples, Giusti renewed his friendship with the poet Alessandro Poerio, whom he had known in Florence, and who fell fighting for Venice in 1849. He also met again his friend, the brother of the poet, the Baron Carlo Poerio, whose virtues as well as his sufferings in a Neapolitan dungeon have since made him celebrated throughout Europe.

" Pompei," Giusti continues, " stands alone of its kind ; but the pictures and the stuccoes remind one of the effeminate days of Rome. I must confess that, judging by the beauty of the frescoes and paintings here, the Arts have hardly yet retraced their steps. It is an unspeakable annoyance to have one of the usual guides at your side to inform you, here Sallust walked ; here Cicero washed his hands ; there Livia combed her hair, &c. What can it signify to me to conjecture all this, when I know for a certainty that the Romans inhabited this place, and left the serious cares of the Republic and the fatigues of war to seek refreshment amidst these delights ? The ruins speak for themselves ; the heart understands, and that is enough. For the rest, the figures or decorations, when they are found entire, appear as fresh as if made yesterday, if the merits of the work did not remind us that we are below ground. As reverence for authority increases in the ratio of distance, so the estimation and care for antique works is greater according as we are removed from the epoch when they were called into existence. As they are consumed by time they appear to grow in greatness, and a ruin, a relic, a fragment, speak more to the inquiring mind than the beauty of an entire monument in its magnificence. . . . The skeletons are all that remain; but as the beauty and strength of a man can be proved by a human skeleton, so the beauty and grandeur of these works is proved by one of these naked and worn remains."

On their way home, Giusti and his mother were halting at a village halfway between Capua and Mola di Gaeta. A party of travellers were seated at the same table with them. In the course of conversation, their Tuscan accent discovered them to be natives of Central Italy, and, hearing they came from Pescia, one of the travellers remarked, " From the city of Giusti?" upon which another added, " Of that celebrated poet?" A long eulogium followed, when a third asked if they were acquainted with him. There was a pause; and Giusti's mother looked at him and blushed, whilst her son himself answered in the affirmative. " Is ne young or old?" " Young," answered his mother.—

"And handsome?" asked one of the ladies present. At this question there was another pause. It was Giusti's turn to blush, as his mother looked at him with a smile. The truth was soon told, to the gratification of the travellers. This little scene of homage, amidst the number of flattering compliments he was in the habit of receiving, gave him double pleasure, because it was offered him in the presence of his mother.

Giusti wrote from Naples to the Marchese Gino Capponi, and to Andrea Francioni:—

"MY DEAR MARCHESE,   " February, 1844.

"Every day here has passed in a succession of wonders, and I have my head so full, so crowded with sights, that I do not know how to describe them. The two days I spent in Rome I only saw stones, but stones which inspired me with an old and a new life; in Naples, until this moment I have seen nothing of works of art; but the men with whom I have become acquainted, and the nature by which I am surrounded, fill me with joy and consolation.

".. . The Poerios have overwhelmed me with kindness, and introduced me to persons of the highest distinction of every kind. This is a country which has in it much that is good, much that is bad. . . . I do not know to which side the balance leans, but at all events one sees and feels here, there is something great and promising. I

M

lament that habit of scanning one another's faults, even where we agree in opinion, which is so injurious to us, and so much regretted by all who love Italy. The old do not trust the young, nor the young the old ; the latter are accused of being too slow, the former of being too precipitate. I am at great pains to converse with every one I meet, and am always confirmed in the old and bitter truth, that there is a want of understanding among ourselves. As I have always been rather the friend of moderation than of popular violence, I cannot tell you with what reverence I listen to the words of certain persons, or with what disgust to the senseless talk of others. Here, too, that bad habit prevails of calling prudence fear, and audacity courage ; but we must treat them with charity, because their wounds are fresh, and their passions dark and present. . . ."

To Andrea Francioni.

"Naples, 28 February, 1844.

" DEAR DREA,

" I promised you to write, and I keep my promise ; but my letter will be short, because the time is hardly sufficient to see the principal things here. I will not tell you anything of the government, because a few days are not long enough for an examination into that question, especially for one who has never had any connexion with it ; and besides, in a country of thieves one must have an eye to one's luggage. Therefore, it is best to keep one's mouth shut.

"Of Rome, I may say I saw nothing but the stones, but stones full of life and history. The Campo Vaccino, the Colosseum, and a thousand other remains of Roman greatness are beyond all imagination. Here I have seen both stones and men. The bay is worth seeing for itself: Pompeii stands alone in the world, as well as the museum of bronzes, and the objects found there and in Herculaneum. The coast from Posilippo to Cape Misenum is a perfect succession of wonders. Pozzuoli, Baia, and Cuma, retain only the vestige of Roman luxury and splendour, but that little is enough to compensate for all we have lost. I examined these places with a weary and almost dull spirit, from my infirm health, which would not quit me; but their sight refreshed my soul. The only annoyance is that tiresome commentary dinned into your ears by the guardians of the several places—a commentary which leaves your brain in the state in which it is left by the commentators on Dante. According to these guides, Cicero is ubiquitous, as you cannot stir a step without being told, 'This was Cicero's villa.' I do believe that, between Rome and Sicily, more stones have been baptized than men. Incredulous as I am, however, of such tales, I know I am visiting places once inhabited by Greeks, Romans, Saracens, Normans, and Spaniards. What a mixture of races! What food for the imagination! What a

range for thought! Another distressing thing is the
restorations of statues and antique bronzes. They
have attached to a wonderful torso of Antinous, arms
and legs which look like gloves and stockings, filled
with flour. This want of reverence for ancient art can
only exist in the dull animal souls of presumptuous and
clumsy artisans; true artists would indignantly spurn
such sacrilege. Michael Angelo alone, in his restorations of the Dying Gladiator and of the Laocoon, has
equalled the chisel of the ancients, yet, when asked to
restore the legs of the Farnese Hercules, he at first
refused; when pressed, he complied; but when about
to fix them in their place, he dashed them to pieces in
anger and expiation: yet he was the sculptor of
Moses, of Night, of *Il Pensiero*, and of other trifles of
the kind. For him who has eyes to see, a fragment is
enough; and he who cannot construct an entire figure
out of this, and fill up what is wanting for himself,
need not go and see. Among more recent works, I
have seen most beautiful frescoes by Il Zingaro, although
misused by time, and suffering from neglect. We use
such treasures as the prodigal does his pockets—taking
care of them when they are empty. There are also many
fine monuments, among which that to one of the three
brothers Sanseverino, who was poisoned by an uncle,
is beautiful and very touching. At San Martino, there
is a painting by Spagnoletto, so fine that it would buy
many of our pictures.

" I began with promising you a short letter, yet I do not know how to finish, although I have not told you the hundredth part of what I have to tell."

The improvement which had taken place in Giusti's health during the journey did not prove permanent, and he had hardly returned to Florence, when he was taken ill, and obliged again to desist from his studies. He accordingly went to Leghorn, to try the effect of sea air, and spent a few weeks there with his friend, Enrico Mayer. From Mayer's house, Giusti wrote to Ranieri, a Neapolitan, celebrated no less for his philosophical studies than for having been the faithful and attached friend of the poet Leopardi :—

"Leghorn, 15 June, 1844.

" MY DEAR RANIERI,

" I had hardly returned to Florence when I was attacked again by my usual indisposition, and I passed April and May between my bed and my sofa. This is the true cause of my long silence to you and to many others, to whom I feel a desire, as well as a duty, to write, without having the strength to fulfil either. I am now at Leghorn, trying sea air and baths, and I shall remain here all August, if I am not caught by the leg by some other demon.

" I was speaking of you to Niccolini, and he praised your writings highly to me, and expressed himself desirous of seeing you in Florence. From that time I have heard no more, as I have been always in the country, far from my friends, far from my studies, far from every pleasure, and only occupied with a search after health, in the absence of which I am weighed down under an insupportable burden . . . I, who never until now gave a thought to the comforts of life, have had to study them with more trouble than I can describe. . . . But let me drop this melancholy subject, and seek consolation in the proverb, After the bad comes the good. . . ."

Whilst at Leghorn, Giusti learnt that, without his knowledge, an edition of his verses, full of errors, had been published. This caused him considerable annoyance, and added to his physical sufferings. Believing that his death was approaching, and that he would not be able to justify his works to the public, he wrote a long letter to Professor Vannucci, entreating him to preserve his reputation after his departure, by disowning for him this publication. The letter was, however, never sent, and a few years later was found by his survivors among his papers. This year Giusti, accordingly, published an edition of his more serious compositions, dedicating the work to the Marchesa Luisa d'Azeglio, the daughter of Manzoni, and the wife of the Marchese Massimo d'Azeglio. Enrico Mayer helped him in the labour of correcting the press ; and often when Giusti was too weak to use the pen, he took it from him, and wrote from his dictation. This edition appeared in 1845, under the title "Versi;" the first which had appeared in print revised and acknowledged by the author. For the two preceding years his health had precluded composition, but in 1845 he brought out his most celebrated poem, *Il Gingillino*, which he dedicated to the poet Alessandro Poerio, in gratitude for some lines Poerio had addressed to him when at Naples, and which ran as follows :—

Il carme tuo pien di' saette vola
Che fanno immedicabile ferita ;
È marchio la tua vigile parola ;
Sulle fronti dei Re s' imprime ardita ;
Nè per la turba letterata sola
Va ; ma su bocche popolari ha vita,
Nella frequente via rapida scende,
Là s' accampa, e dà forza, e forza prende.

Thy verses, like a quiverful of darts,
Fly to their aim unfailing ; and the wound
They make incurable : a watchword they,
Branded in letters bold on brows of kings ;
Nor spoken only by the learned throng
But in the people's mouths they have their life ;
Rapid descending to frequented paths
Where they abide, and give and take new strength.

Giusti's biographer, Frassi, alluding to his poem of *Il Gingillino*, says : "This is one of those poems which will be read, perhaps, when Italian, like Latin, will no longer be a spoken language."

CHAPTER XII.

GINGILLINO is an expression in the Tuscan dialect signifying a man of contemptible character, always busying himself about trifles, and who, whilst professing to hold no opinion, flatters those in authority, and contrives to make his fortune. The Tuscans have a verb *gingillare*—to play the busybody.

The Genii who Giusti supposes presiding at the birth of Gingillino, are described as Turncoat, Turpitude, Cowardice, &c. who sing the Ninna Nanna or lullaby of the infant, with such counsel as might best foster the character of the future sycophant. Twenty years later he is represented about to quit the University, having received honours, which are accompanied by an eulogium from the friar, Professor *Gran Sciupatesta d'Università*—Great Fritterbrain of the University—who adds this piece of advice :

> Comincia coll' esempio e coll' inchiostro
> A difender l' altare a destra mano,
> Ed a mancia il nostro
> Dolce e amorevolissimo Sovrano ;

Vattene, agnello pieno di talento
Caro al presepio e al capo dell' armento.

Begin by your example and your ink
With your right hand the altar to defend,
Whilst with your left uplifted you may shield
Our gentle Sovereign, worthy of our love:
Go forth, young lamb, thy talents promise well,
Dear to the fold and first among the flock.

Gingillino is followed to his door by a party of his fellow-students, who serenade him in an opposite strain from that to which he has just listened from the heads of the University.

Giusti next transports the reader, with his hero, to Florence, where the poet laments the degeneracy of his people, in lines which are perhaps among the most beautiful he has written :—

O patria nostra, O fiaccola che spenta,
Tanto lume di te lasci, e conforti
Chi nel passato sogna e si tormenta ;
Vivo sepolcro d' un popolo di morti :
Invano, Invano, dalle sante mura
Spiri virtù negli animi scontorti.

Oh thou our country, torch which extinguishd
Leaves such light behind, to encourage him
Who dreams of glories past, himself tormenting ;
A living tomb which holds a people dead ;
In vain, in vain from out thy sacred walls
Thou breathest virtue in perverted minds.

The Bargello, or the residence of the police, containing the prison, and used as a place of meeting for lawyers, is next described as a den of infamy.   Here Giusti introduces us again to Gingillino, who receives advice corresponding with that offered by the Genii round his cradle, and is thus directed onwards in the road to success.   Female influence completes his corruption; and the poet concludes by a creed which Gingillino is supposed to recite nightly, instead of a prayer.   He declares his belief in the coin, in the Motuproprio or decrees of the sovereign, in the dynasty, and in the taxes ; he promises to attach himself to the saint or the hero of the day, and hopes to mount to the highest step of the ladder, to obtain a rag of nobility, and die with a cross at his button-hole.

On the 9th May, 1845, Giusti writes to the Marchesa Luisa d'Azeglio from Pescia :—

" MY DEAR FRIEND,

" I will not delay telling you that the letter of this morning has conveyed good news to me: you, who know how attached I am to you, will believe it.   I am not surprised that the journey should have been of benefit to the Signora Vittorina.[1]   Between ourselves, I fear that the air of Pisa for some time past has not suited

[1] The younger daughter of the poet Manzoni, and sister of the Marchesa Luisa d'Azeglio.   She afterwards married Professor Giorgini of Pisa.

her, especially now that we are in full sail for summer ; for complaints such as hers, a climate like Pisa is required in winter, and a mild mountain air in the hot season. We can talk it over together, and should you not be satisfied with this residence, we will find one more suitable, and send the doctors to the devil. In this world every one praises his own saint, but you know that we have spots in the Valdinievole which are really delightful. Pescia is in a hole, but the heights and hills around float as it were in a current of balmy air. Among my dreams is that of having you only a few paces distant from me ; and if it were possible to transport one of the two villas I possess on one of these eminences, I would say, Come and live there, as in your own home. If it will not be too much trouble, write to me by return of post, to say how and where you are lodged, and I will meantime make my arrangements. In these last days, the scirocco and the fog, my two mortal enemies, have been prostrating me, as usual, and I have driven away the dismals and my uneasy sensations by scribbling. . . . This accumulation of sufferings, which have increased in my head for two years, breaking down my bodily strength, has, I feel, liberated my spirit from the burden of material interests. I could be resigned to live as a confirmed invalid, provided the invalid could study, write, and go his own way. In this time of solitude and discomfort I have had leisure to review my life several times. . . . In the careless idleness in which I voluntarily spent three years of my youth, amidst errors of every kind, something began to germinate in my brain. Many years afterwards, a terrible blow which fell on me from very dear hands caused the development of whatever genius had fallen to my share. To a mind probed as mine has been by so many wounds, nothing else was wanting but this final trial to enable me to say—Now no experience can be new. After a fierce inward struggle of several months, I have once again raised my head ; I have sounded my depths, and I find within myself a large share of love, and of passion, and (do not think me vain) of poetry. . . . My body is sixty, my spirit eighteen, and this is the youth which I desire.

"Among many things which I have scribbled, I must name to you *L'Amor Pacifico*, a jest as innocent as water, which might be printed with the permission of the authorities, even in Modena ; *Il Papato del Prete Pero*, in which I treat, in my way, the question touched on by Gioberti, Balbo, and others ; *Gingillino*, a long, very long poem, of the same kind as the *Scritta* and the *Vestizione*, in which I have endeavoured to express all the baseness, all the contumely, of those who seek to rise to offices in the State by dirty and mean conduct. . . ."

Giusti shortly afterwards joined the Marchesa d'Azeglio and her sister in Pisa, and describes his pleasure at this meeting, and the life they led there, in a letter to their father:—

" Pisa, June, 1845.

"MY DEAR SIGNOR MANZONI,

"I have at length seen a dear part of yourself in the good and charming being who has come here to recover her health; and I am so happy, that, in spite of my tribulations, which whisper to me, Make haste and return home, I mean to remain here another two or three days, let what will come of it. Bista, Giorgini, and I pass hours, and hours, and hours, in the house of the Marchesa d'Azeglio; and if there is any nonsense in our heads, or that we can remember, I can assure you we do not keep it to ourselves. Giorgini, who, besides having much talent and knowledge, reads aloud delightfully, every now and then takes up a certain book [1] which lies on the table of these ladies, and then the pleasure is twofold.

"I hope that this climate may be of much service to the Signora Vittorina. She appears to me to have already gained a good deal. Cartoni, an excellent physician, has found nothing essentially wrong, and has allowed her to take sea baths—a proof that he finds her strong enough to bear them. We, meantime, shall continue every morning and evening to administer a laughing cure, and we have already a reinforcement at

[1] I Promessi Sposi of Manzoni.

hand, in a certain Giacomelli, an old comrade, who quite enters into the spirit of our amusements, and is the best madcap that could be desired. Laughter is good for the blood; and I hope that, if the Signora Vittorina is not tired with our prescription, she will find herself benefited by it. What a pleasure it will be to us, if, by emptying our bag of nonsense, the accumulation of years, we may boast that we can send back your darling daughter to you in good health!"

A few weeks later, Giusti writes to Manzoni from the baths of Lucca :—

"MY DEAR SIR,

"As I have learned that my letter of last June has not reached you, I hasten to write to you again. . . . The Marchesa d'Azeglio has already told you that I was at Pisa with Giorgini, who, knowing that I was a prisoner at home, came to unnail me, and deposit me on the Lung' Arno, above the *Caffè dell' Ussero*; where I shook off many of my fancies. She will also have told you of the evenings when Giorgini and I found a certain book on the table of these ladies, and sat down to sip at it, and also to give our opinion upon it. Very respectful, indeed, to sit down to play the syndic at so many miles distance, on one who is so much wiser than ourselves. Tell the author to have patience, and at least give us credit for good intentions. We had agreed to read the book through, when Gino Capponi enticed me away to his villa, and thence to Florence, where he kept me so long that, at last, instead of returning to Pisa, as I wished, I had to go to the baths of Lucca. . . . I will, however, do my best to take a run to La Spezzia; and if Giorgini, who is destined to uproot me from this also, had not gone to Siena, I should have already been two or three days there. The Marchesa writes to me that the Signora Vittorina has found great benefit from the baths, and you will believe how earnestly I hope that she may be restored to the flower she was a year ago. To make all safe, she must pass a winter in Pisa, where the climate is so mild that even the most chilly do not require any other fire than that which the lizards enjoy. I say this in my own interest, as I shall certainly pass the winter there, in the place which reminds me of my *profound* studies, pursued in the streets, and with books hermetically sealed. . . .

"Do me the favour of saluting Grossi [1] for me, and

---

[1] Tomaso Grossi, a Milanese poet, born towards the end of the last century, and considered on nearly the same level with Parini and Manzoni. In 1816 he wrote a poem in the Milanese dialect called *La Pioggia d'oro*. His next poem which excited still greater sympathy was *La Fuggitiva*, the subject being an Italian woman whose lover is carried to Russia by Napoleon, with the great army. The lady in despair follows her lover in disguise, and, because a slave belonging to a subject nation has no country, fights and dies for the stranger. The *Fuggitiva* was first written in the Milanese dialect, but afterwards rendered by the poet into Italian, in which it is said to have lost much of its

tell him I will soon write to him again ; that I love him as a friend of my boyhood, and with reason, since the first verses which made me shed tears, and excited my love for the beautiful, were his of *Ildegonda.* Permit me to add, that Father Cristoforo, with all that comes after him, is a favourite resource of mine, when I feel cold and dried up, and when I find I cannot get rid of the torpor which oppresses me, without tears shed for some worthy object. At those times I can hardly believe that we never saw one another. That book has been everywhere with me ; and I shall never forget how, one day, I was so buried to the eyes in its pages, that I do not know how I ever recovered the better part of myself. Have I not, then, reason to protest, with all sincerity, that

I am most affectionately yours."

Professor Giovan Battista Giorgini joined Giusti at the baths of Lucca, in August, and offered him a place in his carriage, to convey him to La Spezzia, where they met the Marchesa d'Azeglio again with her sister. The ladies were, however, preparing to return to Milan, by Genoa, and persuaded Giusti and his friend to

---

original force. *Ildegonda* raised his fame to its greatest height, and was followed by *I Lombardi alla prima crociata.* As a rival to Manzoni's *Promessi Sposi,* Grossi wrote *Marco Visconti,* and the poem of *Ulrico e Lida* completed his works. —("L' Italia Letteraria ed Artistica, per opera di I. Delecluze.")

accompany them thus far. From Genoa, Giusti writes to Manzoni :—

" MY DEAR MANZONI,

". . . This morning I woke early ; and, as lying long in bed always weakens me, I jumped up, to enjoy the enchanting view from the heights around. A sworn enemy to cicerones, who are only the baptizers of stones, I explored by myself, wandering here and there, as chance directed, looking in the faces of men and at buildings, indifferent whether this palace be called Balbi, nor that wiry, brisk, busy man be Thomas or John. The spectacle of a flourishing city, and of an industrious people, accompanied by a few recollections of what I have read in *illo tempore*, and which has remained in the magazine of my head, to serve when wanted, enabled me to build castles in the air, to indulge fancy, and to enjoy two hours of wandering thoughts, which is a perfect Elysium to any one who has a grain of imagination. As I returned, a servant of the Marchesa d'Azeglio, who remembered having seen Montanelli and me together in Pisa, like two souls in one nutshell, called out to me from a distance, ' Montanelli is up there, at Giorgini's.' A fiddler at a dance could not have put more animation into my legs than these words. It seemed as if something within me had told me that Montanelli would bring me

N

good news; and I was not mistaken. The letter he brought is a precious pledge of your friendship and courtesy, and of the kindness you entertain towards me.[1] Who could have told me, ten days ago, that I should have been so near you, and still more near you in spirit than on the road? When these ladies hooked me at La Spezzia, they knew what bait the fish would take; for they were aware how I had revered you from my youth upwards, and they had heard me say, more than once, that when led astray by youthful follies I was led back by your book. One day, I recollect, I was in a place where the conversation was anything but noble or refined; where all were occupied in drowning their senses, or in sleep; and I was dull, languid, incapable of anything but a yawn. I do not know how a copy of the *Promessi Sposi* had

---

[1] Professor Montanelli, of Pisa, who had just come from Manzoni, was the intimate friend of Giusti. As before stated, he had been made a professor at nineteen years of age, and was a poet, musician, and doctor of law; he had besides contributed articles to Viesseux's "Anthologia." His political opinions were somewhat vague, though always in favour of progress; but his leanings towards the fanciful and mystical, were in contrast with the practical common sense which Giusti, by a rare combination, united with poetical genius. Montanelli's warm heart, gentle manners, and pliable disposition, gave him great influence over the young men of the University. His opinions at this time of his life led him to unite with the moderate party, but he was always opposed to Gioberti's views of the temporal supremacy of the Papacy. In the prominent part he afterwards played in 1848, he separated himself from Giusti, the Marchese Capponi, and others to whom he was warmly attached.

found its way into that house ; I know only that it fell
into my hands ; and that I no sooner came upon Father
Cristoforo than I recovered that part of myself which
I thought lost or left outside. . . .

" I will frankly confess that I have also a great fancy
to read *Gingillino* to you. I wrote it in the midst of
the most atrocious and agonizing spasms I have ever
experienced, and after having had for two years to
lament the absence of my poetic inspiration and even
of common sense. When I first returned to composition, I worked by fits and starts, stopped, went on
slowly, jerked forwards, like a windmill which had been
standing still for ten years, but which was forced to
move because the spring breezes set it going. I wrote
ill or well, feeling my way in the dark, uncertain which
way to go without falling; and when I had finished, and
touched it up, I had to read it over, and to chafe at it
again and again, at one moment thinking it might pass
with its fellows, and the next trembling lest I should
have made a great mistake. I had been buried fourteen months in a corner of our town, half dead ; and,
as I intended to show my nose again in the world, I
wished to bring along with me something to make my
friends recognise me, in case, after such a discipline as
I had undergone, they should hardly tell who I might
be. . . . The thing did not turn out so ill as I feared,
which, believe me, was a great consolation. These
little vanities may be pardoned in a poor fellow who

has nothing else to recommend him, especially when he finds himself set upon a candlestick, against his will, and without feeling any pride in the position in which he is placed.

"I regret that I have not a string of proverbs with me which I have been collecting for the last five or six years in the streets and in booths, and in which you would find real gems of language and of practical wisdom ; of that wisdom which does not figure among gold coins, but which is of admirable service in the smaller traffic of life. . . .

"Giorgini sends you a thousand greetings : you will find him a young man you will like, and who only wants encouragement to make him value himself a little more. Urge him on a little, as he can do much if he will. . . ."

From Genoa, Giusti and Giorgini were persuaded to proceed to Milan, from whence they paid a visit of some weeks to Manzoni, enjoying the society of Grossi, and of other literary and distinguished friends of the novellist. In October Giusti was again in Genoa on his way south, when he wrote to Manzoni to express his sorrow at leaving his hospitable roof, and the friends he had made whilst there :—

"Genoa, 5th October, 1845.

"MY DEAR ALEXANDER,

"I write to you from Genoa, where I have just arrived, and I can hardly believe that I am still able to hold a

little conversation with you. I will not say what I felt
on leaving you, because I could not express all I ought
and all I wish : any one who has lived in your house
as we have, my dear Manzoni, can well conceive what
must have been our feelings when the moment of
departure arrived. May it please God to enable you to
visit Tuscany, and to spend five or six months with us.
It is this hope alone which can diminish the bitterness
of yesterday's parting.

"You would not be surprised at hearing we had
reached Genoa so soon, could you know the rate at
which we travelled—enough to knock ourselves up,
as well as our horses, from that impatience which
seizes one to get away from the sight of places and
objects which recall a happiness we are forced to quit.
A month ago we travelled from Genoa to Milan as
escorts to two charming ladies, who were taking us
to you ; this time we have traversed the country by
ourselves, whilst receding farther and farther from
you.

"I can do no more this evening, and to-morrow
morning we shall start as early as we can. Accept
these lines meantime, only to prove to you how much
affection you have left in our hearts. As soon as
I reach home, I will pour forth a letter to you in my
old way.

"Salute all your dear family, the Marchesa d'Azeglio,
Grossi, Rosmini, Torti, Don Giovanni, and all who have

a claim on our gratitude and love. Adieu my good Alexander, my distinguished friend. . . ."

In November, Giusti came to Pisa to try the effect upon his health of a milder climate during winter. He took up his abode with his friend Giovanni Frassi, his fellow-student when a youth, and who, after his death, became his biographer. Here Giusti was surrounded by an agreeable and choice society of friends. Professor Giuseppe Montanelli, Giovanni Giacomelli, of Leghorn, mentioned in a former letter to Manzoni, and the Advocate Adriano Biscardi. They met alternate weeks at the houses of Montanelli and of Frassi, where reading aloud, the letters they had received from Manzoni, Grossi, and the Marchese Capponi, formed an agreeable variety in their lively evening conversation.

Giusti was occupied at this time with his collection of proverbs, for which he derived much assistance from the Marchese Gino Capponi. He had for many years had his attention called to the purification of his native language, as a means towards the future existence of an Italian nation.

An eminent modern German philologist informs us, "that the sources of Italian are not to be found in the classical literature of Rome, but in the popular dialects of Italy ;"[1] and again, "Many of the Neo-Latin dialects must be sought for in the ancient dialects of Italy and

---

[1] Science of Language, by Max Müller, M.A. p. 59.

her provinces. . . . As soon as the literary language of Rome became established and classical, the first start was made in the future career of those dialects which, even at the time of Dante, were still called vulgar or popular."[1]   The subject had occasioned the foundation of the Academia della Crusca in the sixteenth century, but in the beginning of the nineteenth century had been applied to a political aim, as the Academicians, whilst endeavouring to banish every foreign idiom from the language, hoped likewise to produce a spirit of unity in the nation, and form the strongest barrier against foreign encroachments.   Monti, whose pliable genius seems hardly to have comprehended the word country as applied to his own people, attempted to stem the native stream which threatened to sweep away time-honoured Gallicisms, and accordingly wrote his *Proposta*, in which he endeavoured to prove the fallibility of the decrees of the Academia della Crusca. Manzoni, in an opposite spirit, visited Tuscany for the express purpose of reforming his language and style, and under the tutelage of the Academy, to make it purely Italian.   A few years later we find Giusti devoting himself to the same study, and in order to acquire a more correct knowledge of his native idiom, he conversed much with the common people.   From them he learned and applied words and expressions of purely Italian origin, worthy, as he considered, to

[1] Science of Language, by Max Müller, M.A. p. 183.

be restored to the language of educated persons ; he introduced them in his conversation, and even in his letters to ladies. These studies led to his being subsequently elected a member of the Academia della Crusca.

In February, 1846, he gave an account of his occupations in Pisa, in a letter to Manzoni :—

"MY DEAR SANDRO,

"I intended to send you, by the Litta's, a few lines with my little book, but at that time my ink was dried up. Pisa suddenly filled with Milanese, who spoke of you to me every half-hour, so that I expected every moment to see you appear. But the Milanese departed and the gentleman to whom his friends paid so many compliments when absent, never arrived to make the choir complete. . . . I have undertaken to write a short notice of Parini for a new edition of his works, which is now in the course of preparation. Ask Torti if he can give me any particulars which have been omitted by his biographers. Good wine does not need the sign of the Tavern Bush to recommend it, but a frame improves every picture, provided it be introduced with taste. Torti ought to know his life, death, and marvellous works, and I do not think he is the man to keep it all to himself. Beg him from me to grant this request, and, if he consents, I shall be able to say I have hit two birds with one stone ; for I shall leave authentic notices of Parini, and a letter from this distinguished man.[1] You, too, may help me, but I do not build any expectations upon you. . . .

"Have you seen Fauriel's work on Provençal poetry ? I am reading it now with the greatest pleasure, and it appears to me a book worthy of consideration ; I only wish he had given documents, as it would then not only have been amusing but useful. It is a pity Fauriel did not publish the work himself ; a book given to the world without the last touches from the author is, in ninety-nine cases out of a hundred, a failure. I am aware that these studies were the darling occupation of his life, and I know that he studied, laboured, and gave his writings away to others, that they might have the same enjoyment. For this reason many of his works have been lost, or those in possession of them have not the conscience to restore them. I envy you having known him. He must have been a rare instance among men of literature, open, honest, and more solicitous for the truth than for his own glory.

"Tuscany is all in a ferment. The new Ministers, the surrender of Renzi, and the attempt to introduce the nuns of the Sacre Cœur, have turned the country topsyturvy ; I cannot think how it will end. These gleams

[1] Probably Francesco Torti, a Milanese, author of a treatise on "Dante." Giovanni Torti, who died in 1827, was the cotemporary of Parini.

of light ought to help the people and the rulers to understand one another. To see them stand with teeth set, looking at each other in so canine a manner, would make one suppose that they were equally incapable of acting. What fools we all are when we cease to follow the guidance of reason, and, hoping to recover its trace, we only increase the confusion and intricacy! Europe appears to me just now like a great caldron, a chaotic mass of discordant elements, boiling up all together, and from whence, some day or other, a better state of things will emerge. But what may we not see before the pudding is ready? Let us trust in Providence, who watches over the caldron. I, for one, have not much confidence in those who want to handle the ladle."

Giusti was engaged with his notice of Parini's life from 1846 to 1850, but left the work incomplete at his death.[1] The Lombard satirist, poet, and moralist found a worthy biographer in a fellow-labourer in the same field. Born in 1729, of poor parents, who wished to bring him up as a priest, Giuseppe Parini is stated to have entered life when false taste reigned in literature, as well as corruption in morals; but even here Giusti's true and philosophic mind discerned good in the midst of evil. He thus describes the Italy of that period:—

" People, there were none; citizens, only by name;

---

[1] Recently published with his inedited works by Le Monnier, of Florence.

nobles, without influence, puffed up by pride, effeminate, haughty, idle, and vicious; and yet out of the class of these very nobles came Verri, Beccaria, and Filangieri; names which will always be held in esteem, as long as learning, order, and the growth of civilization are honoured. Science had Spallanzani, Mascheroni, Oriani, and Lagrangia; philosophy, Genovesi; history, Giannone and Muratori, and greater than all, though least known, Vico, who stands forth like a solitary and rugged mountain, where grow neither laurel groves nor flower gardens, but here and there a great oak, and within whose caverns are precious veins of solid metal, which wait to be tested and turned to profit. The masses slept, the few were awake; the princes who, more than the people, were in love with novelty, agitated reforms, but which were to emanate from themselves. In short, amidst much that was superficial was also much that was sound, and on all sides the germs of better men and better times were unfolding. Some say the last century was the century of destruction, I say it was the century for clearing the ground."

The allusions to the state of Tuscany made by Giusti in his letter to Manzoni, refer to events which preceded the revolution of 1848. The death of the Minister, Neri Corsini, the worthy successor of Fossombrini, in 1845, had occasioned a complete change in the Cabinet of the Grand Duke. Corsini was succeeded by Francesco Cempini, Giuseppe Paver, Alessandro Humbourg, and Giovanni Baldassaroni, all of whom had held office in various capacities during the administrations of Fossombroni and Corsini; but the characters of these men raised doubts in the minds of the public, who waited in anxiety for the first acts of the new Council of Ministers.

The policy of the Austrian Court justified the alarm created by the danger of a weak Ministry. The position of Austria in Italy is thus described in a pamphlet already referred to. "Austria planted in Lombardy, derived her title for dominion from an act of injustice, and was therefore constrained to rule by violence. The good government of other countries bordering on Lombardo-Venetia was dangerous as an example: Austria only obeyed the logic of her condition in Italy when obliged to maintain corruption in Naples, misgovernment in Rome, and to keep the Duchies and Tuscany under her rule."[1]

As long as Tuscany thus continued under secret subjection to a foreign power, no substantial reforms could be made in the Government: ostensibly an independent State, she was in reality an Austrian Province. There was perpetual vacillation on the part of the Grand Duke, who started at every shadow; he felt his hands tied whenever he attempted to act for himself,

---

[1] " Toscana e Austria—Cenni politici—Biblioteca civile dell' Italiano, compilata e publicata per cura dei Signori Marchese Cosimo Ridolfi, Barone Bettino Ricasoli, Cavaliere Ubaldino Peruzzi," &c. &c.

and the feebleness and hesitation on the part of the sovereign found its echo in the people, who were nevertheless beginning to be aware that as long as Leopold depended for his safety on foreign support, no good could arise for his subjects, and that self-government, to which they as well as he could alone look for strength, must remain a mere shadow.

An attempt at revolution was made this year in the States of the Church, led on by a man of the name of Renzi, who declared it was not his intention to raise the standard of revolt, but of peace ; not to destroy the temporal power of the Pope, but to establish it by better laws, and a more just administration. The attempt had signally failed, and its authors sought a refuge in Tuscany. Under Fòssombroni's or Neri Corsini's administration they would have been safe, but it was only their personal influence which had allowed Tuscany to receive political offenders within her boundaries ; the iniquitous law of extradition continued in force here as in other parts of Italy, and after the deaths of these two Ministers, the Grand Duchy became treacherous ground. Renzi and his companions were, however, permitted to pass through Tuscany, and sail for France, on condition of never returning. Renzi broke this promise, and on his re-appearance was thrown into prison. His personal character excited little sympathy, but when shortly afterwards, he was delivered over to the Pope, all the Tuscan people were filled with indignation, at discovering on how insecure a foundation their boasted toleration and privileges rested. Confidence in the Grand Duke, even where it existed before, was now completely shaken. Another act followed to fill the measure of his misdeeds. A proposal was made by the Government to admit the nuns of the Sacre Cœur into Pisa. As these nuns only confess to Jesuits, this was supposed to be merely a cover for the introduction of this most dangerous Order. Professor Montanelli was the chief instigator of a petition to the Government to prevent their intrusion, and this petition was the first legal, organized, and open resistance offered to the acts of the Italian governments subject to Austria.

Giusti writes on the occasion to the Marchese Gino Capponi, who, it appears had given his support to the act —

" Pisa, 3d March, 1846.

" MY DEAR GINO,

" We were all happy in having done a good action; but since receiving your letter our Jubilee has greatly increased. I have read it to as many as I could, and, in accordance with the desire of those to whom I have shown it, I have left copies of it with all who wished for it. Montanelli embraces you again and again; the Marchesa Arconati shed tears of joy; all bless and thank you. Cease to say, my dear Gino, that you are dead;[1] you live in yourself, and you live still more in our hearts.

" The first merit of this act is due to Montanelli and to Rinaldo Ruschi (the gonfalonier or mayor of Pisa); after him (you may tell all who wish to know it) that everybody hastened to take part in it heartily. Ask yourself if I did not rejoice, and if I do not now rejoice, to hear you blest for those few lines. One word such as you know how to say when your heart dictates it, is worth a thousand of ours.

" I write to you in the house of the Arconati,[2] surrounded by twenty people who wish you were here, to tell you that which the intensity of my feelings perhaps forbids my expressing as I should like.

" Accept an embrace from all, including the ladies. Adieu!—this has been a happy day."

[1] The Marchese Gino Capponi had been afflicted with blindness.
[2] Count Giuseppe Arconati and his family were Milanese, residing in Pisa, and highly esteemed by the moderate party in politics. He had been condemned to death by the Austrian Government in 1821, and, in spite of the amnesty of 1838, Tuscany was forbidden by Austria to harbour him in 1846. Gualterio, Part II. Od. 1. p. 144.

CHAPTER XIII.

OCCUPATION OF FERRARA BY THE AUSTRIANS—DEMAND FOR A
NATIONAL GUARD—LETTERS.

AMONG the friends and correspondents Giusti had acquired in the house of Manzoni, we find Tommaso Grossi, the Milanese poet, and author of the novel of " Marco Visconti," one of the few compositions in modern Italian literature which has become popular in England.   Giusti writes to him from Florence :

" Florence, 25th June, 1846.

" MY DEAR GROSSI,

". . . . How many events have taken place since last we wrote to one another ! If I were to count them, there would be no end of their number, and therefore I had better let them alone, and turn to the marriage of Vittorina with Giorgini. I augur well for this union for many reasons. I hope Vittorina will recover her health in Tuscany, and that the new ties of wife and of mother may compensate to her for being so far from her father. Giorgini will find his centre in her, and that sweet and happy refuge needed by a young heart and intellect, which sees too clearly into the ways of the world. A man with the talents of Giorgini, and who feels himself in possession of a gem like that girl, may do much for himself and for others. All his relations are enchanted with Vittorina, and I am not surprised; but they will be more delighted with her when she becomes one of their family.

" I pass my life in idleness; my health is not worse, but I assure you I pay a very heavy price for existence. It is true that our lives are not at our own disposal; Nature pretends to give them gratis at the beginning, and then sends in her account.

" Some time ago I wrote to Torti, and sent it by the Marchesa d'Azeglio; but it cannot have reached him, as I have had no answer. I requested him to tell me all he knew of Parini. There is yet time, if only for notes I mean to add to the work. Try and persuade him to comply for my sake.

" I write to you from Florence, where I have been living a month in the house of Capponi; I have been with Gino ever since Easter, and now I see that I shall pass most of the summer with him. We are alone here in these great rooms, large enough to contain a crowd of people, but the master of the house is enough for me, and would that it had pleased God that he were enough for himself. Believe me, the more you know this man, the more you feel his value, and

O

the pain of seeing him cut off and almost separated from himself. Born of a truly illustrious family, rich, learned, possessing a noble mind, and a most noble heart; in excellent health, strong, handsome, in the flower of his age, you see him reduced to a struggle not to bend beneath the misfortunes which have rained upon him, and which would make him despair were he not the man he is. When we see such things, we have no longer a right to complain of our own trials. God knows best what He has ordered."

On the 5th of December, of this year, the Genoese celebrated the centenary of the expulsion of the Germans from their city in 1746; and rejoicings, and fireworks, throughout Tuscany, and even in the Romagnas, expressed the sympathy of the people in all parts of Italy with the cause of independence, and their hatred of foreign intruders. The Tuscan Government, however, took alarm at these repeated demonstrations in favour of nationality, which, associated with the late resistance offered to the attempt to introduce Jesuits into Pisa, determined the Ministers to lay a fresh embargo on the press. The consequence of this act, however, was a wider circulation of seditious papers by secret means, as well as menaces of robbery and arson. Disturbances occurred in Monsummano, Borgo a Buggiano, Pistoia, and other places; and agitators, pretending to be Liberals, were everywhere to be found in the disguise of priests and lawyers.

On the 16th of June, Cardinal Mastai succeeded Pope Gregory, and assumed the name of Pius the Ninth. He began his reign by reforms in his household, and a system of stricter economy. A few days after his accession he was seen attending mass, in a church in the neighbourhood of Rome, in so simple and unpretending a manner as to form a contrast to his predecessors, and the people augured well from such a commencement. He gave audience to all persons, and pardoned several of those condemned for political offences. Not a day passed without some act of beneficence or charity. He likewise called a council of prelates, to consider the introduction of railroads into the States of the Church, which it had been sacrilege to mention a few months before; and he promised to show favour to scientific men, and to encourage scientific meetings: finally, he issued an edict of a general amnesty, which raised his popularity to its greatest height. In the provinces, however, the legates who had been appointed by Pope Gregory began to demur at these proceedings, and either altered or postponed the publication of the edict, diminishing its value, or rendering it a dead letter. An inundation of the Tiber, which took place in December, gave another opportunity for the Pope to exhibit his philanthropy, by calling upon his Roman subjects to aid their suffering brethren; and the beginning of 1847 was hailed as the dawn of the first new year of an auspicious reign. The acts of Pius, however, began to create a feeling of uneasiness in the princes of the other Italian States, and he was watched with jealous eyes by the Court of Austria.

Hatred of Austrian rule, and of Austrian interference throughout Italy, had become so strong, that it was necessary for that Power, if she meant to retain her hold in the country, as well as to obtain that increase of territory at which she was aiming, to augment her physical force—the only force, except that of intrigue, by which she had maintained her position in the Peninsula—whilst, at the same time, to repress every effort for reform and progress. The Austrian Government, therefore, was still further incensed by a demand for a national guard in the States of the Church. The Pope wavered between refusal and consent, as, though unwilling to offend an ally and protector, he could not perceive the danger to himself or to Austria in an institution for the preservation of order, and for the defence of the country from foreign invasion. The influence of two priests, Graziosi and Father Gioacchino Ventura of Sicily, succeeded in defeating that of the Austrian Minister, Count Lutzoff, and Cardinal Ghizzi; and the edict for the organization of a national guard was issued on the 6th of July. To punish this act, though emanating from a nominally independent sovereign and

the head of the Church, the Austrian Government resolved to seize on a city belonging to his jurisdiction.
Under the pretence of protecting Pius from the revolutionary projects of his own subjects, eight hundred
Croats, and sixty Hungarian troops, with three cannon,
were sent to take possession of Lagoscuro and Franco-
lorio, the two passes of the Po ; and on the 17th of
July they entered Ferrara by the gate of San Giovanni,
with fixed bayonets and banners flying. The people,
who were enjoying a holiday, and were busy inscribing
their names on the list for the national guard, were
taken by surprise, and offered no resistance. The
troops next demanded quarters from the legate and
the municipality, but were refused. The legate declared the act to be a violation of the treaty between
the Emperor and the Pope, and wrote to Rome for
orders. Matters remained thus for twenty days : the
people displaying their animosity by liberal demonstrations, of which the Austrian commander vainly complained to the legate and to the archbishop. An
Austrian soldier, returning late one evening to the
town, declared that he had been insulted by the
townspeople, which furnished pretext sufficient for the
general in command to place sentinels in all parts
of the city. Austrian patrols paraded Ferrara by
night ; and those citizens who did not submit to
military rule were insulted. Meantime, a message
arrived from Rome, approving the conduct of the

legate; the messenger was likewise the bearer of communications to Vienna and to other courts, protesting against the act of Austria. Metternich's only reply was, that the Emperor had a right to retain garrisons in Ferrara and Comacchio, whilst orders were conveyed to the troops from Marshal Radetzky, to occupy all the gates of the city. But the expected result, that of striking terror into Italy, wholly failed; and far from being panic-stricken, the Italian people were roused to indignation at so flagrant an act, in violation of the rights of an Italian State and of a Pope who had just begun to prove himself worthy of the name of an Italian sovereign.

The agitation which had prevailed in the Roman States, from the time of the accession of Pius, had spread to Tuscany, which had long been preparing for reforms. Discontent at the existing Government was openly expressed in the Cafés and drawing-rooms of Florence, and the walls of the houses were found every morning covered with placards emanating from the clandestine press. The police, which was at that time under the direction of a man of the name of Giovanni Bologna, whilst making themselves odious to the people, were too imperfectly organized to be of use to their employers, who even hampered their actions, from a jealous fear lest the power of the *Buon Governo*, as it was called, should interfere with their own. Meantime, the leaders of the moderate party perceived the necessity of coming forward, to prevent the whole Government falling to pieces.   The current of agitation could not now be stemmed; it could only be allowed to run off by opening channels of reforms and good laws, so much needed in a country where the principa error lay in the rulers having begun to mould a free State, and stopped short, leaving the constitution incomplete.   The moderate party were sincerely desirous to preserve the sovereignty and the Lorraine dynasty, by suggesting the only means of safety.   Towards the latter part of February some of the wisest and most distinguished citizens in Florence took council together how to act.   The three who first met for this purpose were the advocate Vincenzio Salvagnoli, Baron Bettino Ricasoli, and the Abate Raffaello Lambruschini.   They proposed to lay a memorial before the president of the Council, Francesco Cempini, exposing the deplorable state of affairs, and to suggest reforms in the administration, and, above all, a wise law by which the press should be allowed greater freedom, and thus offer no apology or pretext for clandestine publications. The Marchese Gino Capponi refused to join this conclave, because he objected to the few thus taking upon themselves the initiative for the many, and he preferred on principle an open, steady action, to secret meetings and consultations.   Some time afterwards he joined other friends, whose views were like his own, and who advocated making a less demand upon the Govern-

ment.   This party were ignorant of Ricasoli's projects,
which were only known to Capponi, and they thought
it wiser not to expose themselves to rejection or
disappointment, and that the time had not yet
arrived for energetic enterprise.   They proposed to
overcome the evils caused by the clandestine press, by
counter instructions, and by teaching the true principles
of political economy ; they thus hoped to combat the
follies of communism, whilst preparing the public mind
for the enjoyment of liberty, and dispelling the fears of
the Prince and of his councillors.   The moderate party
was thus split into two ; the leaders of which, Ricasoli
and Capponi, whilst acting separately for the common
end, were ready to unite their efforts again when the
occasion should present itself.   Montanelli, meantime,
advocated the use of the clandestine press, condemned
alike by Ricasoli and Capponi, and even claimed the
merit of being its founder.   Capponi was supported by
the Marchese Cosimo Ridolfi, the Advocate Leopoldo
Galeotti, the Advocate Ferdinando Andreucci, the
Marchese Vincenzio Antinori, the Advocate Marco
Tabarrini, Count Guglielmo Cambray Digny, Giuseppe
Giusti, and the Cavaliere Vincenzio Peruzzi, the Gonfalonier of Florence.   These citizens drew up a petition to the Government for permission to edit a journal,
in which they proposed to enlist the services of the
most eminent writers in Tuscany ; the aim of the
journal was to be moral rather than political, and

chiefly to treat of political economy, industry, education, and similar topics, with an appendix containing notices of literature and art.   It was likewise proposed that the Government should be requested to grant a separate censorship, with fewer restrictions on this newspaper than was commonly allowed to the Tuscan press.   To this last proposition, however, Ridolfi objected as unjust, and a demand for privilege.   After the principles had been discussed and agreed upon, Capponi dictated the petition, which was presented to the Grand Duke, but was rejected on the unexpected ground that a new law was in the course of preparation, which would grant far greater freedom to the press, prevent the necessity of a special permission for the publication of the proposed journal, and give universal satisfaction.

This surprising announcement was the result of the labours of the other section of the moderate party, who, believing in the urgent necessity of a general reform, and greater liberty to the press, had unceasingly endeavoured to persuade the Grand Duke and his ministers to further concessions ; and thus the efforts of Ricasoli, Salvagnoli, and Lambruschini had succeeded, before Capponi and his friends could present their petition.   Ricasoli had spoken in plain terms to the President Cempini, pointing out to him that if all constituted States felt the necessity of reforms, nowhere could they be so much needed as in Tuscany, where the good work of the Grand Duke Leopold I. having been interrupted by his being called to the Imperial Throne, the old corrupt system of his predecessors had been abolished, whilst the new system was as yet incomplete: Tuscany, besides, had the elements of reform and of self-organization, and therefore it was the more easy to frame a statute, constituting a representative or Parliamentary Government. In the Memorial drawn up by Baron Ricasoli, the principal causes of discontent were thus enumerated. The number, ignorance, and inutility of the clergy. The monks, who neither instructed others nor themselves ; their idleness and incapacity ; private instruction discouraged, and public instruction imperfect ; a want of primary as well as of secondary schools, and the University was compared to the top of a pyramid without a base. Imperfectly trained and intriguing officials in the Government ; who, always inert, always discontented, their pretensions increased in a ratio with their incapacity ; ignorance and irregularity in the officials in the provinces, to the injury of the public service, and prejudice of the State, weakening the respect for Government as well as morality ; the want of a better organized administration: Cosmo I. had founded the State ; Leopold I. had reformed it : the organization was left to Leopold II. The municipalities wanted more power, and were only used as machines by which to raise money, under the Finance Minister ; whilst internal custom dues made intercourse difficult between cities of the same State.

Besides these grievances, the whole conduct of the interior Administration was defective, including the power confided to obscure subaltern officials. A sincere and upright desire for reform was confounded with sedition and rebellion, enthusiasm with evil intentions. The means were wanted by which the sovereign could be made acquainted with the real necessities of the country, or to assist him to provide for them, and enforce a prompt execution of the laws. The constitution of the Government itself was unsound, and impediments were thrown in the way of the right of petition. A municipal code, a code for the regulation of the customs, another for the regulation of ecclesiastical affairs, and a civil and penal code, were all needed ; the judiciary system was incomplete, and the censorship of the press, instead of being conducive to public morals, was only an impediment in the way of progress and knowledge. . . .

The answer to this petition was the publication of a law on the 7th March, which was far from fulfilling the promise of its announcement. By admitting criticism on the acts of the Government, the evil it was intended to mitigate was increased ; for by enabling the people to discuss laws after they had been irrevocably passed, discontent was promoted, and the authority of those in power weakened, without benefit to the State. Any concession at that moment was, however, hailed as a boon, and the people collected beneath the windows of the Palazzo Pitti, to express their gratitude to their sovereign, whilst newspapers immediately appeared, directed against old abuses, and demanding more reforms.

On the 3d of August, the young men of Pistoia celebrated the anniversary of the death of the favourite Tuscan hero of republican memory, Francesco Ferruccio. Giusti thus describes the excitement in his city on the occasion, in a letter to Francesco Farinola, the son-in-law of the Marchese Gino Capponi :—

" MY DEAR CHECCO,

" I found Pescia in a state which would make Leghorn appear, in comparison, a perfect mortuary. This does not, however, stagger me in my deliberate conviction—indeed it confirms me in it—that the Tuscan people will not be guilty of disorders, unless driven to extremity. If treated judiciously, above all, if that bad custom of bestowing things by halves be given up, there will be no cause for complaint. With the occupation of Ferrara almost before their eyes, and with the Pope arming his people only a few miles off, how could Tuscany avoid feeling the reverberation? It is to expect impossibilities. On the other hand, the Government itself calls upon us to awaken to a new life, and this new life must necessarily differ from the old. What sort of doctor would that be, who, to restore us to health, would keep us in bed like invalids? I would never flatter the passions of the multitude, but I would never calumniate nor misapprehend the reviving spirit of the nation. An ill-intentioned person, one of those mollusca, a species which abounds on land as well as in the sea, might, in a letter dictated by malice or indolence, make you in Florence believe that this part of the country was all in convulsion, because the people sing, and hurry in crowds to listen to newspapers; these, as you may perceive, are monstrous acts, enough to terrify even the seven sleepers of Ephesus. I, who am a looker-on, and studying how matters stand here, can tell you that all this takes place without the slightest disturbance, and half a word spoken in earnest, is sufficient to quiet them in a moment, and send them to their homes. If you wish to know why the public tranquillity is undisturbed, it is because the chief magistrate of this district looks to the reality rather than to outward appearances; because there are no secret agents to stir the fire, and because the enthusiasm is real. Appoint a magistrate of an irritable, suspicious temper, without a head, without conciliatory manners, intolerant by word and deed, and you would see a simple innocent affair at once turned into a real subversion of everything, as has nearly been the case in other places. I do not mean to hold up Pescia as an example, but only to insist that from small dangers we may take warnings for great. During the sepulchral time which intervened from 1833 to 1846, I have often heard the custom of reading out newspapers in shops and public offices, as practised in other countries, lauded to the skies; but now that this custom begins to prevail with us, will it be of any continuance? All nations, whether their voices be cracked or nasal, in times like these which sound the réveille, croak, bark, or screech their patriotic hymns; and we, who belong to the country of music, and of silver voices, shall we not sing ours? 'Keep quiet, do not pretend to know anything; when the opportunity arrives, then you may speak, act, and show yourselves capable of understanding and of sustaining your rights.' This is the programme and the new order of civilization which is perpetually droning in the noddles of certain tortoises, who like the spirits in the Inferno of Dante, whenever they see the people make a step forward, conclude, judging of them by their own slow pace, that they are running a race. I have the more right to say this, as I have been praising up moderation and caution." . . .

About the end of the month of August, the people of Florence, following the example of Rome, demanded a national guard; some of the students, who were supported by the eminent surgeon, Professor Zannetti, and by a few others, drew up a petition on the subject to the Grand Duke. As difficulties were always thrown in the way of the presentation of petitions, Professor

Zannetti himself undertook to see the Minister of the Interior, Paver, and inform him that this expedient had been resorted to by some faithful citizens, in the hope of preventing dangerous assemblies of the people, and to beg him to use his influence with the Grand Duke in their favour. Paver, though in his heart adverse to the demand contained in the petition, dared not refuse.

Meantime Leghorn was in a state of commotion; the Livornese assembled tumultuously, and demanded a national guard. Their example was soon afterwards followed in Florence, the people collecting beneath the windows of the Palazzo Pitti, with the same demand. The Grand Duke at length yielded, and on the 4th September the petition was granted. The following morning, upwards of twenty thousand persons, of every age and condition, adorned with the Tuscan colours, marched through the greater part of Florence, and, after again assembling before the Palazzo Pitti, and cheering the Grand Duke, returned peaceably to their homes. In the evening the cathedral was crowded with worshippers, when the archbishop offered up a thanksgiving for the auspicious event.

A rumour was now circulated that a change was about to be made in the constitution of the Cabinet; but this hope soon vanished, when the salaried officers of the Crown were reinstated with the sole addition of one unsalaried minister, the Marchese Gino Capponi; but this appointment was so popular, as to reassure the people respecting the future measures of the Government.

Another important subject engaging public attention during the summer of 1847, was the position of the Duchy of Lucca. In 1805, the Republic of Lucca had been granted a free constitution by the Emperor Napoleon, which lasted until 1814. At the Congress of Vienna, the five Powers were desirous of creating a State for the ex-Empress, the Arch-Duchess Maria Louisa. They accordingly restored the ancient Duchy of Parma, and bestowed it upon her, for her lifetime. It was, however, necessary to offer some compensation to the Spanish Bourbons, thus deprived of their hereditary dominions, and Lucca was assigned to their representative, Carlo Ludovico, with one condition, that he should preserve the Constitution granted by Napoleon, and with the promise that on the death of Maria Louisa, Carlo Ludovico was to be restored to Parma, and Lucca to revert to Tuscany. Such were the conscientious scruples with which the contracting Powers dealt with royal and plebeian interests. In order not to be less generous towards other Italian princes, it was stipulated that when Tuscany obtained this accession of territory, a small district, called the Lunigiana, was to be taken from the Grand Duke, and to be bestowed on the Duke of Modena, as a counterpoise for the acquisition by Tuscany of the important position of Pietra Santa, now included in the Duchy of Lucca.

But no sooner had the Duke of Lucca entered on his sovereignty, than the Constitution became a dead letter. A council of state, nominated by himself, and convoked at his pleasure, was the only restraint the Prince admitted upon his power, whilst the treasury of Lucca was squandered for the indulgence of his amusements and vices. An English jockey, of the name of Ward, having obtained his favour, was raised to the office of Prime Minister, and he managed the finances so as to supply all the exigencies of his master. In June, 1847, the Grand Duke of Tuscany had consented in form to accept the custom-duties of Lucca, together with the duties on salt and tobacco, and on the lottery, whilst becoming, in return, surety for the public debt, which had been reduced from eight hundred thousand to six hundred thousand scudi.[1] This transaction had caused an increase of burdens in Tuscany, which had to give more than she could receive from her new source of revenue. The Lucchese meantime had preceded the Tuscans in obtaining a national guard from their Prince ; an event which excited universal interest, and was described by Giusti in a letter, in which he likewise alludes to the recent appointment of his correspondent, the Marchese Capponi. It is dated from Pescia, the 3rd September, 1847 :—

[1] A scudo is worth five francs sixty centimes, or four shillings and eight pence.

P

" MY DEAR GINO,

" I rejoice with the country, and with those who
have conferred this fresh responsibility upon you.   I
shall wait to rejoice with you, when you can tell me
the shoe does not pinch. . . .

" This is what has occurred at Lucca.   The son of
the Duke caused some arrests to be made in the night,
assisting in person, and urging them on, like a school-
boy.   The next day, wiser heads than his ordered those
arrested to be released from prison; but when the
Prince, on his return to the city in the evening, was
received with hisses and stones, he hastened after the
messengers who had been despatched to Viareggio to
liberate the prisoners sent there on the previous day,
and forbade their being set at liberty.   This happened
on a Tuesday.   Wednesday morning there was a great
hubbub in the city.   The chief officials resigned, and
the people crowded before the ducal palace, in which
the Ministers were sitting in council, to deliberate
what means to adopt.   At four in the afternoon, a
deputation of the Council started from Lucca to wait
on the Duke, who was at his villa in the neighbourhood,
and who had not made his appearance at the Council,
as he had promised.   Hardly had the mob learnt where
the Ministers were going, than they immediately formed
in procession, and followed the carriage, their numbers
increasing as they went along, until they arrived before

the villa, to await the answer of the Duke. The Duke issued the *motu proprio*, which you have read, and which, being carried to Lucca, converted that city from a perfect hell to paradise. The news was sent on to Pisa and Leghorn, and yesterday (Thursday) Livornese and Pisans poured into Lucca by thousands; the rejoicings were universal, and without the slightest disorder. They say that the Duke and his son have gone to Massa, but that their return is expected to-day. I think the people did very wrong to accompany the deputation of the Council; but when a city is all in commotion, who can prevent the mob giving the slip. Speaking dispassionately, they may have committed a few follies, but they have been the first certainly to get the better of that profligate rogue. . . .

" I must inform you that our provinces are likewise determined on obtaining a national guard, and I repeat that there is much to be said on both sides respecting this measure. Remember that the Government wishes to lay the responsibility on you. The people are at the boiling point, and it would not be amiss to subject them to discipline, and give them something to do. I confess this matter gives me much anxiety. I can answer that there will be no rising in the Valdinie-vole, but who can say as much for other parts of the country? Without boasting of being a popular man, I may tell you that I have spoken a few words which have set the people here on the right track. . . ."

On the 8th September, the feast of the Nativity of
the Virgin, the Grand Duke and his cortége went, as
was customary, to attend mass in the church of the
Santissima Annunziata. They had all, on this occasion,
laid aside the hated Austrian colours, and assumed the
red and white of Tuscany. The people lined the whole
way from the church to the Piazza dei Pitti, and followed
the Grand Duke to his palace with cheers, which Giusti,
in his new poem, the *Congresso de' Birri*, supposes to
have been listened to as a knell by the agents of police.
The poet was that very day writing from Pescia to
Francesco Farinola, as follows :—

                                  " Pescia, 8th September, 1847.

" MY DEAR CHECCO,

" *Requiem æternam.* At last the old rags are gone.
The *Gazetta di Firenze*, now that a national guard
has been established, has begun to speak out, and has
become loquacious, like Don Abbondio when he learnt
the death of Don Rodrigo. But the *Gazetta di
Firenze* is not the only Don Abbondio who has appeared now that this measure is carried. This is the
time for the resuscitation of ghosts and extinct mortals,
who start into life, after having wholly disappeared
since the year 1830.

"There is a movement and activity, a distribution
of banners and cockades impossible to describe. And
what order, what peace, what happiness, on the faces

of every one! The people allow themselves to be led like lambs, and the crowd who are present, when the newspapers are read and discussed in the Café's, show incredible calmness and docility. To-morrow I shall be in Florence, to introduce five or six Pescian people, who are to represent us at the convention of the Tuscan Communes. We did not know in time what was preparing in Florence and in all Tuscany, but we had pledged ourselves to celebrate the institution of the national guard with the whole Valdinievole on Sunday. The banner of our Commune will be in Florence, and will join that of the men of Pistoia. I shall return that same evening, or at latest the following day, but I do not know if I shall have time to see you all. . . .

"And what does Gino say? I am told that the rejoicings in Florence were very grand. I believe that the rejoicings next Sunday will be grander still; but after that day we must return to sobriety, and think seriously of our duties."

On the 11th September, a second great rejoicing took place for the institution of the national guard, a rejoicing not confined to the capital, but throughout Tuscany. A procession was formed in Florence, composed of the inhabitants from all the provinces, as well as of companies of the citizens ; and, amidst shouts of joy, were heard the names of Pius the Ninth,

of Gioberti, and of the Florentine patriots of old,
Ferruccio, and Piero Capponi. Even priests and riar
joined in the celebration of this event. Not less than
fifty thousand persons met in the Piazza dei Pitti to
greet the Prince. Such was the joyful welcome given to
the first dawn of a better government, and of the hope
it held out, that the nation might become independent
of foreign dictation.

Among other poems of this year, Giusti produced
Il Congresso de' Birri (the Congress of Police Agents).
Beginning with a description of the assembly, which
he compares to a meeting of Parliament, composed
of right, left, and centre, he gives the oration of a
violent speaker on the left, who advises that the pesti-
lence of free opinions should be stopped by cutting
off a few heads, as by nursing this fungus of liberty, or
allowing it to grow and to compromise the State and
the monarchy, the vessel will be swamped, to the sound
of lullabys. Why speak smooth words to a people
who would play the masters, or suppose that beasts
can have right and reason?——

> Lisciare un popolo
> Che fa il padrone ?
> Supporre in bestie
> Dritto e ragione ?

Concluding by advising, as the soundest of maxims, the
galleys and the headsman :——

> Ecco la massima
> Spedita e vera
> Galera e boia
> Boia e galera.

The next speaker is from the centre, an easy personage, in love only with his salary; he blames the violence of the orator on the left, reminding him that the times are gone by when the word Italy was only known to the learned few, since now every nurse teaches it to her nursling. Dungeons now do more harm than good, as the liberal, after fattening there, comes out as a martyr, and those who put him in are denounced as assassins. The speaker declares that he would not have uttered opinions such as these in public, and that in the streets he plays the cannibal; but in that Chamber, there are no liberals, and every honest man may therefore say what he likes :—

> In piazza fo il cannibale;
> Ma quì, Signori miei,
> Quì, dove è presumibile
> Che non sian liberali,
> Un galantuomo è in obligo
> Di dirle tali e quali.

He advises in the present crisis that they should be ever on the watch, ready to act when they discover in what direction the country leans, and, without caring for Prince or Republic, be on that side which secures for them the best means of livelihood. The centre applauds this speech, the left condemns, when a third Demosthenes rises on the right. The new speaker observes, the question is not one of salary, but of retaining the power in their own hands; and the first thing necessary is to prevent the ruler and the ruled from understanding one another, for should a reconciliation take place, farewell to the golden age. . . . When a State is sound and all agreed, what part can the police play?

> Quando uno Stato è sano e in armonia
> Che figura ci fa la Polizia?

Time was when the police were the base instruments of justice, but since kings have taken them into favour, and made them their ministers and confidants, they, the servants of servants, have at once become masters of their masters. As he is speaking, the sounds of cheers for a Prince in unison with his people, reaches them from the streets below, with shouts for Italy and the national guard. All turn pale as death, and the genius of that enlightened agent of police dies upon his lips.

Ten thousand copies of *Il Congresso de' Birri* sold in three days.

To Alessandro Poerio.

"MY DEAR SANDRO,

"After so many months of silence, your letter was a great consolation to me, and the more so that it was accompanied by a few lines from Montanelli, in which he informs me of the immediate publication of his newspaper. What do you say to this sudden wakening up of our Government? For a whole month, good measures have succeeded one another so steadily, that we are filled with wonder. This wonder generates suspicion in the cautious, doubt in others, and those who feel secure of the times and of themselves, who have neither suspicion nor doubt, confess they are puzzled. I will, if you like, give you the history of what I partly know to be true, and have partly guessed. When Baldasseroni[1] and his colleagues rose to the highest offices in the State, they disappointed the ambition of several who were standing open-mouthed, secure of a mouthful. After the first discomfiture, those who had been thus mortified united against their successful rivals, and enlisted all they could on their side : these consisted of the scum of sub-officials who had suffered or been dismissed, or who were envious ; the phalanx of newsmongers, whose name is legion, and a portion of the liberals, who threw themselves into the *melée,* either from the effervescence of youth, or from over-deference to the opinion of those who instigated them, or from that disposition, which all share more or less, of looking doggedly at the authorities that be, whilst crying up to the skies men, whom they believe to

---

[1] Baldasseroni, one of the Ministers who succeeded Neri Corsini. He had formerly been Director-General of the Customs.

have discovered the remedy, simply because they have not yet been tried. Thus the attack being organized, the sharpshooters began to pick out the new Ministers by obscure notices, which were followed immediately by the clandestine press, giving them no breathing-time. To increase the fever, the Government committed the blunder of giving up Renzi, and then the skies opened upon them. The abuse, the discussions on their conduct, were universal and endless. Tuscany became like a man with a nervous disease, who after a torpid and lethargic sleep, wakes up excited, and almost in convulsions. Pisa protested against the introduction of female Jesuits; and Florence, Siena, and Pistoia, were roused to demand reforms; when, to decide the balance, there arrives Pius the Ninth. The Ministers, attacked on all sides, gave way; the Grand Duke was confounded; and the police, accustomed to gather their advantage from every disturbance, from mistakes and panics, as much in the people as in their rulers, raised their crests. The Grand Duke, it seems, partly from the fear of his own people, partly from seeing his statues few in number compared with those bearing the name of Pius, began to coquet a little with the Austrians, and a little with the police, who are in reality identified with himself; and they say that the ghost of the former president, Ciantelli, was seen in the palace, and that he had been there retained from 1833 as a quondam pensioner. Meantime, months rolled on, and the Ministers who had been attacked, perceiving that the attack had failed, and fearing for themselves as well as for the country, that the Austrians or the police might gain the upper hand, wished to reinstate themselves in public opinion, and to take revenge on their assailants ; but aware that the Grand Duke was the only power they could move, which was able to act, they set to work hand and foot, particularly Baldasseroni, who was younger and bolder than the rest, and by the single act of the new law on the press, they got rid of their adversaries, silenced those who accused them of having been seduced by a love of power, and once more encouraged the true friends of the public weal, who in the confusion had kept in the background, and almost in a corner. I will not dilate upon every detail, the gossip, the blunders, the commentaries made and acted upon this occasion by all of us, who are well known, *ab antico*, for opening our mouths and speaking without reflection. Enough, that even the most incredulous began to come down from their pinnacles, and to inhale the first breath of a new life. That which is most encouraging is, to observe that whilst all confine themselves within the limits of prudence, common sense, and moderation, a man, however honest, if he stand still with folded hands, will not be secure from the accusation of lukewarmness and idleness.

"The wheels will creak at first, but afterwards, by God's help, they will turn easily ; I am only afraid lest the ambitious spirits I have before alluded to should reappear in the guise of liberal newspaper writers, and, under the colour of enlightening the country, should attempt to unhorse those now in the saddle, whilst saying, 'Get you out there, I want to get on,'—'*Dicendo ! esci di là,/vo' star io.*' But in that case, we will ring other bells,[1] and the Government as well as the people must be defended from secret machinations. The *Alba* (the Dawn), a newspaper which ought to appear among the first, from the name that has been chosen, speaks out loudly and distinctly, and when it is set agoing, I hope to see it advance steadily and rapidly. We are now expecting *l'Italia* and the *Patria* in Florence. The *Fenice* is to appear in the course of September, a journal in swaddling-clothes, directed by Viesseux, in which, if my health allow me, I shall have the honour of assisting. But to confess the truth, I am less anxious about the journal, than to continue in my old trade, to which the older I grow, the more I become attached.

"I am sorry you do not feel as well as we all wish. . . . I can assure you that I purchase life at a high price, but I pay it, and am silent; the more, that my complaints would now be disbelieved, because no one would suppose from the envelope that the enclosure is so sad.

[1] Alluding to the old war signal of the Florentines.

" Remember me again to the dear Baroness,[1] and to your dear brother ;[2] my mother, also, who frequently speaks of you, sends her remembrances. . ... I am now publishing, without being obliged to ask permission from the censor, seven more compositions : *Il Poeta Cesareo, La chiesta del Passaporto, La Guerra, Il Consiglio a un Consigliere, La Rassegnazione, Il Delenda Cartago, Una Messa in Sant' Ambrogio.* The first two are rather feeble productions ; of the remaining five I hope better things.   I shall also publish here, either in the first three numbers of the *Fenice,* or in some other journal, or collected in a small volume, three poems, *L'Etere solforico, Strofe a Gino Capponi, Il Giovinetto.*   I have other scrawls in hand, which I do not see when I shall finish.   But, my dear Sandro, I am failing.   Right or wrong, I was one of the first to call out ; now that all call out, my throat is dry. Patience !   Many would not have done what I have done, but I have more still within me to do.   Others will do it, and better than I.   But do not you be disheartened ; you have genius, knowledge, courage ; you are willing, and you are an honest man.   What more would you have ?"

How little the Grand Duke trusted his people, in spite of this show of liberality, may be seen in a letter

[1] Baroness Poerio, mother of Alessandro Poerio.
[2] Baron Carlo Poerio.

he wrote immediately after the 4th September, 1847,
to his daughter, married in Bavaria. He there desires
her to assure the Emperor of his unalterable attachment to his person, and to the interests of his house ;
that he had been made aware of the preparations
for a revolutionary manifestation, to take place in
the theatre of the Pergola at Florence, and to avoid
this he might have feigned sickness, but that it
would have been of no use, as the people would have
sought him in the palace. He therefore considered it
expedient to show himself, and to pretend to sympa-
thize with this explosion of popular feeling, which would
soon blow over, and everything would then return to
its former condition.[1]

[1] See Giornale, *il Diritto*, 21 Luglio, 1859.

CHAPTER XIV.

POEM—ALLI SPETTRI DEL 4 SETTEMBRE, 1847—CHANGES IN THE CABINET—LUCCA—LETTER TO GENERAL COLLEGNO.

IN another poem of the year 1847, Giusti addressed what he called the Spectres of the 4th September, *Alli Spettri del 4 Settembre*, 1847, in which he denounces those who had kept themselves concealed in dangerous times, and now made their first appearance, like ghosts among living men.

The poet took for his motto a quotation from Manzoni's novel *I Promessi Sposi*, in which Don Abbondio is described recovering his power of speech upon hearing of the death of Don Rodrigo. He calls upon the Don Abbondios, or time-servers of this period, to take courage, since, secure from danger, they may now waken up from their sleep and from their fears. He represents the crowd of those who are neither believers nor unbelievers, leaving Limbo to join the people in the cries for Liberty, and seen towards dusk joining company with real liberals, who are consulting together and arranging the festivities for the following day, or found walking in the processions, after

the banners of the people. When they see the Grand
Duke reconciled to his subjects, and the police put
down, they breathe freely, and lose the fears which
have haunted them from their cradles; they then hasten
to place themselves first in the procession, and to make
more noise than all the rest, whilst *distributing the
July sun*—a Tuscan expression, signifying an affectation of generosity, whilst bestowing what belongs
equally to all.

> Bravo ! coraggio ! Il tempo dà consiglio :
> Consigliati col tempo all' occasione ?
> Ma intanto che può fare anco il coniglio
>   Cuor di Leone.

Don Abbondio calls out that even when he lay
concealed in times of danger, he had always been
a republican. The Poet compares him to a mollusca
enclosed in his shell, to a fungus without a root, to a
mask, a shadow, a creature without substance, and
to a butterfly just emerged from the state of larva.
Bearing himself like a half-intoxicated orator, he reigns
supreme over the audience of a Café, his head filled
with absurd ideas about government : he addresses
hearers, who utter a perfect Babel of opinions, if
not of tongues, and who pride themselves on their
ugly moustaches, whilst discussing cigars and punch.
Among them is an unknown spectre, the ghost of a
late spy, and looking on at this disorderly assemblage,
he finds some consolation for the loss of employment.

Fool! the poet continues, if the Theban orgies are renewed in this place, these are not the people who are born to a new life, but only a portion of the mob, despised by the majesty of Italy. He describes them as fickle in their affections as in their hatred, to-day raising their hero on the altar, and crowning him with honours, to-morrow abhorring him and casting him into the mire :

> Lieve all' amore e all' odio, oggi t' inalza
> De' primi onori nell'ara eminente
> Diman t'aborre, e ne fango ti sbalza
>> Sempre demente.

The disconsolate jealousy of the North may vainly rest its hope in such supporters, for concord is rising among the valiant and chosen sons of Italy :

> Invano, invano in lei pona speranza
> La sconsolata gelosia del Norde.
> Di veri prodi eletti figliolanza
>> Sorge concorde.

Then, addressing those who really compose the people, Giusti ends with these words :

> Tu modesto, tu pio, tu solo nato
> Libero, tra licenza e tirannia,
> Al volgo in piria, e al volgo impastoiato
>> Segna la via.

Thou who art modest, pious, and alone born free, between licence and tyranny, teach the way to the

Q

vulgar who would hasten on, and to the vulgar in harness.

When the law for the organization of the national guard appeared, the rulers still hesitated to place arms in the hands of the people ; they therefore produced so incomplete a project, that the late rejoicings were converted into complaints against the Grand Duke's advisers, on whom the odium of this half measure fell. Don Neri Corsini,[1] himself one of the Ministers, declared his opinion that the late concessions were dangerous unless a step farther was made, and the liberties of the people with the privileges of the crown consolidated by a statute granting a parliament. He ventured to suggest this idea to the Grand Duke, but his proposal only drew down on him the anger of his sovereign, who declared that to grant such a constitution to Tuscany was as much as to invite Austria to send troops into the duchy. Corsini was obliged to retire from the Ministry, but the Grand Duke and his advisers thought it necessary to concede something to the people, and accordingly a change in the Cabinet was resolved upon. Count Luigi Serristori was appointed Minister of War and Foreign Affairs, and the Marchese Cosimo Ridolfi accepted the office of Minister of the Interior, in place of Paver ; the new Cabinet, however, included several of the former Ministers.

[1] The late Marchese Lajatico, brother of the Prince Corsini.

Their first act was an alteration in the law respecting the national guard ; but their attention was speedily called to Lucca, as the treaty between the Duke of Lucca and the Grand Duke of Tuscany, of June, 1847, had proved of so little advantage to either party, and was so burdensome to Tuscany, that the Tuscans were desirous of anticipating the union of Lucca to the Grand Duchy, and thus at once relieve themselves, as they hoped, from a burden their sovereign had incurred, and the Lucchese from a ruler who was as tyrannical in his government as he was disgraceful in his life. The Duchess of Parma could have no objection to a proposal by which she could neither lose nor gain. The Duke of Modena would at once acquire an accession of territory, and the Duke of Lucca himself, by receiving a sum of money in compensation, would be enabled to retrieve his wasted patrimony. On the 5th October accordingly, Carlo Ludovico, of Bourbon, resigned the sovereignty of the Duchy of Lucca, which immediately passed into the dominions of the Grand Duke of Tuscany, who sent the Marchese Pier Francesco Rinuccini to take possession of it in his name.

The advantage which the Tuscans had expected to derive from this exchange was, however, wholly cancelled by the amount of the sum which they found themselves pledged to pay from their exchequer, as a compensation to the late Duke of Lucca ; for they had not only to give him his former stipend, but to grant him an additional income of nine thousand scudi a month, whilst they forfeited to the Duke of Modena, Pontremoli, Fivizzano, with the whole district called the Lunigiana.   The inhabitants of this district were thus coolly handed over to the most unscrupulous of masters, who obtained with the mountains of the Lunigiana and the Garfagnana, the key to Central Italy.   This transaction took place at a juncture when there was an alarm of war with Austria, with whom the Duke was sure to be allied.

The Tuscans at first only regarded the fact of the acquisition of the Duchy of Lucca, and rejoiced at their success, but the Lucchese, who not only perceived the danger, but who were discontented at their capital being converted into a provincial town, saw only cause for lamentation.   The right to their Constitution conferred by Napoleon I., and confirmed by the Treaty of Vienna, had indeed been left in abeyance by the ex-Duke, but had at least been acknowledged ; it ceased with their incorporation into Tuscany, then governed as an absolute monarchy.

On the 14th October, the Grand Duke and his family arrived in Lucca, but did not receive as favourable a reception as they expected.   Many of the Lucchese nobles retired to their villas, to avoid appearing to approve of the change, and when the Grand Duke named a junta to carry on the government, all the members of which were nominated from the first

nobility, the honour was declined. Meantime the
inhabitants of Fivizzano and Pontremoli, who had been
sacrificed to Modena, were in still greater excitement
and indignation. They had long known what was to
be their fate on the death of the Duchess of Parma,
but this anticipation of their misfortunes, fell cruelly
upon them. Petitions and protests from these districts
were presented to the Grand Duke on his arrival at
Lucca, and as he left the Church of San Martino, a
deputation of the inhabitants of the Lunigiana surrounded him, and entreated him not to abandon them.
They reminded him they had been united to Tuscany,
under his family for two hundred years, and complained bitterly, that just as they had begun to share
the advantages of recent reforms, and the new institutions, they were to be robbed of all, and their hopes
quenched. The Lucchese united their prayers to those
of the inhabitants of the Lunigiana, and the Grand
Duke promised to do all in his power to consult their
interests.

Meantime Leghorn was the first city in Tuscany to
express sympathy for these poor people, and the
example was followed by Siena, Pisa and Florence ;
all declaring they were willing to place their fortunes
and their persons at the disposal of their sovereign, to
save the inhabitants of the Lunigiana from so cruel a
destiny. Giusti describes Leopold's reception at Lucca
as follows :—

" DEAR FRIEND,

" The welcome the Lucchese gave the Grand Duke on the 14th was neither cold nor hot in the morning, but during the day, when they saw him go out on foot, dressed like other people, many cheered, and some reproached themselves for not having applauded him more. The Lucchese naturally regret their city having been reduced from a capital to a provincial town, and I think the Duke ought to show himself there the more frequently, and remain among them some time. If I am not mistaken, this is what most of them desire ; not from any servility, if I except some half-dozen courtiers, but from that gratification which, without being able to assign a reason, men naturally feel at the pomp and splendour of their native city.

" Before the Grand Duke left Lucca, he invited the Lucchese national guard to the review, ordered at Pisa for the following day. Towards evening, clandestine papers were dispersed in Lucca, which are said to have been sent from Leghorn, in which the Pisans and Lucchese were exhorted to fraternize with the Livornese. We ought clearly to understand the nature of these intrigues said to proceed from Leghorn. I repeat, however, that such occurrences ought not to be imputed to the whole population of Leghorn, but rather to the audacity and intrigues of the few who have succeeded in imposing silence on the many, and who, in the eyes of Tuscany and of all Italy, throw obloquy on an industrious, thriving city, abounding in traffic, and inhabited by a frank, energetic, warm-hearted people. I appeal to all who have known Leghorn formerly, to say if that people are disorderly, turbulent, or violent. For my part, I have found them much the reverse, and I declare and maintain that to impute all that has recently occurred, to Leghorn, is as much as to impute to the whole population the assassinations which of late years have contaminated that city. As the assassins were only few in number, so the disturbers of the public peace now can only be few. How is it that eighty thousand souls allow themselves to be overruled by a handful of factious persons? But you know the power of vague ideas, or of a panic from causes unascertained, of suspicion and of terror artfully desseminated over the minds of the multitude, and how dexterous and daring agitators are, in making use of these mysterious weapons. The Livornese, after the first excitement is past, have frequently given proof of a desire to maintain tranquillity, and as often the agitators have returned to excite them again. At one time they spread a report that the Germans were at their gates, at another in the silence of night they tolled the bells, and the bloodshed and feverish excitement which followed was all the work of a few reckless, ambitious men, who now strive to throw the blame on others by falsehood and calumny, and who have perverted, ruined, and thrown disgrace on an innocent population. . . . Leghorn herself will justify these words, when she is allowed to breathe freely. But for the present, let whoever is the friend of truth cease to talk of Leghorn, and dare, for once, to point out the parricides of Leghorn.

" My remarks on Leghorn apply nearly equally to Lucca. The misfortune of Lucca is, that she has been maltreated and trampled under foot, for years, by a branch of the Spanish Bourbons,[1]—who may God scatter from the face of the earth ! The Spanish Bourbons are all cunning ; they are wilfully ignorant, proud by race, and mean by disposition ; superstitious, licentious, covetous, and prodigals. If an unhappy people have been subjected to the meanest, if not always the most corrupt, of the family, you may imagine to what a condition they must be reduced. Allowing for this, who has not heard of the industry and activity of the Lucchese ? If you examine into the state of their cities and land, you would think that, instead of the Bourbons, Washington had been there. The Lucchese might in many ways serve as a model to neighbouring States. The public roads in Tuscany were always bad, whilst those of the Lucchese were kept

---

[1] From the time of Charles of Bourbon, succeeded by his brother Philip in the Duchy of Parma, 1733 ; they were sons of Philip V. of Spain by Elizabeth Farnese. The ex-royal house of Naples are the descendants of Charles.

like garden walks ; Florence is always in want of drink-
able water, whilst Lucca has had magnificent conduits
for twenty-three years, which carry health and plenty
into her bosom ; the Via Calzaioli is like a narrow
gorge, whilst in the centre of Lucca the two principal
streets have been widened at a considerable outlay, and
to the great embellishment of the city. Lucchese
industry and agriculture are proverbial ; and the
Lucchese, by their skill, so to say, force the land to
conquer nature herself. Lastly, that country is one of
the most populous in the world, and if it be an un-
doubted fact that the inhabitants enjoy prosperity, it
may likewise be maintained, that in actual wealth they
can compete with any country in Europe. But in this
lovely plant you may detect the worms which are gnaw-
ing at the root. The worm of foreign fashions, partly
imported from abroad by Carlo Lodovico, who is a
retailer of dishonour ; but also rained down on the
country from the Baths of Lucca, which disseminate
money and scandal ; next, the worm generated and attaining its full growth in the houses of the nobles, who
are the proudest of masters and the humblest of servants ; lastly, the worms of certain desperate characters,
and of those threefold apostates who angled for liberty
in 1831, angled for salaries and titles from 1831 to
1846, angled for office at the change of government in
1847, and are now returned to angle for popularity.
These, in a few words, are the ruin of Lucca. . . . "

A violent attack on the police in Florence on the 25th October, was followed by a decree from the Grand Duke abolishing that corps. Meantime the Duke of Modena, without waiting for the completion of the act of cession by the Grand Duke of Tuscany, sent commissioners to take possession of the Lunigiana in his name. There immediately followed commotions in the principal Tuscan cities, where the people were eager to hasten to the aid of their brethren in the Lunigiana. On the evening of the 9th November, a crowd assembled in the Piazza di San Marco, from whence they proceeded outside the Porta di San Gallo to a public park, where speeches were made, and lists opened for subscriptions to petitions, to be allowed to to go in aid of the inhabitants of Fivizzana. The petitioners then marched to the house of the Gonfalonier, who carried their petition to the Grand Duke : in his reply he expressed his thanks for their generous proposal, but declared that he had no intention yet of having recourse to arms. The following morning accounts reached Florence of atrocities committed by the soldiers of the Duke of Modena in the Lunigiana, when the people again assembled beneath the windows of the Palazzo Vecchio, demanding arms. The Minister, Ridolfi, assured them that the Grand Duke was actuated alone by motives of prudence, and he warned them that their conduct not only endangered the cause of the people of the Lunigiana, but even of Tuscany.

Satisfied by this explanation, after loud cheers for the Grand Duke and for the Minister Ridolfi, the people quietly dispersed.

Meantime the Ministers were accused of tardiness and indifference in the formation of the national guard. On the evening of the 13th November, the Tuscan militia were sent to Pietra Santa, to sustain, as it was said, the dignity of Tuscany, and as a protest against Modenese encroachments. The Gonfalonier and the municipal officers were ordered by the Grand Duke to consult together respecting a reform in the Municipality, and for this purpose some of the citizens, who were independent of the Government, were joined with them. Among them, were the Marchese Carlo Torrigiani, the Advocate Vincenzio Salvagnoli, and Leopoldo Galeotti, Count Luigi Serristori, though he had hitherto been reputed worthy of his office as Minister of War, disappointed public expectation, by only increasing the army by 900 men, whilst sending General Giacinto Collegno to visit different places of Tuscany, to ascertain which were best adapted for military operations.

General Collegno, a Piedmontese by birth, had been distinguished in the wars under Napoleon, in which he had given great proofs of courage. The choice of so able an officer was therefore approved of as one of the wisest that could have been made; but more energetic preparations were required from the Minister.

Meantime the controversy between the Grand Duke

and the Duke of Modena for the occupation of the Lunigiana had terminated by the intervention ·of the Pope and the King of Sardinia. The umpires apologized for the Duke of Modena not having shown sufficient regard towards the Grand Duke, on the ground, that it is always an advantage in similar cases to enter at once on possession of ceded territory; but the wishes or the interests of the people who were thus, like slaves or cattle, transferred with the land, to a new master, do not appear for a moment to have entered into the consideration of either umpire.

On the 28th November, Giusti wrote to Collegno from Monte Catini :—

" MY DEAR COLLEGNO,

"I have for many reasons rejoiced whenever I saw your name in our newspapers ; but now that you have consented to bestow on us a part of your military knowledge, acquired by practice and study during so many years, I do not only rejoice, but I thank you from my heart. Let talkers talk ; what we want are written instructions like those you have given ; and if you continue, as I believe you will, to impart your views to us, we ought to invoke a blessing on your head, and even love you more than we do now, which is not a little. You must devote a few lines to teach us the best method of training the youth of the country and of small villages to the use of arms. They are, in general, willing enough, but we are in want of instructors, and are entirely without practical views on the subject. Empty declamations about the war have put vague ideas into the heads of the people, and, if nothing worse, have prevented several, especially in the country, from volunteering to inscribe their names on the lists of the national guard.[1] I have seen some persons taking the most idiotic among the people aside, and explaining to them in detail all the affairs of the country, whilst they are as yet incapable of assisting to any purpose, even in the possible contingency of having to protect the frontiers. I assure you, that if your paper were read to them by one capable of giving explanations when required, they would understand and accept it *ipso facto*. The people have little science— they are not the worse for that—and they have much common sense. Big words confuse their brains, like those of every good Christian ; but explain facts to them with the simplicity of truth, and they are yours, body and soul. You will have to combat the mania for uniforms, which, at a time when we want all the implements of war, appears to me only worthy of milliners. Many decline promotion because of the expense of the uniform, and still more because they feel it puts them to real inconvenience. It is no longer ago than yesterday

[1] Because eager to be sent to the theatre of war, rather than stay at home to defend Tuscany in case of invasion.

that a worthy and brave fellow said to me : ' If they
make me an officer, I shall be obliged to refuse, because, though I have enough to live on, I cannot spend
seven or eight hundred lire, without becoming a
burden on my family.' This man might happen to
be the only man, or almost the only man, in the
country to whom so important a trust could be confided. Any one making a tour through Tuscany,
would find hundreds of similar examples. I have seen
a company of national guards under arms, without
uniforms, and who had not only a military air, but
even the appearance of their muskets and belts, all
alike, and their dresses different, seemed to make them
look more what they really are. In time, we shall
accomplish all we wish, at least I hope we shall accomplish much ; meantime let us attend to the essentials.
There is another unfortunate circumstance, which I can
only touch upon slightly, because I may as well handle
a burning coal. There has not been sufficient stress
laid on that most wise saying, ' New men for new
things.' Pages to draw tears of shame might be written
on this topic, and, believe me, though I have done
nothing since last September but cry out, Peace, peace,
peace ! that if complaints and murmurs are heard, the
people are neither so impatient nor so unreasonable
as some suppose. But all this between ourselves. In
public I affect to see everything *couleur-de-rose,* and
I make this a duty, not to call down stones upon the

pigeon-house. The Government, either because when they began to move in the right direction they had no fixed plan, or that they were forced to advance by rapid strides, do not appear to me to have acted judiciously. They ought to have begun as they did begin, with a reform in the Council of State, and a free press, because, by thus submitting their acts to the people, they were obliged to interrogate public opinion. But afterwards, instead of granting a national guard, they ought first to have abolished the police system, the cause of so many crooked deeds, and of so much disturbance ; they ought, as soon as possible, to have given greater vitality to municipal reform, and then, when political and communal administration had been purified in their elements, and in their chiefs, have instituted the national guard, and confided the choice and the formation to persons free from all connexion with the dead past, and who, therefore, would not have infected the new body from its birth, with the putrid taint of its predecessor. But now that matters have advanced thus far, nothing remains for us by which to remedy the evil, but to make it our sacred duty to behave like honest men.

"And how are you yourself? The last news I had of you were very good, and I believe that this fine season must have helped to restore you to your full vigour. Besides, this new life which has arisen among us, and which we have so long dreamt of, almost without hope, must be an excellent medicine to your rejoicing heart.

" Salute your wife, the Arconati, and Berchet, and continue, I beg, to let your voice be heard ; you know how dear it is to Italians ! "

To Giacinto Collegno.

" Pescia, 7th December, 1847.

" MY DEAR COLLEGNO,

" Continue to assist our country, you who are so capable of doing so. For my part, I shall continue the trade I have always hitherto followed, except with a few modifications required by the times. If I had been one of those liberals who excommunicate all others without exception, and who remain nailed to the year of their political baptism, professing a kind of *statu quo* of republicanism, that which has lately occurred would have made me very ridiculous.

" The project of an escape to Pontremoli, in case of an invasion was known to me. Pity them, they are suffering from the remains of a chest complaint. One turn of this earth has thrown us from a muddy plain wrapt in fog, upon the top of a high mountain ; and, accustomed as we are to a dense atmosphere, we have not yet lungs to breathe a rarer air. Therefore, if you see the Government and the people just at present subject to fits of coughing, lay the blame on the oxygen. To resist Austria for one quarter of an hour, appears a gigantic undertaking. . . . The great car of our Jove thundering from Vienna, may sometimes happen to fall on a nest of hornets. This was proved in the case of that poor cardinal at Ferrara, who has been more severely handled than we. Let the outlets of the country be fortified, and let arms be sent, with men capable of teaching how they are to be managed, and it will be seen that our natural bulwarks do not want defenders. Fivizzano and Pontremoli are there to speak. The Fivizzano people acted like true Tuscans, and, I lament to say let themselves be caught like blackbirds. The people of Pontremoli resisted, and have escaped.[1] Now it depends on the Government and on all of us to cease to be like the Tuscans of old, and to act like the inhabitants of Pontremoli. There is a report here that Austria is caressing the German people, to maintain them on her side, and to persuade them to come down on us. Will the magnanimous Hungarians and Bohemians allow themselves to be driven here to extinguish the sacred fire at which they themselves are again being tempered? And shall that generous chafing of the spirit be considered in their case the chafing of men, and in ours the chafing of beasts? Is not the cause of the people one and the same throughout Europe? Prussia and Bavaria do not act with Austria; the Sclavic nations give signs that they wish to manage their own affairs, and what will come next? Is one nation in progress to be sent against another nation in progress?

[1] Pontremoli was allowed to remain temporarily with Tuscany.

R

Then there is another consideration.   Although Austria
has plenty of men, she can never send them so far
from the Alps as to the centre of Italy, as long as she
needs more than her own numbers to defend her possessions foot by foot, especially those of Lombardy and
Venetia; and the same may be said of the Duke of
Modena, and of that woman who reigns in Parma;
whilst Rome, Tuscany, and Piedmont, may distribute
as many bayonets, and as long as they like, without
fear.   I do not say this to induce certain persons to go
to sleep, but to put cowardly fears out of the heads of
others who allow themselves to be over-persuaded and
disheartened.   To return to ourselves: the Tuscan
character is extremely plastic, everything depends on
knowing how to bend it in the right direction and to
keep it there.   *Laisser aller* and they fall to pieces;
take pains with them and a little puts them in the right
way.   Besides, allow me to mention one fact to you, of
which I have been for years convinced: we have plenty
of ability, but as it is not steadied and directed by
long-established institutions in the State, the critical
spirit which leads us to dissect everything with the
utmost minuteness, and to examine it under every
aspect, instead of producing foresight and delibera-
tion, causes perplexity and discouragement.   We are
born sceptics, with whom an excess of light dazzles
the brain, or we are like rope dancers, expert in
walking on a line, but always in the air.   As a last

resource, and almost as if turning against ourselves, in the close struggle between the wavering judgment and the heart, which has not power to move of itself, we turn everything into ridicule :—*Mea culpa, mea culpa, mea maxima culpa*—and we are most ready to pick out faults in others, when the moment arrives in which we ought to decide how to act, to nail ourselves down to some one thing, and to resolve with certainty on some one measure. If we do not want the requisite ability, we want self-reliance, and therefore the courage to act. This is why we have so often resigned ourselves into the hands of individuals ; as, for example, Charles of Valois,[1] the Duke of Athens,[2] Malatesta,[3] and other more modern rogues ; and yet we have always ended by declaring we could have done better if we had been left to ourselves. When we have been roused, and have made the prodigious effort of using our own paws to scratch with, we have found ourselves more lively and prompt in action than we had given ourselves credit for ; as, witness, the transformations we effected six months ago. We must continue these efforts, and if, after repeated attempts, we discover that we are a spoilt and useless piece of goods, then, and then only, let us abandon ourselves to our old fetters. I have an example to offer you of the truth of what I

[1] Charles of Valois entered Florence, 1494.
[2] Walter de Brienne, Duke of Athens, 1344.
[3] Malatesta, commanded at the Siege of Florence, 1530.

am now saying, in my own poor self. When, last
September, we began first to speak of military exercise, I asked myself, in the midst of so much bodily
suffering, sluggish in spirit, and with the weight of
thirty years on my shoulders, what was the use of
my joining the corps only to make myself ridiculous ?
But shame conquered pusillanimity, and after eight
days' trial, I began to feel another man ; and now I
would rather resign my mattress than this gun, which I
never supposed I should have been able to shoulder.
The first time that I had to act as sentinel, in that
monotonous walk backwards and forwards my thoughts
flew back to the bright years of my youth, wasted in
trifles, and my eyes filled with tears of sorrow and of
joy, to find myself where I was. This is the cause
which detains me here ; and as I know that none of
you will take it amiss, I will tell you frankly, that
this is the first time that I have not felt any weariness
when away from you.

"Tell me if you have ten minutes to bestow on me.
I want four percussion guns of the best kind, and fit
for use. If there are any to be had in Florence, you
will do me a great kindness in purchasing them for me
as soon as possible. I do not mind paying eight or ten
francs more or less, provided they are perfect. We have
none here, and we must handle such, and accustom
ourselves to the weight ; I wish to be the first to import
them into this part of the country."

CHAPTER XV.

LETTER TO THE PRUSSIAN AMBASSADOR—TREATIES WITH AUSTRIA—
REVOLT AT LEGHORN—F. D. GUÉRAZZI—WAR IN LOMBARDY.

THOUGH so ardent a patriot, Giusti was without the
bitterness of party spirit, and without personal animosity. In January, 1848, he writes to the Prussian
Ambassador at the Court of Tuscany, who entirely belonged to the retrograde party in politics :—

"MY DEAR REUMONT,

"I am glad that I have convinced you that the love
of my country does not so far blind me, as to make me
despise my fellow-creatures, because I follow a different
banner. I am opposed to all such intolerance, which
some hold up as heroism, and I wish that all people
on the face of the earth were at peace, without recrimi-
nation, without oppressing one another, and without
fighting, like greedy and savage beasts. God has
created each and all; let every one be contented with
that which he has, and, without invading his neighbour's
fields, remember the world was made for all.

" I thank you for your praise. You confer a pleasure and honour on me by acquainting your countrymen with our state of feeling. I say *our*, because so many in Italy are of my opinion, or rather, we are many who think the same way."

In December, 1847, a treaty was signed by the sovereigns of Modena and Parma with Austria, by which they consented that their States should be included in the line of defence of the Italian provinces belonging to the Emperor : they, further, acknowledged his right to advance Austrian troops upon the Modenese and Parmese territories, and to occupy their strong places, whenever required for the common interest, either for defence or as a military precaution. The two Duchies likewise engaged not to conclude any military convention, of whatsoever nature, without the previous consent of Austria.

The news of this convention was enough to excite the apprehension of neighbouring States, and on the evening of the 6th January, Leghorn rose in tumult, demanding arms from the Governor : after a vain effort to tranquillize the people, he summoned the Gonfalonier, who was however equally unsuccessful. The Livornese repeatedly called for the Advocate F. D. Guérazzi, and upon his showing himself in the midst of the mob, and addressing them, they quietly dispersed. This scene was repeated upon the following morning, when the Governor proposed to send a deputation to the Grand Duke, composed of several of the citizens, and among them the most popular man of the day, Guérazzi. The people, meantime, were still further excited by the circulation among them of a paper, calling upon all Tuscans to arm, whilst accusing the Ministers of being cowards and traitors; and warning the people that their country would soon be occupied by the Austrians. If this paper was seditious, and therefore dangerous to the cause of liberty, it found its apology in the encroachments Austria had so recently made, by her treaty with Modena and Parma, on the borders of Tuscany. The alarm of internal division, however, when the danger from without was so imminent, struck not only the Government with consternation, but all the well-wishers of their country, and the Ministers appealed to the loyalty and patriotism of the Tuscan people to stop the rash violence of the Livornese; the Communes throughout the country responding to this appeal, resolved to rally round the throne, and endeavour thus to avoid civil discord; but these patriotic offers of succour from all parts, received by the Grand Duke, were mistaken by the hot-headed leaders of the revolt for a hostile league, and served to irritate rather than terrify the Livornese into submission. The Government accordingly determined to send troops to put down the insurrection, and the General of the Forces was accompanied by the Minister of the Interior,

the Marchese Cosimo Ridolfi.   The Minister thought
it best to stop short at Pisa, and to announce his
approach by indulgent edicts, which, upon his arrival
in Leghorn, were followed by two of greater severity.
The following night several arrests were made, and
among those thrown into prison, was the Advocate
Guérazzi, who was loaded with chains, and sent to the
fortress of Porto Ferraio.   Similar arrests likewise took
place in Florence ; the next day, all Leghorn was in a
greater state of commotion than ever, at a severity which
appeared needless, since the peace of the city had already
been restored.   The friends of Guérazzi were especially
loud in their complaints, and an apologetic edict from
the Minister proved unavailing to silence them.   Two
months later a decree of the Grand Duke declared the
insurrection of the Livornese had had no other object
than to procure that form of government which had
since been proved acceptable ; the prosecutions were
accordingly stopped, and the accused set at liberty.

This was not the first occasion on which Guérazzi
had taken a prominent part in political disturbances,
although he had hitherto been chiefly known as a poet
and romance writer.   In all his works he had aimed at
nourishing ideas of patriotism, and of the unity of Italy,
and in his most celebrated novel, the *Assedio di
Firenze* (Siege of Florence) he had spread the fame of
Francesco Ferruccio, the republican hero of the sixteenth century.   Though tedious to a foreigner, from

its length, the work is important from its popularity at a time when the Italian mind was making an effort to awaken from a long sleep, and to disengage itself from those toils which prevented its free development. There are passages in the book vigorous and powerful, worthy of the hand of a great master, and which almost redeem its fault of prolixity, though they cannot make amends for the delight with which the author seems to revel in scenes of crime and bloodshed. The reader, justly or unjustly, traces in it the mind of a man who, whilst describing exciting scenes which do not move his own feelings, has no standard within himself by which to measure the effect of his words, and is therefore apt to exaggerate and disgust, where he only meant to awaken pity and just indignation. But Tuscany, in her lethargy, perhaps needed such to rouse her, and as in most works of fiction, when genius holds the pen, that which is evil in the book appears to have left but a slight impression, compared with its merits in the author's noble delineation of the character of Francesco Ferruccio, and the patriotic ardour which breathes through all the pages of the "Siege of Florence." As a literary man and a patriot, Guérazzi was at this time esteemed by Giusti, and by others of moderate views in Florence, even though they might disapprove his acts when he meddled with politics. The son of a woodcarver—who appears likewise to have been a man of education and acquainted with the best

classical authors of Italy—Guérazzi had studied law at
the Pisan University, from the age of fourteen.   He
there knew and admired the English poet, Lord Byron,
who became his oracle and prophet.   At this early age
he was considered by the police of sufficient importance
to be banished, for having read aloud, in a Café,
Neapolitan newspapers, at that time liberal, and his
appeal against this sentence, with his bold and remarkable reply, after justice had been denied him, showed a
singular precocity in a lad of fourteen.   "I pity you,
sir," said young Guérazzi, addressing the Chief of the
Police, "if holding a place which obliges you to commit
an act of injustice which you have not the power to
repair, your conscience allows you to retain office."
On leaving the University, he returned to Leghorn, and
began life with brilliant success as an advocate.   In
1828, as a member of the Academy of Leghorn
(*Academia Labronica*), whilst pronouncing an eulogium on a brave Livornese soldier, he introduced
observations obnoxious to the Government, and was, in
consequence, banished for the second time.   Mazzini,
then a young man, walked from Genoa to Monte
Pulciano, the place of Guérazzi's banishment, to express
his sympathy with one who had had the courage to
attack those in power.   In 1831, when twenty-seven
years of age, he was allowed to return to Leghorn, but
was almost immediately afterwards arrested, and accused
of having fomented a disturbance in the city, which he

had, in reality, tried to allay. He was thrown into prison, where the scenes of vice and horror he witnessed, can only be compared to those described at the same period in Neapolitan dungeons. Released, as he had been imprisoned, without trial, he found his house and papers had been searched, and his affairs ruined. Spies were placed round him, and in 1834 he was again seized, and sent to a prison at Porto Ferraio, in the island of Elba. He was there allowed the use of the library left by the Emperor Napoleon, and he spent his time writing his celebrated novel. On leaving prison, he found that he had lost his father, his brother, and the only woman to whom he was ever attached. Returning to his profession, he adopted the orphan children of his brother, and it was not until 1847 that the more important part of his public career commenced.

The circumstances of his precocity as a boy having nurtured a spirit of early independence, and of persecution having placed him ever on the defensive, had produced their natural fruits in a character which might, under different auspices, have been an honour to his country. Self-sufficient, proud and daring, he identified his country's wrongs with his personal injuries. With ambition greater than his talents, a love of power stronger than conscience, jealousy of others, combined with the cool calculating spirit of self-interest, truth and falsehood were alike employed by him as means to an end; and this man of real genius, but unstable morality, prepared to lead the democratic party in the revolution, which was impending over his country.[1]

The Grand Duke had appointed a special council, to propose a new law for the press, and a reform in the Council of State, as well as to suggest any reforms esteemed practicable in the reorganization of the Municipality, when news arrived of the Constitutions granted to Naples and Piedmont. On the 17th February, Leopold, yielding to the wishes of his people, resolved to follow these examples, and he published a new Statute for Tuscany, granting the people a parliamentary representation. Science, as well as property, was to be represented, and the members of every religious persuasion were equally to enjoy their rights as citizens. This new and greatest boon was received in Florence with banners flying, and all the noisy demonstrations by which a people show their gratitude for rights conceded as favours by their sovereigns. A few days later, the French Revolution of the 24th February took all Europe by surprise; Louis Philippe and his family had fled to England, and the French nation had proclaimed a republic. The news caused a panic at Vienna, where the finances had long been on the eve of bankruptcy, and where the liberal demonstrations in Hungary had already occasioned some alarm.

[1] Most of the above account of Guérazzi's career has been taken from " L' Italie est elle la terre des morts," par Marc Monnier, p. 386.

On the 18th March, Lombardy broke out in revolt, and on the 22nd, Field Marshal Radeztky was driven out of Milan, and Count Zichy, the Austrian Governor in Venice, had been obliged to take his departure.

The affairs of Tuscany meantime were steadily advancing, and Giusti, in a letter to Professor Montanelli of Pisa, written early in the year 1848, acknowledges how much the country was indebted for its present hopeful condition to the first bold step taken by him :—

To Giuseppe Montanelli.

" MY DEAR BEPPE,

"The time has now arrived to give everybody their due, and I will therefore venture to say that the Tuscans ought to acknowledge their debt to you, for one of the first steps they made in the road which has opened before us. When, two years ago, Pisa was all in a ferment at seeing the crane arrive, which heralded the storm of Jesuits, I can bear witness to how much you did to avert the calamity, by placing yourself, without either passion or violence, at the head of the malcontents, and regulating their actions with much prudence, much firmness, and at considerable personal risk. Now, every one could do as much ; but, at that time, it is our bounden duty to confess, that if there was plenty of talk about freedom, there was no freedom of action. It is indeed true that the applause came from all sides, that every one was full of wonder, and that some had a presentiment of the great changes which have since occurred and were then approaching. . . ."

The inhabitants of the Valdinievole were desirous that Giusti should offer himself as a candidate for election for the approaching Parliament, but he declined to stand, excusing himself, partly on the plea of bad health, but partly on a naturally retiring disposition. Another honour was, however, conferred on him, when he was chosen major of a battalion in the national guard. Meantime, the revolutionary party had been gaining rapid successes in Lombardy. Brescia, Pavia, Bergamo, Como, Cremona, and Lodi, had driven out the Austrian soldiers, whilst Vienna itself was in revolt, and all Germany had caught the infection of liberalism. But in Germany, the people had only to contend with native misgovernment; in Hungary, and still more in Italy, they had a strong foreign army to expel. On the 21st March, the Florentines again assembled before the Palazzo Vecchio, demanding arms to go in aid of their Lombard brethren. The Gonfalonier, Baron Bettino Ricasoli, addressed them, promising to acquaint the Grand Duke with the desire of the people. But the Ministers had not the power, if they had the will, to provide sufficient arms in a few hours; and they still hesitated to take such a step without the consent of the other powers, and thus draw Tuscany into a war with Austria. The people then became excited, and called again for a change in the Cabinet, when the Ministers themselves descended to the Piazza in front of the palace, and the Marchese Cosimo Ridolfi harangued them, concluding his oration in words to this effect:—"Whilst we are speaking, the great struggle is being decided on the plains of Lombardy; banners are therefore already prepared for our brave volunteers, since every delay may prove a source of remorse."

The youth of the city accordingly hastened to subscribe their names for the army, and the Grand Duke published the following edict: "The hour to complete the resurrection of Italy has unexpectedly arrived, nor can any man who loves this, our common country, refuse to her the succour she implores. I have often promised, when the times should become opportune, to second the impulses of your generous hearts with all that lies in my power, and here I am, ready to fulfil that promise. I have given the necessary orders for my army to march in two squadrons to the frontiers without delay. One corps is destined for Pontremoli, the other for San Marcello. The city will be meantime confided to the national guard. Those volunteers who desire to follow the troops of the line will receive immediate organization, and will be placed under able captains. But, amidst your ardour for the Italian cause.

do not forget that moderation which adorns every enterprise. I, with my Ministers, am watching over the country, and I shall meantime endeavour to hasten the conclusion of an Italian league, which I have always desired, and for which I have begun forming treaties."

Though the troops were to be sent to the frontiers, to satisfy the demands of the people, the Grand Duke had as yet made no declaration of war against Austria. The following day the Marchese Ridolfi declared by another edict, that there was no necessity to hasten the departure of the troops, as all the events of the war were hitherto propitious for Italy. Nevertheless, the greatest ardour was displayed in every city in Tuscany, and in none more than in Pisa, where the professors placed themselves at the head of companies of the students. Volunteers flocked in from Leghorn, Siena, Lucca and Pistoia, all eager for the fight. The march to the frontiers was unfortunately conducted in a disorderly manner, from the hurry in which the volunteers started for the field, and from their arriving in great numbers in places on the road where nothing was prepared for their reception. Meantime, the Duke of Modena had fled from his dominions, and the inhabitants of Massa and Carrara were eager to be united to Tuscany ; the Grand Duke convoked his Ministers to consider their demand, and on the pretext that having been abandoned by their sovereign these people might cause disturbances in adjoining provinces, it was decided to occupy them temporarily.

On the 29th March, Carlo Alberto had crossed the Piedmontese frontier, the first Italian sovereign to go to the aid of the Lombards; and on the 8th April was fought the battle of Goito, in which the Austrians were defeated and driven back. But the Modenese, meanwhile, were vainly expecting their Tuscan auxiliaries, and began to consider the delay as ominous; therefore, when the Tuscan volunteers at length arrived, they met with a cold reception. They only remained half a day at Modena, and by the orders of the Grand Duke occupied a district between Modena and Reggio, there to await the arrival of the Pontifical and Piedmontese troops. On the 26th April, Carlo Alberto, after a series of victories, crossed the Mincio. The Piedmontese army then consisted of 60,000 men, under Generals Bava and Sonnaz, and was accompanied by Victor Emmanuel, Duke of Savoy, the eldest son of the King. The Tuscans were commanded by General d'Arco Ferrari, and between the troops of the line, the volunteers, and one regiment of Neapolitan soldiers, mustered 6,950 men. The Parmese and the inhabitants of Piacenza had sent 1,670 soldiers, and Modena as many; 17,000 Pontifical troops under General Durando had crossed the Po, and 15,000 Neapolitans, led by General William Pepe, were on the march to join them from the South, whilst the Tyrolese and Venetians

s

in the North, had already furnished a contingent of several thousand.

In this time of ever-increasing anxiety, and in which the fate of Italy hung in the balance, Giusti describes the impatience of the people, in the following letter addressed to his friend Adriano Biscardi :—

" MY DEAR ADRIANO,

" We busy and courageous people who stay at home, every time that news arrives of the Italian army, and that we do not find that Mantua, Peschiera, Legnano, and Verona, are taken, Radetzky captured alive, the Croats cut to pieces, and the last remnant of the Austrian soldiers escaping right and left by the Tyrol and Friuli across the Alps, call out that Carlo Alberto has lead at his heels, that the Pope is irresolute, and that neither Naples nor the Grand Duke are capable of doing anything.[1] Fear is impatient, my dear Adriano ; fear, which, eager to get rid of that which keeps her upon thorns, expects men and events to move at the speed of steam, and thinks every hour a thousand, because she stands still with her hands folded. Fear sees a mere pond in the Lago di Garda, a brook in the Mincio, a soldier's barrack in Verona, and in Legnano a wafer on the map. Fear believes that at a word

---

[1] Subsequent events proved the fears of the people to have been better founded than Giusti at this time supposed.

eighty thousand men can be put on a war-footing, and that it is a mere trifle to send them off a couple of hundred miles, whilst to provision the army, we have only to take up our baskets and go to market. Men and horses have Mercury's wings at their heels; cannons move of themselves, and, already primed, plant themselves on the right spot; and every soldier has a forager in the ravens which fed Elijah in the wilderness. What are bridges, trenches, a wide and deep stream to cross, to Fear seated in a Café? A month's work may be accomplished in a day, but the work done appears to have taken a year. In short, we warriors of the immovable columns are like bells, which call others to church and never go themselves. If we were as clever as we think, words such as these would sound more appropriately from our mouths: here are we at our ease, watching over, or pretending to watch over the welfare of the country; whilst our countrymen, our dear brothers of September, are far away, exposed to the common enemy, ready to suffer and to fight: we sit down to table, thanking God, and from the soup to the salad we eat away without a fly to trouble us; whilst they, with their loads on their backs, have to gnaw a morsel of dry bread, ready for action between every mouthful, and have to shoulder their muskets before they have done swallowing: we, with our well-polished shoes, go our rounds, avoiding ditches and mire; they have to walk mile after mile, over the gravelly beds of rivers, or up to their knees in a bog; and after a substantial supper, chatting and smoking, we go to our comfortable beds, whilst these poor fellows either throw themselves on a heap of straw, or lie stretched on the bare ground, under the canopy of heaven: our severest fatigues and greatest hardships are to mount a staircase, to read a newspaper, to talk nonsense, and to wear our uniforms; whilst our brothers have to make forced marches, to ford streams, and to obey orders; they have to bear the burning scourge of the sun, to endure rain and wind, and to suffer all the unmerciful wear and tear of the terrible vicissitudes of war. Yet in our idle talk we pronounce the night and the repose enjoyed by men in active service, as interminable. When at the cost of their sweat and their blood they have forced a body of the enemy to retire, or have advanced a step, or opened a breach, they pitch their tents with the joy those feel who have fulfilled a duty, and who are prepared to do as much again on the morrow; we, who read the account of these actions in a paper three fingers long, measure their valour and dangers by the length and breadth of the newspaper, and with long faces wait for the next account in the succeeding number. I am getting angry, and so conclude with—

> " *Poeta.* Eroi, Eroi,
> Che fate voi?
> *Eroi.* Si ciarla.

Poeta.   E poi ?
Eroi.   Si scrive.
Poeta.   Ed io
         Dal canto mio
         Faccio lo stesso.
Eroi.   Va bene.   Adesso
         Tamburi e trombe
         Cannoni e bombe.[1]

" It would not be amiss if we were to show ourselves more discreet, patient and modest."

[1] *Poet.*   Heroes,
          Heroes,
          What are you about ?
Heroes. We talk,
Poet.   And what next
Heroes. We write.
Poet.   And I
          For my part
          I do the same.
Heroes. All right.   Now for
          Drums and trumpets,
          Cannons and bombshells

CHAPTER XVI.

A BAND of volunteers from Pescia started in April to
join the Tuscan army, which was ordered to encamp
before Mantua, and guard Le Grazie and Curtatone.
Giusti writes, on the 29th of April, from Pescia, to
Benvenuto Checchi, a friend in Florence, engaged with
the organization of the Pescian volunteers :—

" DEAR LELLO,

"A letter from the Prefect of Pistoia, addressed to
the Lieutenant-Colonel, announces that the Grand Duke
will come in person to Pescia to give away the colours,
as soon as all are ready. It is necessary that, on his
arrival here, he should not only find the colours, but
the man destined to carry them. The Lieutenant-
Colonel, therefore, desires me to write to you that
he will remit to you an attestation, by which it will
be shown that you were selected for that post, and
that he is constrained, with regret, to assign the

honour to another. My dear Lello, you know the regard we bear you; but ask yourself, if we are not reduced to the necessity of being in readiness for the reception of the Prince, who has thus unexpectedly announced his visit. The Colonel or I will come to Florence in a few days, and we will try our best to help you. Meantime, exhort our beloved fellow-citizens to show themselves worthy of the enterprise in which they are about to engage; and assure them that we will do all in our power to serve them, and shall always regard them as brothers. Let them remember that the honour of their country is now in their hands, and let none lag behind. More will arrive on Monday; and thus Pescia will have furnished her contingent to the Italian army."

He writes again on the same subject:—

"MY DEAR NICCOLINO,

"I hoped to have joined you at the head of a column of volunteers; but my health is always worse in the spring, and I feel that the offering of my poor carcase to the army would be like Cain's offering. I send in my place Captain Angeli, an able-bodied young man, who has a willing spirit, and whom I beg you to befriend, if ever you should fall in with him in Lombardy. Happy are you whose strength allows you to be present where the need is greatest! You are the legitimate sons, the

true firstborn of this beautiful land. We must all
bow down before you when you return among us rejoicing, and glorying in the redemption of your country.
Every time we see our brethren starting to join you,
our hearts are divided between fear and hope, and are
drawn first one way, then another. . . ."

On the 29th of April, Pius IX. issued his famous
Encyclica, the first blow to the hopes of Italy, and the
commencement and origin of disasters which rapidly
followed. A petition had been addressed to the Pope,
on the 28th of April, praying him to declare war
against Austria, as by allowing his armies to go to the
frontiers whilst maintaining peace with the common
enemy, his subjects who had crossed the Po, fighting
under his banners, if captured by the Austrians, were
exposed to be treated as common assassins instead of
prisoners of war. Pius assembled a Consistory of
Cardinals on the 29th, and there read his Encyclica,
in which, employing the formula of the old Court of
Rome, he denied all sympathy with the Italians waging
war against Austria, and declared that his general,
Durando, " had crossed the Po contrary to his orders,
which had been limited to the protection of the
frontiers."

This weak, hypocritical, and cowardly declaration, on
the part of one to whom all had looked up as the
leader, almost creator, of the new order of things, was

felt like a deathblow from one end of Italy to the other. It is at all times painful to have our faith and hope betrayed, but in this instance it was doubly so, as it not only destroyed the people's faith in the virtue of the Pope, the embodiment of their religious faith on earth, but likewise crushed their hopes for the deliverance of their country, by calling down upon Italy the hostility of every Catholic power in Europe.

The Tuscans encamped before Mantua were in such stress for provisions, owing to neglect on the part of their commissariat, or of others who should have kept them supplied, that they were obliged to borrow from the Piedmontese. Their general, D'Arco Ferrari, was slow, hesitating, and inefficient. On a false report that the Austrians had made a sortie from Mantua, he ordered a temporary retreat upon Goito; and by this unfortunate movement he exposed two Tuscan officers, Colonel Melani and Major Landucci, quartered near Le Grazie, to an attack from the enemy, in which, after a valiant defence, Landucci, one of the most able of the Tuscan militia, was slain. Just as the discontent against the General was at its height, Don Neri Corsini arrived in the camp, and, after having examined into its condition, he persuaded the Grand Duke to recall D'Arco Ferrari, and to send, as his substitute, General de Laugier.

On the 10th May, Giusti writes to the Marchesa D'Azeglio, from Pescia :—

"MY DEAR MARCHESA,

"God bless you for the letter you have written me.
If you were surprised at not hearing from me for five
months, you may imagine how much more surprised I
was not to receive a line in answer to three long
letters. . . . I regret the loss of these letters to you
and to Grossi, the more so as they would now appear
almost prophetic. . . . My dear Louisa, I confess my
self-love is hurt, and I shall long feel vexed that these
letters have not reached you. As far back as last
January I was certain that the Austrians had lost
Lombardy ; and our friends can bear witness that, in the
midst of the general panic, I laughed in the face of our
executioners. If the Arconati, Berchet, Collegno, &c.
do me justice, they will tell you that I have often
argued the point with them. . . . If you ask me whence
my confidence proceeded, I answer, it proceeded from
the utter contempt in which I always hold those who
trample on their fellow-creatures. I think you may
have heard me say, that I consider the tyrant to be the
real victim. The truth of this axiom, which I have
maintained ever since I had the power of thought, has
been demonstrated to me by a thousand facts which
have passed before my eyes ; and, whenever I see any
one making a bravado, and stalking over the heads of
his fellow-men, I immediately sing the *requiem œter-*

nam. If not to-day, to-morrow—but sooner or later he who sows death will reap death.

"You will imagine my vexation at not being able to head the column of my Pescian Volunteers, who are already half way to the Italian camp. I had taken every pains to form them, with more pleasure than I can express. I need only say it was like raising a troop for the protection of my own hearth. We overcame a thousand obstacles, we encountered and sustained numberless battles, partly whilst refuting the follies of certain persons, and partly whilst conquering the dilatoriness of others. . . . Newspaper writers howled and howled and knew nothing of the matter. To the honour of truth, I must tell you that we had no other aid but the good will of these youths, and the prompt succour of the Government, which, as you will see by the papers, is attacked on every side. . . . I thank God that my people of Pescia can show themselves where all Italy now is. Unhappily, I cannot accompany them, because I have not health to meet the hardships of a campaign. It is better to remain here, than expose oneself to the risk of having to turn back. . . . I never go to bed without thinking of those poor fellows on the Adige and on the Mincio, suffering and fighting for us, and I almost feel remorse at finding myself under cover, whilst they are passing their night in the open air, on a miserable heap of straw. You will believe, I have not the heart to put on my uniform, as

I cannot bear to be seen in that costume only for show. . . . I would give all my verses, and all my past life to be in the shoes of the húmblest volunteer in Lombardy. Among other honours, they have just made me a member of the Academia della Crusca, a very fit post for a carcase like mine. I believe they intend making me a deputy also ; but if they expect that I shall stir a straw to gain votes, they are green indeed. I have protested that I do not feel myself capable of the work, and I have pointed out the persons for election in my stead. I have ever loved my country from duty, and with sincere affection, and not from any vainglory, or desire to be conspicuous, and now is the time to prove my sincerity in the light of day. . . From the hour we began to revive, I have never relaxed my efforts to forward everything. But the time is now past when I felt the necessity of speaking out to our oppressors, and I have begun to tell truths to those who are slaves under the cloak of liberty ; a more dangerous office than, the first, and, in fact, one few take upon themselves. . . . I have written nothing for the newspapers, nor will I, because I have my reasons for keeping clear of them ; but, believe me, that to play the journalist on the highway is not a less arduous or less fatiguing enterprise. At Florence, in our days of trouble, I have been fourteen hours together on my feet, and with these legs ! February, March, and April, have been field months for all of us, from one cause or another.   In fact, I have written nothing, I have read nothing, and if deprived of my post of major of battalion, I shall be at an end altogether.   The revolution in Lombardy so turned my head that I hardly knew where in the world I was, and I repeat for the hundredth time, that I am vexed you should not have received the letters I wrote under the first excitement.   I ended with remaining three days in bed, with a bilious attack, but I bore it patiently, because my hopes were fulfilled, and I could have died without regret.

"I have been to see Vittorina, and I have kissed that angel of a baby.   What a lovely creature !   God has rewarded Bista for his noble act in joining the ranks of our valiant countrymen in Lombardy.   I wrote lately to Manzoni, and told him of his dear granddaughter.   Tell him to answer me ; it is so long since I saw his handwriting.   I will give you my verses if you come here, but now they belong to the past, and I do not care to speak of them.   Perhaps I may write no more, and it is immaterial whether I do or not.

"Remember me to Grossi, Castiglia, Collegno, Berchet, and the Arconati, and tell them all to be of good courage—the snake is scotched.   Adieu, my dear Louisa, rejoice at having suffered for so honourable a cause, and believe me that, as soon as I heard of your expulsion from Milan, I loved and esteemed you more than ever."

On the 15th May, the Neapolitan Parliament had been convoked, and that same day the hopes of the Neapolitan people were extinguished. A hideous massacre took place in the streets, ending with the King's resumption of his despotic authority a few days later, and his recalling the troops which had been sent to Lombardy with General Pepe. Thus the King of Naples and the Pope had alike proved faithless to the cause of Italian liberty and independence. Their treachery, which at the time caused greater bloodshed, and ultimately, defeat, and which postponed the liberation of Italy, was perhaps a necessary event to make the future unity of the nation under one head possible ; as well as to justify the acts of the Italians in the eyes of those who, acting on the principle that nations are the property of individuals, have the power if they have the will, to crush all free action in the people of Europe. Italy had, and still has much to endure, before fulfilling Giusti's prophecy that his native country would, sooner or later, be delivered from her foreign bondage, and from the rulers who were dooming her to a moral death among nations ; but, in his own words, those who sow death must reap death.

Union among the people was now of greater importance than ever, but union at such a juncture can only be purchased by the sacrifice of individual interests and views to the stronger party, if not to the actual majority in the nation. The arrival in Milan of Mazzini, the leader of republican ideas, and almost simultaneously, in Turin, of Gioberti, who not only desired a monarchical head, but dreamt of Papal supremacy, helped to increase dissensions and mistrust, already generated by human errors or weakness, by the ambition or lukewarmness of the leaders, and the impatience and rash inexperience of the people. Disturbances took place in Milan ; Carlo Alberto was prevented attacking Peschiera by delays in the arrival of his siege artillery, thus giving the Austrians time to strengthen their position ; whilst the King's adversaries spread reports, which were daily gaining more credit, that he was waiting to prosecute the war, until Lombardy and Venetia should acknowledge him as their king. Anxious to vindicate himself, Carlo Alberto resolved on attacking Verona, but on his approaching that city, met with a severe repulse from the enemy at Santa Lucia. Not discouraged by this defeat he again advanced, but by spreading his Sardinian troops over too wide a surface, and separating them from the other Italian troops, who were placed in detachments all over the country without the means of communication, each army could be attacked and destroyed without hope of succour.

The Tuscan troops were encamped as before described, when on the 29th May they were attacked at Curtatone by Field-Marshal Radetzky, who left the fortress of Mantua with 35,000 men, and a numerous train of artillery. The Tuscan camp consisted of 4,867 men, most of them raw volunteers, peasants, young men from the towns, and students from the universities, with their professors, and was only provided with eight guns. Radetzky, however, met with a spirited resistance. The Pisan students especially signalized themselves, as they rushed into the thickest of the fight, where fell many youths, the hopes of their families, and with them the distinguished Neapolitan, Professor Pilla. The Neapolitan battalion, quartered with the Tuscans at Montanara, likewise displayed great valour. The combat lasted six hours, in which time the Tuscans had to resist a force of three times their number, whilst the accidental explosion of their gunpowder, which happened twice during the battle, added to the horrors of the scene. Their retreat soon became a rout, but even amidst the confusion, marvellous instances of courage were displayed. Colonel Ghigi, after losing an arm, rushed among the fugitives, and endeavoured to rally them, calling out to them to unite their scattered forces and retreat like brave men. An artilleryman of the name of Gaspari, the only man in his corps who had not been wounded, tore off his burning clothes, and half naked, continued to direct those guns which were yet manageable, against the Austrians. Among the surgeons who were in attendance upon the wounded and dying, was Professor Ferdinand Zannetti, of Florence. He shared with the common soldier the perils of the field, and wherever there was greatest danger, he was on the spot, showing an example of dauntless courage and humanity. Many might be mentioned with honour, but the only well-known name was that of Professor Montanelli, of Pisa, who was wounded in the fight. When Radetzky heard what had been the number of the Tuscan force opposed to him, he expressed his surprise at the daring courage they had displayed.

The following day, the 30th May, the remains of the little Tuscan army were ordered by the King to retire to Brescia, where they were received with every mark of welcome. But the force was entirely broken up. Letters arrived from Tuscany, recalling all who survived of the gallant band of young volunteers, and none were left in Brescia but the wounded and sick. Another great victory gained by Carlo Alberto, at Goito, over Radetzky, on the 30th May, again raised the hopes of the Italians. In this battle the Austrians lost 3,000 men, the Piedmontese not 400, but the King and the Duke of Savoy were both slightly wounded. The citadel of Peschiera surrendered, and Carlo Alberto was joyfully saluted as King of Italy. On the 1st June he entered Peschiera, and the news of this double victory spread joy even in Tuscany, where so many were mourning for sons and brothers who had fallen at Curtatone. In Florence the Grand Duke, with his Ministers, went to the cathedral to return thanks to God, and there were rejoicings throughout the city.

T

CHAPTER XVII.

THE fortunes of war had begun to change, when, a few days after Peschiera had surrendered to Carlo Alberto, Vicenza fell into the hands of the Austrians. This disaster was followed by the fall of Padua, and of other Venetian cities, whose inhabitants, by the advice of General William Pepe, retired into Venice, there to abide a siege, which commenced on the 18th June, 1848.

The elections for the Tuscan Parliament, which was to meet on the 26th June, were meantime advancing, and Giusti, in spite of his resolution not to stand, was elected a deputy. Some changes had been made in the Ministry: the President of the Council, Cempini, had retired, and had been named President of the Senate, and the Marchese Cosimo Ridolfi had taken his place in the Cabinet; the Procurator-General, Cesare Capoquadri—already mentioned in this biography as the Advocate with whom Giusti commenced his career as a lawyer—had been appointed Minister of Justice, and the Advocate Ferdinando Andreucci Minister of Public Instruction.

On the morning of the 26th, the national guard
lined the way by which the Grand Duke was to pass
from the Palazzo dei Pitti to the Palazzo Vecchio;
and, accompanied by his Ministers, by the senators and
deputies, the Sovereign entered the Great Cinque Cento
Hall, a room built at the instigation of Girolamo Savona-
rola, in 1494, for the reception of the Great Council of
the Republic.   In the speech from the throne, the Prince
assured his people of liberty at home and independence abroad; he thanked God for having permitted
him to grant them a constitution heralded by reforms
and civil franchises, so well deserved by the Tuscan
people; he informed them that he was at peace with
all nations, except Austria; he urged on them the
necessity of prosecuting this war with vigour, so as to
lead to complete victory; and he concluded by in-
voking the blessing of the Almighty on their mutual
labours.

The first question which occupied the attention of
the deputies accordingly was, the conduct of the war.
The Ministers were interrogated as to the number of
the Tuscan forces sent into Lombardy, and what
advance had been already made towards the conclusion
of a league of Italian States.   Don Neri Corsini undertook to reply, and explained that the reason why the
Tuscan forces had not sooner been brought into action
was owing to the imperfect state of discipline of the
troops, and the neglect of the late Ministers in not

providing what was required for the army; he further
informed the Parliament that, though several treaties
with the Italian States were pending, nothing had, as
yet, been concluded. To this followed a series of in-
consequent queries, wasting time, and making demands
on the Ministers, impossible to fulfil. One of the deputies asked, if Italy could be delivered from the Austrian
yoke without Tuscan aid? to which Giusti was provoked to answer, "that without a spirit of prophecy,
none, not even the Ministers themselves, could reply to
such a query; but that to conduct a war directed by
many parliaments, a variety of assemblies, and vocife-
rating newspapers, was, indeed, a desperate undertaking."

The finances next came under consideration; when
it appeared, by the statement of the late Minister
Baldasseroni, that the various expedients tried ought to
have produced an income of six million of lire; but
that the resistance to an extraordinary tax made by
those engaged in commerce, and the unwillingness
shown by the citizens to lend upon their capitals, had
made it difficult to raise half that sum; whilst, by the
7th July, the expenses of the army alone would amount
to upwards of four hundred thousand lire. These
statements were followed by angry recriminations, and
several days were thus consumed before coming to
a resolution on the reply to be sent to the speech
from the Throne. Unhappily for the leaders of those

revolutions which first break the ground of long-established system, it is only through errors, and sometimes through violence, that experience is gained, and the soil prepared for other labourers ; still more unhappily, for that generation, as well as for their rulers, free institutions are seldom conceded until the hour of extremity has arrived ; when those accustomed to govern, being obliged to confess their incapacity, throw the responsibility of the most difficult questions on men who never, until that moment, have been trusted with the conduct of affairs.   The Florentines soon began to lose patience with the garrulity of their Parliament ; and newspapers, and the leaders of the people, vented their discontent in sarcasms, throwing ridicule on the new institutions, and thus bringing them into discredit with the multitude.   The Livornese were, as usual, the first to break out in disturbances, declaring themselves in favour of Carlo Alberto, as King of Italy, in place of the Tuscan government of the Grand Duke.   The arrival of Father Gavazzi, a priest who played the part of demagogue as well as reformer, added to the excitement.   In an harangue to the people, he upbraided the rich for not sending their horses to drag the artillery to the theatre of war ; he called on the priests to raise the standard of Italy, and on all to give their substance and their persons to drive the Austrians from the country.   Riots took place in various parts of the Grand Duchy, at Empoli, Fucecchio, Pisa, Lucca, and

Cortona ; and accusations in the Chambers, against the Ministers, became more frequent and noisy.

Meantime, the news from Lombardy were daily more disastrous. Confusion reigned in the camp of Carlo Alberto, and the Austrians were steadily regaining the ground they had lost. Though the King's army was in reality as numerous as that commanded by Radetzky, Carlo Alberto, from not concentrating his forces, always met those of the enemy with unequal numbers. The heat had become excessive ; and the soldiers were already exhausted from fatigue, hunger, and thirst (as, from whatever cause, the Italian army was scantily provisioned), when they encountered the Austrians in the Val di Staffalo, and once more beat them back ; but on the following day, the 26th July, Radetzky attacked the diminished army of the King, with reinforcements drawn from Verona, and totally defeated him in the battle of Custosa, near Valleggio. The combat lasted eleven hours, with enormous loss on both sides. Carlo Alberto retired to Villa Franca, from whence he ordered a retreat upon Goito, and thence proposed a suspension of arms to Radetzky. The conditions offered in reply were, however, too humiliating for the King to accept, and he continued his retreat to Cremona.

The news of the defeats in Lombardy spread consternation everywhere, and on the 30th July Florence was again in commotion, the people demanding a change

of Ministers. The movement in Leghorn had as yet met
with no response in the capital ; therefore, when a native
of Nice, haranguing the mob, declared the Tuscan
dynasty deposed, he only met with derision, and was
treated as a madman or fool. A storm of thunder
and lightning, accompanied by rain, finally dispersed
the crowd, and sent all to their homes. In the evening,
however, the disturbances recommenced ; the national
guards were called to arms, and the deputies hastily
assembled. . Towards night the Grand Duke issued
a proclamation, entreating the citizens to keep the
peace, and promising to take immediate measures
to provide succour for the war in Lombardy. The
Ministers went in a body to the palace to offer their
resignation, which Leopold hesitated to accept ; but
the next day they informed the Parliament that they
had only consented to retain office until the sovereign
was able to provide their successors. No sooner was
Florence restored to tranquillity, than Leghorn was
again in an uproar ; but, happily, the news of the
resignation of Ministers arrived to restore peace there
likewise.

The Grand Duke invited Baron Bettino Ricasoli to
form a Ministry, but he was unable to succeed, and the
former Ministers therefore continued in office a few
weeks longer. Meantime, England and France offered
their mediation between Carlo Alberto and Austria ;
but before the proposed terms could be submitted for

approval by the contending parties, the war in Lombardy had become still more disastrous for Italy. The King had retreated to Milan, and had undertaken to defend that city against Radetzky. But here the committee of defence and Carlo Alberto quarrelled; accusations and recriminations were followed by attempts to counteract one another's schemes, and thus any effectual resistance to an army like that of Radetzky's was rendered impossible. After the King had promised to defend Milan to the last, the people discovered he had already begun to treat for a capitulation, and Carlo Alberto had to escape in the middle of the night from the infuriated Milanese, leaving the Lombard capital to be once again the prey of the Austrian. Radetzky threatened to follow his victorious course into Tuscany itself, and was only arrested by the mediation of France and England, and by being reminded of the respect due to an Austrian Prince.

The Duchies of Modena and Parma were, meantime, occupied by Austrian troops; but, whilst the Duke of Modena hastened to return to his States, and announced to his people that by *Divine Grace* their sovereign was restored to them, Carlo Lodovico, who had succeeded to his hereditary dominions on the death of the Arch-Duchess Maria Louisa, allowed Radetzky to govern Parma by martial law.

In Tuscany, the Grand Duke had at length prevailed on the Marchese Gino Capponi to undertake the formation of a new Cabinet, and the respect and affection with which this truly noble-minded man was regarded by both sides in the Chambers, made the choice acceptable to all. Guérazzi was now the acknowledged leader of the democratic party ; neither he nor his supporters had forgiven his imprisonment by the Marchese Ridolfi, nor did he refrain from attacking his opponent's conduct ; but the late Minister found an eloquent defender in the advocate Salvagnoli.   The debate was at its height, when the entrance of the Marchese Capponi checked the rancour of party spirit ; and at the sight of one whom all agreed to reverence, but whose infirmity deprived him of beholding the faces which were gladdened by the sight of his, the deputies with one accord rose to greet him with a loud cheer of welcome.

The discontent of the people was not, however, allayed, and the Chambers were persecuted by petitions urging them to represent to the Sovereign the necessity of creating an army and of imploring aid from France. Forming themselves into what they called committees of war, the leaders urged the Prince and the nation to prepare for an expedition into Lombardy.   Refugees from Lombardy, Parma and Modena, flocked into Tuscany, and a second visit of Gavazzi to Leghorn, in defiance of a prohibition from the Grand Duke, added to the excitement.   The people hastened down to the port, and escorted the priest in triumph to the city ; that evening and the next morning he addressed them on the treachery of princes, their ministers, and their armies ; alluding to the recent conduct of Carlo Alberto in Milan ; and he called on poor and rich, women and priests, to lend their aid for the prosecution of the war of liberation in Lombardy. As his intention was to proceed to Bologna, permission had been granted to him by the Tuscan Government to visit Florence on his way; but after these orations, the permission was withdrawn. On his attempting to proceed in defiance of the prohibition, he was stopped and turned back, which was no sooner known in Leghorn than fresh tumults broke out. To the credit of the Livornese, it must, however, be told, that whilst seeking for arms and ammunition, the public bank and private property were alike held sacred, and there was no attempt at pillage. A council of citizens was elected to provide for the safety of the city, and among those named was the advocate Guérazzi. This committee persuaded the people to send a deputation to Florence with five demands : that the Tuscan people should be armed without further delay, for the support of the war in Italy ; that the national guard of Leghorn should be reorganized ; that a navy should be formed ; that the tariffs should be better regulated ; and, lastly, that the price of salt should be lowered.

A disturbance had meantime taken place at Lucca, upon the arrival of De Laugier, late general of the Tuscan forces, who was insulted by the mob, and would have been murdered, but for the interference of the national guard. On the 30th of August, the prefect of Florence issued an order forbidding meetings of the people, which presented occasions for seditious persons to conspire, thus obliging the Government to make arrests. The tumults in Leghorn not subsiding, but rather increasing in numbers and importance, the Grand Duke called out the national guard throughout Tuscany, and met them in a camp near Pisa ; but a report having got abroad that they had been summoned to act against their fellow-citizens and not for the defence of the country, Leopold had the mortification to find on his arrival a comparatively small force on the field.

In the midst of these difficulties, the Marchese Capponi sent for Guérazzi, and requested him to interpose his authority with the Livornese and persuade them to return to obedience. Guérazzi's eloquence had the desired effect, the people removed their barricades, and returned to their usual occupations, leaving the care of the city to the council of citizens. The Ministers at Florence, however, refused to acknowledge this provisional government. In the Chambers, the advocate Salvagnoli, in a long and eloquent speech, denounced the insults which had been levelled against the Parliament, and pointed unmistakably, in his description of disturbers of the public tranquillity, to Guérazzi. Don Neri Corsini charged the Livornese with plunder, an accusation which was refuted by the

Livornese deputies, and its injustice commented on by
the newspapers of the day.   A proposal was next made
in the Chambers to increase the standing army by 4,000
men, but the measure was steadfastly resisted by the
Advocate Capoquadri in the senate, on the ground that
large armies are subversive of liberty.   Other reforms,
especially those belonging to the municipality, were
proposed and carried in the Chambers, by the Marchese
Capponi.

Professor Giuseppe Montanelli had about this time
become one of the most prominent leaders of public
opinion.   Wounded and taken prisoner at Curtatone,
he had, at the request of the Tuscan Parliament, and
of the Ministers, been restored to his country, where he
was received with the greater enthusiasm that he had
at one time been thought dead.   Elected a deputy to
the Chambers, he made his appearance, pale, and with
his arm in a sling, to thank the Assembly for the interest
they had shown in his fate.   Whilst his courageous resistance to the introduction of Jesuits into Pisa, and
his having joined the ranks of the Tuscan volunteers in
the war, had alike made him popular, his intimacy with
the Marchese Gino Capponi, with Giuseppe Giusti, and
with others of the moderate party, served as a guarantee for his political opinions ; he was accordingly
selected by Capponi for the difficult office of Governor
of Leghorn.   The appointment was not as popular
as might have been expected, as Guérazzi at that

moment was the favourite of the Livornese ; but the day before the arrival of the new Governor the streets were placarded with the words, "Down with the Capponi Ministry—Long live the Ministers Montanelli and Guérazzi."

On the 8th October following, when the people as usual were congregated in the great square at Leghorn, calling for a resignation of Ministers, Montanelli addressed them from the windows of the palace, and promised to represent their wishes to the Grand Duke. Not satisfied with having thus far taken upon himself to act independently of the will of the Ministers who had appointed him Governor, and to whom he was responsible, he proceeded in a few days later to address the people to this effect : " I differ from the Ministers in this, that they intend to prosecute the treaties with other Italian States for a Confederation and Diet, whilst I consider that we ought to make an end of all treaties, and let the Tuscan Government set an example to the rest, by assembling without delay the representatives of Italy, the chosen of the people, to meet in Rome, in Turin, or even let it be in San Marino ; but let them determine our destiny by a general union and a common will."

The meeting of a constituent assembly at Rome, which finally became the eager desire of the Republican party, had not met with the approval of the sovereigns of the different States of Italy, and at that moment an idea was still pending of a Congress composed of the representatives of the various European monarchs, to meet in some foreign city, and there decide the fate of the Peninsula, whose disturbances threatened to embroil other nations.

The Marchese Capponi, accordingly, had given instructions to the Marchese Ridolfi (who had been sent to Paris and London, to watch over the interests of Tuscany), to claim for the Duchy a representative in the meeting of European Sovereigns. He likewise enforced on him, that if it were found impossible to oblige Austria, after her recent successes, to abandon Italy altogether, he should use his utmost endeavours to obtain from that power the cession of Lombardy to Piedmont, and to place the Lombard crown on the head of a son of Carlo Alberto. With regard to Venice, if the question lay between an Austrian Archduke and Francis of Modena, to prefer the latter ; but, if possible, to preserve the Lunigiana and the Garfagnana for Tuscany. . . .[1]

But meantime Austria herself was in the midst of revolution. Vienna had risen, and the Emperor had fled on the 6th of October. These news filled the Italian people with fresh hopes, and in no city were the rejoicings greater than in Leghorn. The Governor sent a telegraphic message to Florence on the 20th October, acquainting the Government that the Livornese threat-

[1] Ranalli, Istorie Italiane.

ened another revolution, unless a democratic ministry were appointed. The Minister's only reply was to recall Montanelli himself to Florence. He there confirmed by word of mouth what he had sent by telegraph. The Grand Duke accordingly yielding to the desire expressed by many of the citizens, accepted the proffered resignation of the Marchese Capponi, and of his colleagues, and commissioned Montanelli to form a new cabinet. Montanelli's first act was to hasten to Capponi, with the request to accept office under him, a proposal which was refused, not from any resentment at the provocations he had received, but by the advice of his friends ; and Montanelli was equally unsuccessful, in an application which he made to Professor Zannetti. The new Minister thus reaped the fruits of his own acts, and found himself alone in a crisis from which there was no escape. His rapid advance in literary honours, and the popularity he had acquired by the courage displayed in his first step in public life, appear to have over-balanced a mind where imagination predominated over judgment. Singular inconsistencies are to be found throughout his career. In early life an admirer, if not a member, of the society of Young Italy, he was at the same time a strict observer of Church discipline, and in this respect might have belonged to the extreme Roman Catholic party allied to despotism. After the accession of Pius IX. he became an enthusiast for the idea of a theocracy, as initiated by Gioberti. In his Austrian prison, after the battle of Curtatone, and when separated from all external influence, he became a confirmed republican. Attachment to that form of government appears instinctive in the poet and man of letters, who is born and bred in a land where all that is great and good belongs to her republican memories—all that is weak and corrupt to her monarchs. The republicanism of Montanelli was not, however, confined to a belief in the superiority of one form of government over another, but, like Mazzini, he wished to impose his ideas on Italy, without regard to the cost. Such a man was better fitted for a poet, historian, or prophet, than a statesman, and he fell an easy prey to one with equal ambition, who combined with more practical talent fewer scruples, less generous impulses, and less sincerity of purpose. Montanelli separated from his more judicious friends, rather than relinquish his hope of forming a Cabinet, turned to Guérazzi, and with some difficulty persuaded the Grand Duke to accept the services of a man who was peculiarly obnoxious to him. Guérazzi readily grasped at office, and from that hour secured for himself a predominance in the Cabinet, which left his chief only the name and the responsibility of power.

CHAPTER XVIII.

UPON the fall of the Capponi Ministry, Giusti wrote as follows to the Marchese Francesco Farinola :—

"Montecatini, 18th October, 1848.

"MY DEAR CHECCO,

"By my not making my appearance last Saturday, you will have concluded I was unwell; and, indeed, my dear friend, my health is much worse. I will not trouble you with a detailed account of all my sufferings; enough, that a wearing cough has returned, proceeding from biliousness, which leaves me no peace. You can easily suppose what has been the occasion of this return of illness. I am ready to pay this tribute of friendship to Gino, for certainly had my friendship been less, I should not have felt the blow as I did, when I read of his and his colleagues' resignation. It was so unforeseen, so unexpected a shock, that I thought it a dream for some time, and I read and reread the advertisement in the Gazette, like one stunned. Even

U

whilst writing to you my hand trembles, and I can hardly tell why. I have passed two nights without sleep. My dear Checco, I require to summon up all my courage not to despair; nevertheless, I feel it a duty, and more than a duty, a necessity, for me to return to Florence, to my post beside my poor friend, before whom we shall all bow down, when Tuscany has recovered her senses. But I do not know when I shall be able to move; therefore, I beg you to tell him, and those among his colleagues who care to hear it, that they must not accuse me of cowardice, or of holding back; that I have been with them in thought during these trying days, and that one of my severest trials has been to have been forced to remain here. I do not write to Gino, because I will not add to his troubles. His own sorrows and those of his country are enough. Write me a line, I beg; I long for news from Florence, and I cannot exist without hearing from you. If you could only hear how, in this little town, they cry out against the infamous conduct of certain persons, and how they do justice to honest men! It is impossible but that Tuscany will repent. Adieu, dear Checco. One line, one line, will satisfy me."

A report had been circulated of the death of Giusti, and in the comments on his character which followed, he was censured for having changed his opinions, influenced by his attachment for his friend the Marchese

Gino Capponi.   He thus exonerates himself, in a letter
to Professor Atto Vannucci :—

"MY DEAR VANNUCCI,

"You will have seen the *Dies Iræ* they have sung
on me, in the same metre in which I myself sang it
thirteen years ago on the Emperor Francis the First.
This *Dies Iræ* could not have appeared more *à propos*,
as I indeed feel very ill, and am almost more dead than
alive.   Having made a jest of others, it is only fair that
others should make a jest of me, and it is courteous to
attack me with the weapons with which I am most
familiar.   This *Dies Iræ* has, however, induced me to
make a conscientious examination of myself, the more
necessary as that song has reminded me there is no time
to lose.   I have spent my life in attacking those in
authority and their supporters, at a time when authority
was free to give me a kick in return, and (let it be
said, without vanity) I did so when others were either
silent, or spoke in a whisper, or bowed before those
in power.   Now that all may freely indulge in these
attacks, I do not think it any great display of moral
courage to stab a dead man.   As to the charge of
having changed my opinions, what do *you*, who know
all about me, say?   I myself am not aware of having
done so, but a man may find opinions, like wrinkles
and grey hair, growing, without knowing whence they
came.   It can only be thus explained: that whilst

others have advanced, I am where I was years ago, and because they do not see me beside them, they infer I am lagging behind. I do not say this is the case, but that it may be so ; at any rate, they may thank me for having made the road, when they were standing still.

" Perhaps they think, seeing me a deputy, and yet saying little or nothing, and not knowing what to angle for, that I have become a worthless piece of goods. In this respect they are right, for I am as much made to sit in Parliament, or to be an official man, as the statue of the Giant in the Piazza [1] is made to play the postman. They ought to have said this to those who insisted on electing me ; the whole district can bear witness to the fact, that having taken it into their heads that to compose a law and to compose a poem were one and the same thing, they insisted on having me here. Please God they may change their minds, and send me home again! I do not say this from indifference or indolence, but because I do indeed feel in this place like a chicken among the flax [a fish out of water].

" But in one of these commentaries on my conduct, I perceive that I have drawn down on myself the disapprobation of the writer, by the friendship which binds me to Gino Capponi. In 1836, when I first knew Capponi, I was told I had made the acquaintance of a true gentleman, and, perhaps, of something more than

[1] The statue of David, by Michael Angelo, in the Piazza della Signoria, in Florence, opposite the Post-office.

a gentleman ; and as he appeared such to me, I acknowledge that I endeavoured to cherish that acquaintance. In twelve years' time, and long before we reached the jubilee of universal fraternization, our friendship had so far ripened, that we had become like brothers ; in fact, for four years past, we have lived under the same roof. I refrain from speaking of the intellect and heart of this man, because we are too much one, and it is not well to praise ourselves. But this is the less necessary, as I can appeal to the opinion of Montanelli, who loves him much ; to Panattoni, who calls him the patriarch of liberty ; and to Guérazzi, who four years ago dedicated a book to him.[1]   I need not say how much benefit I have derived from his conversation, from his advice, and his example, because I have already said all this publicly, and because I know that he does not like my speaking of it. In short, if they think his friendship is injurious to me, I may regret their holding such opinions, but I cannot separate myself from him, although during the two months that he held office, and when I was at his elbow the whole time, he never condescended to make me his secretary.

"Another thing which is said to have made me change, is my rank of major in the national guard, because the

---

[1] All who are here mentioned belonged to the democratic party, who were now attacking Giusti because they believed his opinions were influenced by those of the Marchese Gino Capponi.

nomination belongs to the sovereign. Another man was indeed presented to the Grand Duke, of great talents and capacity, and for whom I have always entertained esteem and friendship ; but all the time that he was major, my constituents wished for me in his place. I hope you will not think me a vainglorious fool, but, for the sake of truth, I must inform you that for three months my constituents grumbled to have me, and were never contented until they had seen poetry in epaulettes. I was at first vexed at being a source of dispute, but I soon perceived, without having envied any one or aimed at honour, I should have to pay the costs of the feast. By going from shop to shop ; by having *tête-à-tête* conversations with this one and with that ; by telling them that my habits, my health, and I don't know what besides, would always keep me in the rear of my troop, I succeeded in appeasing them, and got out of the affair. If numerous occupations had not obliged the other major to resign, I should not have been placed on rank and file, for I had convinced my constituents I was in the right, and they had become reconciled to my view of the matter ; they thus gave me the greatest proof of affection I had ever asked from them. The whole inhabitants of this district can bear witness of the truth of what I am now saying, and they can likewise declare that we have always been good friends, and shall always continue so.

"But now that I think of it, it is quite possible that

I may have been set down as a turncoat, for having been elected an Academician della Crusca. We have yet to learn, my dearly beloved colleague, if those fifty lire all but five crazie a month were the bone which is supposed to have stuck in my throat. It would indeed be choking on an ant's egg, but we have seen worse things happen. Let us seriously reflect on this accusation, and pray remind me of it the first time that we meet in the Palazzo Riccardi, for the purpose of throwing light on the dictionary. You are aware what pains you, Arcangeli, and I took to be permitted to wear the Academician's gown! If the Academia della Crusca, then, has turned me from white to black, you must share the blame, since some one who peeped into the ballot-box saw that you gave me a favourable vote.

"But enough of this nonsense. What I have now written is partly to open my heart to you, and partly that you may be made aware of all my titles, and that not a single one may escape your memory when you direct an envelope to, the Advocate, Major, Deputy, and Academician della Crusca : enough to make ten Codini." [1]

Giusti writes again to Professor Vannucci :—

[1] Codini, a name applied to the retrograde party in politics, from the old pigtail, the absence of which, in the days of the French Revolution, was considered a sign of liberalism.

" MY DEAR VANNUCCI,

" I could not write the lines for you. Look at Leopardi's poem on Italy, and from the words he puts into the mouth of Simonides,[1] take the motto for the chapter which treats of the dead at Curtatone and Montanara. There were only two natives of Pescia, Luigi Marchi and Cesare Scoti ; the first was an officer in the troops of the line, the second a sergeant ; both of them belonging to good and respectable families, and both very young.

" As I have always been the enemy of systematic opposition, I cannot approve of those who set their faces violently against anything, especially if influenced by private animosity more than by a desire for the public welfare. The opposition, indeed, a few days ago, gave the worst example, by abusing right and left ; but the man who is firm in his principles ought not to allow himself to be shaken by every little jolt. He who treats Montazio with contempt, should not fly into a passion upon receiving a blow from Montazio. Do you remember our conversation when the new Ministers were first appointed ? I, who never have asked, and never would ask anything, of any one, who am, and always will be, the warm friend of my poor Gino, and who in

[1] " Beatissimi voi, ch' offriste il petto alle nemiche lance
    Per amor di costei che al Sol vi diede."

no way share the opinions of the present Cabinet ; even I exhorted certain persons not to run on as they were doing before ascertaining the facts, and I declared my own intention of keeping aloof, since over-hasty judgments appear to me both unjust and imprudent. I was not listened to, because the man who belongs to no party is disliked by all, and is bastinadoed by the reds as well by the blacks and yellows. The day before yesterday, I was amused by having to stand being censured in the morning, because I would not allow that Capponi was a Jesuit, and that same evening I had to give a man a slap in the face for abusing Montanelli. I hardly know how to steer between these extremes. I have always loved my country ; I have never lost hope of her resurrection, even when she lay prostrate on the ground. I have rejoiced from my heart when I saw her rise again. I have believed, perhaps with too much of the poet in me, that she might by degrees regain her ancient glory and her ancient greatness ; or, to express it better, that she might attain to a height of civilization to which, in spite of romance writers, she has never yet attained. On the other hand, I have always detested the intrigues of secret societies, ambition of every complexion, and hypocrites in every garb ; and I have found consolation in the calm satisfaction of having spoken out everywhere, and at all risks. . . . I am now determined to maintain my liberty, and as I ascertained that they intended to re-elect me a deputy, I warded it off, by

alleging motives of health, which are indeed most real :
I thanked them heartily, and got out of the scrape. As
I am not good for much, unless it is to stammer out a
verse, I ought not to have accepted the first time ; but,
as the whole district are aware, they insisted upon it.
I was made a deputy as I was made an Academician della
Crusca, and between the Academy and the Chambers,
I do not know which has had most to complain of in
their learned poet. The poet will now be both dunce
and Academician. If the new Ministry and the new
Chambers establish the well-being of the country, I
shall cry, 'Long live the Chambers!' and 'Long live
the Ministers!' If they make a mess of it, I shall be
disappointed, but I will not carry fuel to the fire. Every
one has a right to declare his opinion, but an honest
man ought to abstain from joining the herd of newsmongers, who disturb the country. Remember me
kindly to Giannone, and tell him that we shall soon
meet again. You know how earnestly I desire to see
him in the enjoyment of a competence and of an
honourable subsistence, and that I will do my best to
help him to it. Adieu."

The first act of the new Ministers had been to dis-
solve the Chambers. The election for another parliament was appointed to take place on the 20th November. In spite of many endeavours having been made
to influence the votes, nearly all the former members

were returned. Disappointed at this result, certain ill-affected persons got up a riot in Florence, during which the mob attacked the houses of Salvagnoli, Capei, and Ridolfi, and broke the windows. As no armed force was sent to put a stop to this violence, the Ministers were accused of having instigated or countenanced it. Only late at night a proclamation appeared, threatening the rioters with punishment.

Florence was in this state, when news arrived of the assassination of the Pope's Minister, Pellegrino Rossi, and of the flight of Pius to Gaëta, on the 24th November. Italians from all parts of Italy poured into Tuscany, requesting to be enlisted as soldiers, and greatly adding to the embarrassment of the Ministers. The Grand Duke proposed to form them into a squadron, to be called the Italian cohort, but with Tuscan discipline and rules. The election of Prince Louis Buonaparte as President of the French Republic was the next subject which engaged public attention, and was thus commented on by Giusti, in a letter to Professor Vannucci, written from Pescia, on the 25th December, 1848 :—

" France appears to me to have gone a step back. The election of Buonaparte is, I believe, to be attributed to the little faith that exists in the Republic, and to the dread of Socialism, and of Communism ; to the hatred these same Socialists and Communists bear to Cavaignac ; and likewise to Orleanist and Legitimist cabals. What a harlequinade ! "

CHAPTER XIX.

LETTER OF GIUSTI — THE CONSTITUENT ASSEMBLY — FLIGHT OF THE GRAND DUKE — THE BATTLE OF NOVARA — ABDICATION OF CARLO ALBERTO.

" DEAR FRIEND,

" As the proverb says, ' In due time we shall all learn to walk ;' I, too, believe that in these days a State may be changed with little noise and no bloodshed ; but it must be a State over which despotism and popular licence has swept by, not a State which has just been withdrawn from absolute power. Look at England ; the greatest changes take place there at intervals, which only occasion more or less words. Cromwell smoothed the way for all this, and now they plough with the ox and the ass. Then turn to Spain ; her revolutions have not been without violence, and, perhaps, all the victims have not yet been immolated ; for the ill weeds sown by Ferdinand and Isabella, and cultivated by Philip the Second and the Reverend Fathers of the Inquisition, have supplanted all the flowers of liberty in her fields. Yet, observe, the Spanish people are far in advance of us in the single fact, that by their resistance to Napoleon, they recovered during that war their feeling of nationality. I do not care who gives the impulse; when a nation that has been divided within itself reunites into one body, whether the miracle be performed through the eloquence of a Gracchus or the sermon of a friar, I thank God for it; because from union springs strength, from strength self-reliance, and from self-reliance the resolution to govern ourselves. I do not despair of the man who, though free to regulate his own affairs, does not contrive to regulate them well; for when I say, regulate them well, I do not mean by that, all is to go on as smoothly as would-be philosophers teach, almost as if to rule a people were as easy as to arrange the furniture in a room: such men, as long as there is nothing but talk, are the *ne-plus-ultra* of wisdom, but when the time for action arrives, they cannot lift a spider from its hole; and though hardly able of themselves to build a doll's house, they bark at giants struggling against fate, lying crushed under mountains which have been raised against them. From what you call ruins, the land has arisen again; changed, indeed, but whether for better or for worse, property divided among many hands, an increased population, and other results may best inform you. If it had not been for the French Revolution, you and I should be loading the Post with an academical pamphlet upon the foundation of a new colony in Arcadia, instead of writing such letters as this; yet, at the name of Robespierre you make the sign of the cross, and you weep over the train of Louis the Sixteenth's servants, as if, when they were snatched from this world, all was desert and empty space. You count the numbers sent to death in the name of the people, and you forget those sent to death in the name of God, or rather, to express it better, in the name of that *I* and *mine* which peep out in the *Motuproprio* from the mask of *we* and *our*. By your laws you pardon the man who may kill his enemy to save his own life (and, remember, kings have never had any scruple about cutting off heads, to preserve their thrones), and yet you expect that the people, when they defy their tyrants to the last drop of their blood, are to sheath the sword, and pardon."

Early in the year 1849, Gioberti, who had been appointed Minister to the King of Sardinia, sent Ferdinando Rosellini to Florence to propose a form of Constituent Assembly for the settlement of affairs in Italy. His idea was to unite the nation in a confederation, without disturbing the established Governments of each separate State. Montanelli objected to this proposition, that it set no limits to the power of the sovereigns, who would thus have the destinies of Italy at their disposal. He was accordingly regarded by the Grand Duke and his advisers as an obstacle in the way of the unification of Italy, and Guérazzi took advantage of the opportunity, to offer himself to form another Ministry; whilst, in order to propitiate the sovereign, he proposed to include in it the Marchese . Cosimo Ridolfi. But, meantime, Gioberti had sent a second scheme for consideration, in which he suggested that, at the conclusion of the war, every State should send representatives to two Constituent Assemblies—one general, for the settlement of the affairs of the Peninsula ; the other local, to determine the future Government of each separate State. Before this idea could be digested, a third proposal arrived from the Sardinian Minister, annulling his first of a Constituent Assembly for the nation, and suggesting a separate alliance between Piedmont and Tuscany, by which both States should act independently, or in opposition to the Republican Government now directing the affairs of Rome. With this last proposal of Gioberti's arrived the news of the Roman Triumvirate having proclaimed from the Capitol a summons for a Constituent Assembly to meet in the ancient metropolis of the world, in order to decide the fate of Italy. This news reached Florence in the middle of the night, and the people hastened with torches to the open squares of the city, loudly calling on the Ministers to move in Parliament for a law by which members should be elected for the future Italian Constituent Assembly. The next morning a crowd collected in the Loggia de' Lanzi, an arcade on one side of the Piazza della Signoria, to listen to addresses urging a

petition to be presented to the Chambers. The
people then proceeded in a long procession to the
Cathedral, which they found empty, as all the priests
had retired, to avoid being forced to offer up a thanksgiving on the occasion. Aware that their absence was in
consequence of an order from the Archbishop, the people
were threatening to lay siege to his palace and to seize
his person, when they discovered he had already fled.

The Ministers met to deliberate how to act. The
Chamber had resolved not to delay complying with the
wishes of the people, but the dignity of the Government
forbade their yielding to outdoor pressure. The Grand
Duke himself was the greatest obstacle in the way of
the proposal of a Constituent Assembly to meet at Rome.
Montanelli vainly endeavoured to persuade him to yield
to necessity : but Guérazzi had greater success, as he
assured him he had nothing to fear ; that if the Austrians
should conquer, a prince of Austrian blood would be
respected ; and that if they were defeated, his having
submitted the question of his right to the crown to the
arbitration of his own people would fix it with glory
upon his head. Having obtained the sovereign's assent,
Montanelli addressed the Deputies in a speech which
drew down thunders of applause. A majority demanded
that the law should at once be discussed ; it accordingly
not only passed the Deputies, but was carried without
a dissentient voice in the Senate.

The Grand Duke had no sooner consented to the law

being presented in his name to the Chambers, than, under the pretence of visiting his family, who had preceded him by a few days to Siena, he left Florence. The Gonfalonier, or mayor, Ubaldini Peruzzi, and the commander of the national guard, Ghigi, with Montanelli, hastened after him, in the hope of obtaining his signature, and persuading him to return with them to Florence. Montanelli, immediately on his arrival in Siena, obtained an audience, but found the Grand Duke in bed, on pretence of illness, but really from terror. Words of mutual regard and confidence passed between him and his Minister; but all Montanelli's arguments and persuasions failed to convince the Prince of the wisdom and duty of returning to his capital. Despairing of sucess, Montanelli wrote to Guérazzi, but on the morning of the 7th February he found, to his surprise, that the Grand Duke had risen from his bed, and, apparently well, was starting on a drive for the benefit of his health. Assuring the Minister that he would sign the law upon his return, he departed in the direction of the Maremma, beyond the gates of the city. That day passed, and the following morning arrived, and none knew whither the royal family had fled, when the director of the Post-office brought two letters to Montanelli—one, private, in which the Grand Duke informed him he did not intend to abandon Tuscany, but recommending his servants to his care, with a request that they might be allowed to follow him

x

with his baggage : the other letter, meant for the public
eye, alleged certain reasons for his flight, declaimed
against the proposal of a Constituent Assembly, which
would endanger his crown, and declared, that having
only the good of the country in view, and a desire to
avoid civil war, which motives alone had induced him
to allow the law to be proposed, the Grand Duke
felt himself compelled to refuse his approbation of
a measure which would have called down the thunder
of the Church on himself and on many good Tuscans ;
further, that as he foresaw his refusal would cause disturbances in Florence, he thought it best to leave the
capital, and even Siena, that it might not be said the
city had through him been plunged in civil discord.

Montanelli returned with these letters to Florence.
The Chambers were paralysed by consternation and
were in doubt how to act.   Whilst the Minister was
reading the Prince's letter, the people rushed into the
Palace and demanded the dissolution of the Parliament, and a Provisional Government to be composed
of Guérazzi, Montanelli, and a third member, of the
name of Mazzoni.   Guérazzi, desirous that all should
be done in accordance with law, ascended the tribune,
and addressed the mob ; and, whilst reproaching the
leaders with their invasion of the privileges of that
Chamber, assured them their desires should be fulfilled
without the necessity of resorting to violence.   The
Chambers were then allowed to proceed to business.

The proposal of a Provisional Government was moved, and was seconded by Don Neri Corsini, with the amendment, that to the three above named should be added, the Gonfalonier Peruzzi and Professor Zannetti; but, as both of them declined, the three first were appointed.

A junta was immediately formed for the protection of the royal palaces, and all contained in them. The Tuscan Ministers at foreign courts were recalled, and others appointed; accordingly, Professor Atto Vannucci was sent to Rome, and Carlo Fenzi, a young man, son of the banker of that name, to Venice. A less happy choice appears to have been made in a man of the name of Frappolli, not a Tuscan, who was sent to the Congress at Brussels. The next act of the Government was the introduction of certain reforms. The salt-duty was reduced, the pensions already assigned to the soldiers wounded in the late war were immediately paid, and the royal palace of the Crocetta was converted into an hospital for men. Many changes were made in official persons; some were dismissed, others sent in their resignations. A junta of public safety was likewise instituted, to assist the prefects. The greatest danger arose from a mutiny among the soldiers garrisoned in the fortresses of the city. Guérazzi and Montanelli hastening thither themselves, entered within the walls at considerable personal risk, and, in spite of menaces and insults, Guérazzi addressed

x 2

the men with his usual eloquence, which, with an exhibition of firmness and mildness, succeeded in stopping the mutiny. The Government finally issued a decree, that all not inclined to serve under the new order of things might return to their homes.

The Grand Duke, meantime, had escaped to the port of Santo Stefano, on the coast of Tuscany, from whence he addressed a protest against the Government established in Florence. Popular insurrections had already recommenced. On the 11th the railroad between Florence and Leghorn was interrupted, and the telegraph wire was cut. The triumvirs, who did not place entire confidence in the national guards, attempted to supply the place of the soldiers disbanded from the fortresses, by a troop formed of the refugees from all parts of Italy ; they finally summoned to their assistance a Council, in which were included the Gonfalonier Peruzzi and Professor Zannetti. The reforms they proposed in the national guard were, however, limited to a change of offices, deposing those appointed by the Grand Duke, and appointing others. The people insisted on Professor Zannetti accepting the post of commander-in-chief, an office uncongenial to his former studies, habits, or tastes, but which he accepted in that spirit of pure patriotism by which he was at all times actuated.

But even he did not escape the carping criticisms of party spirit, as may be seen by the observations of Giusti, who wrote to him on this occasion as follows :—

"1849.

"MY DEAR FRIEND,

"I have twice been to the Palazzo Riccardi,[1] without having been able to see you ; I have, therefore, determined to write to you that which I have no opportunity of expressing by word of mouth.

"Your name is the target of two opposite factions— one suspects you of being a republican ; the other, of being a codino. Maintain order, and let both parties talk as they like.

"The questions which every honest man should ask himself at this moment are simply these : Can he do without the Constitutional Sovereign ? If so, let him go ; if not, let him accept him. Will the Grand Duke return the man he went ? So much the better. Will his sojourn at Gaeta have changed him ? So much the worse for him rather than for us ; there will always be time to begin over again. It is vain to deceive ourselves, the Roman Republic rests on an uncertain foundation ; we have the Germans at our doors, and that which is called a reaction is nothing more than a desire for peace and safety. If we listen to the codini, they will tell us we shall never breathe freely until the battlements of the Palazzo Vecchio are surrounded by a festoon of the bodies of republicans ; if we listen to the republicans, they will tell us, that we shall get on very well if that same festoon be composed of codini. The national

---

[1] Palazzo Riccardi, the quarter of the national guard.

guard, which ought not to belong to any party, may beard both parties, and save the country. . . ."

Before the Grand Duke had finally quitted Tuscany, he wrote to General de Laugier, who was then at Pietra Santa, that he had refused the aid proferred him by the Piedmontese, but that he desired him to assemble all his Tuscan forces, and with these, whilst avoiding bloodshed and civil war as much as possible, to advance into the country: in plain terms, to reconquer Tuscany whilst sparing the feelings of the sovereign, who, from a safe place of refuge, could shift the pain or the guilt necessarily incurred for his restoration to power upon other shoulders. General de Laugier found himself in a position of much difficulty and danger. His troops were beginning to vacillate, and he could hardly maintain discipline. The triumvirs, hearing that De Laugier was attempting to restore the Prince by arms, proclaimed him a traitor to his country, and set a price on his head. General Apice was appointed to the command of the Tuscan forces, and, accompanied by Guérazzi, started for Lucca, where the triumvir addressed the soldiers. Meantime De Laugier issued proclamations protesting that, though he had intended to support the rights of his legitimate sovereign, he had neither been supported by the soldiers nor by the people ; his army, in fact, was reduced to 250 men, and his finances were exhausted.

Guérazzi was received at Pietra Santa by a deputation from Massa, offering to mediate with De Laugier,
and stating that the general and his remaining soldiers
were ready to capitulate. The triumvir accordingly
promised pardon to all, except De Laugier, who, if he
fell into his hands, he intended to consign for trial by
a court-martial, which had been created in Lucca. But
De Laugier's little army was now in open mutiny, and
their general had nothing left him but a flight into
Piedmont.

On the night of the 21st of February, bonfires were
suddenly seen blazing around Florence, and there was
heard a discharge of musketry. Soon afterwards a
rabble, armed with pikes, approached the city, led by
an Englishman of the name of Smith, and a Neapolitan
calling himself Ricciardi. All Florence was alarmed ;
the gates were closed, and every one hastened to arm
for the defence of the city. The Government, still
more panic-stricken, made this night's riot a pretext for
fresh arrests, and a court-martial was instituted for the
trial of the offenders. The soldiers, however, refused
to sit in a tribunal which they were ashamed to
sanction, but others were less scrupulous. Though no
act of positive cruelty followed, there were many unjustly condemned to loss of employment, and among
these, Professor Giovanni Battista Giorgini, the husband
of Vittorina Manzoni and the friend of Giusti. The
whole body of the Professors at Pisa protested against

this sentence, but were only threatened with being included in his condemnation.

On Guérazzi's return from Lucca, he was received with the honours of a conqueror; and soon afterwards, Professor Zannetti threatening to resign his command of the national guard, if martial law were not abolished, the triumvirs revoked a decree by which civilians had been rendered amenable to the summary treatment of a military jurisdiction.

Meantime, the war in Lombardy had recommenced in March, and had terminated that same month, by the fatal battle of Novara, in which the Piedmontese, after a hard-fought day, were totally defeated. The terms of a truce offered by Radetzky were so insulting, that Carlo Alberto, summoning all his generals, informed them, that having failed in this last effort for the liberation of Italy, he would not be an obstacle in the way of peace; he therefore resigned his crown to his son, Victor Emanuel, and bade them all farewell. Under the name of Count de Barge, he returned to Turin, and from thence proceeded to Nice, which he reached on the 25th March, 1849.

CHAPTER XX.

THREE LETTERS BY GIUSTI ON THE CAUSES WHICH HAD LED TO THE DISASTROUS TERMINATION OF THE REVOLUTIONARY MOVEMENT IN EUROPE, WRITTEN BETWEEN THE YEARS 1847–1849.

To Signor —— Doria.

"1847.

"I AM anxious to write to you on a subject which, without causing me alarm, has for some time past suggested food for serious reflection on the state of our country. You are aware, that in consequence of the events of 1820 and of 1830, a great many of our countrymen are abroad, who give themselves out as proscribed, and who fasten on to the tail of real victims, either to gain the credit of martyrdom or to make their profits. I do not allude to the exiles of 1821, as I know little or nothing about them; and, judging by the ten or twenty I have seen, I should not say there was any necessity for being on one's guard against them, as they are either harmless, or men who might now be made useful. The exiles of 1831 are known to me for more reasons than I have time to state here. Enough, I was at that period so young, that I was not admitted into their secrets, and all I have since gathered con-

cerning them in the course of these seventeen years, has
been more owing to chance than from prying into their
affairs ; so that, having always professed liberal opinions,
and yet never belonged to any society, I am now at
liberty to speak my thoughts openly, and none can
reproach me with an abuse of confidence.

" I look upon exiles, torn from their country, like
trees rooted up from the soil whence they derive their
nourishment.   They leave a great part of their roots
behind them, and, though felled to the ground, they
always retain a semblance of life—a life which does not
draw its vigour from the bowels of the earth, but is
scantily fed through the leaves, by the air which circu-
lates round them.   Without further metaphor, I maintain, that, whilst the heart of the exile continues at
home, he is imbibing ideas received in his distant
asylum, without, however, adapting himself to his new
country.   Hence the feverish anxiety to return, the
thirst for liberty, made more burning by hatred and the
desire for revenge : and hence theories which are
neither wholly nor partially fitted for our country.
Added to this, these exiles, especially those who are at
the head of the movement, neither inquire nor receive
any information of what is taking place here, except
from their own partisans ; and these partisans, either
because they do not comprehend the changes the
country is undergoing before their eyes, or because
they are unwilling to admit to themselves or to their

chiefs, that the world is slipping from their fingers ; or perhaps, also, from party vanity, maintain and foster in the minds of their distant friends the ideas they carried with them when they were forced to leave their country. Yet all this time they have been standing still, and the world advancing. Exiles always start from the same point ; whilst the people, who have remained behind, are gaining ground upon another road, and see new fields for action before them. They, therefore, consider us slaves and themselves free, or they call our efforts sluggish or insane ; or, if they do not thus condemn us, they fancy that it is they who have given the impulse to a people who walk by themselves. Thus, one way or another, each going at his own pace, we find ourselves in a few hours at the antipodes. The calendar is with us at 1848, whilst with them it always returns to 1831.

"Thus much is true, that now, when Italy has begun to comprehend herself, and has renewed her life like a healthy plant, the exiles in Paris speak of their plan for remodelling her, either because she has not been remodelled according to their particular views, or because they feel they have had no great share in the change which has taken place. Last March, I saw a circular from London, the substance of which was, that to effect anything on a solid basis, we, in the country, ought to rely *in* all things, and *for* all things, on our friends abroad ; that for this end we ought to make one common purse, and place that purse in London, to provide for our necessities from thence. My dear sir, if I had not seen the letter with my own eyes, there is not a living soul who could have made me believe so extraordinary a fact ; and, I remember, after having read the paper in the presence of several persons, who had shown it to me to ask my opinion, I remained silent, my head sunk on my breast, struck dumb, and like a man of stone. I saw beyond it a project to excite the country to arms, and I caused a copy of it to be given to me, that I might be assured I had not been dreaming, for I felt hot and cold with pity and shame. If they could rest satisfied with writing letters and scheming, one might have some patience with them ; but the worst is, they wish to urge us on towards an uncertain goal by violence, such as was tried in 1793, or by disorderly means, such as are now practised in countries differing in every respect from ours. The imprudent clamour raised by certain persons and certain newspapers may be traced back to them ; *they* occasioned the excitement which awoke reprisals in various parts of Italy ; it is owing to them that many have drawn back, almost vexed with themselves for having lent a hand to anything so foolish and of so little moment, and that others have met to agitate in the streets and meddle, to suit their purposes, troubling the waters, which perhaps at that moment were flowing pure and limpid. Some, aware of the evil, but unacquainted with the solution of the enigma, go so far as to declare these persons are washing the hands of Austria ; and men, who up to this time have been considered honest men, are accused of being paid by her. The accusation is false, but the report pardonable. The mistaken opinion which any individual may form of another may arise from prejudice or preconceived notions respecting him, but the mistaken opinion of a whole people is more probably owing to an inexact representation of a truth than to a falsehood. The intrigues of Austria and the acts of the society inimical to her lead to one and the same end, though with opposite intentions ; that is, they both hinder or stop progress. Therefore Austria and the secret societies are one and the same ; hence follows the idea, that the leaders are paid by Austria. This is the opinion of the majority, whilst the minority declare that the members of secret societies, unconsciously, and without being paid, serve the ends of Austria admirably. Austria and the secret societies are alike now dead, but Austria is departing, and the members of the societies are coming among us. I am almost surprised that, with all their desire to interfere in our affairs, they have not yet arrived. What are they about in Paris, when the fighting in Lombardy has been going on for twenty days ? The journey from Paris to the vicinity of Verona and Mantua is an affair of five days, and even I do not suppose that these restless spirits wish to arrive when all is accomplished. But whether they arrive sooner or later, what will they say, do, or bring us? The language spoken in their days has given place to a wider and more comprehensive language; the *modo tenendi* of that time is no longer adapted to us; the merchandise they bring us from abroad we have ordered to be carried to the lazzaretto or, at any rate, put in quarantine. I am convinced that the more sincere among them, when they see their country again, and find it wholly renovated, will lay down the old Adam and sit down to table with us. The rest must be divided into two categories—the category of those who are under a delusion, and the category of those who wish to delude others. I would let these last alone, for my stomach revolts against them; but we must watch over those who are under a delusion, and keep them in sight—watch over them to be ready to recall them to ourselves, which would be a great gain; keep them in sight, that they may not make any escapades. We want such sincere, good men, who will give heart and soul for the cause. We must find a home for the improvident, civil and military posts for those who have talents and courage, and, above all, we must sincerely appreciate the dangers they have confronted and the sufferings they have undergone, and never, in the slightest degree, reproach them for the errors they may have committed. I am never tired of preaching this to all for the common peace and benefit, and I desire that in every corner of our beloved country the necessity should be felt of not imposing our own opinions on others, and likewise of never rejecting any persons, whosoever they may be."

To Lorenzo Marini.

"Florence, 8 April, 1849.

" MY DEAR LORENZO,

" Our affairs have gone down head foremost, and are in a much lower condition than in July, 1848. The nation is not dead, nor is the idea departed this life which first roused her and induced her to attempt her redemption ; this idea, driven to seek refuge within the soul, is preserved there immutable—a living thought, purified and refined by misfortune, it will burst forth again when stronger, more universally acknowledged, and more irresistible. You know I never hoped blindly, but you also know I never despaired, not even in the years of apparent slumber, between 1831 and 1847. Nations, like individuals, when passing from one period of life to another, are sometimes seized by a kind of wonder and stupefaction, which makes them appear weaker than ever at the very moment when they are on the eve of a resurrection to a new life and renovated health. On the other hand, a people who have been struck down by misfortune, after the first grief, the first despair is past, turn to look around, and when examining themselves discover the mistakes and faults which have brought them low ; learning wisdom whilst taking heart once more, they prepare with greater prudence and greater confidence to repair the evil, and to recover the position which belongs to them. Consider how useful sickness is to young men in curing them of thoughtlessness and the intemperance of early youth, and that the fact of having mismanaged our private affairs, of having been deceived, cheated, and robbed, teaches us to keep better account of our possessions, and to guard and defend them from the claws of others.

"Two things have chiefly damaged us—too little and too much confidence in ourselves. The first made us too slow, the second too rash. The first nourished and supported a numerous herd of unbelievers, of vacillators, and of men who, by always backing, fell behind : the second let loose the wild and disorderly haste of the presumptuous and marplots, those who only played at battles; those who, before they had ascertained the course in which the vessel had to steer, and without compass or lead to sound its depths, plunged into a tempestuous and unknown sea. "You are overdoing it!" cried those who were standing with their hands before them. "You don't do enough!" bawled out others; and fretted to be in action. Between the do-too-much and the do-too-little, we did not know what to do, and made matters worse than before. Next time, if we take advantage of past blunders, we shall rest contented with effecting what is possible; and we shall bear in mind that the world is looking on, and that best is a foe to good.

"The Piedmontese army has been ruined by two opposite factions : by the faction which wanted to turn back, and which called Carlo Alberto mad because he persisted in his idea of renewing the war, and by the faction of demagogues who exhorted the soldiers not to fight *for* a king or *with* a king ; they dreamed, and persuaded others to dream, of a general rising, of a people's war, and other fancies of the kind. What was the result ? The war was resumed, but in so unwilling a spirit, that out of sixty thousand men who took the field, only twenty thousand could fight ; and the Italian army was, therefore, annihilated in three days. Do not forget that, to our eternal shame, the two Republics of Rome and of Tuscany have never been brought to life ; that Genoa is all in commotion, and Piedmont in confusion and disorder ; remember the insecure and vacillating condition of central Italy, with the imminent danger here of an Austrian invasion, and that we are now undone ; and then, if you can, form an idea to what state we are reduced.

"Here we are hesitating between the Republic, and returning to what we were before. It is painful to renounce opinions and our own act, but we have to reflect that the Germans are marching in the direction of the Tuscan Apennines. Guérazzi, with the Ministers, and with a majority in the Chambers, as well as a majority in the country, holds on by a thread, or gives signs of capitulating and making a virtue of necessity. The pack

Y

of members of political clubs, the greedy, the turbulent, the desperate, with a small number of honest men, who are wholly under a delusion, sharpen their weapons to be prepared for the last extremity, and are ready to shake the foundations of Guérazzi's power, as they did that of Ridolfi, and of Capponi. Towards the end of a revolution, those who are most alarmed for themselves are the most ready for desperate acts. The most audacious schemes are always started by men who, conscious that they have more than any contributed to change the State, fear they will be the first to suffer the penalty. Depending on the proverb, that where all are to blame none are punished, they endeavour to involve others in their guilt rather than perish alone, and thus prove they are better friends to themselves than to their country. A man of sense or feeling, when he perceives that the country cannot be saved in his way, will save it in the best way he can, by renouncing his own opinions if necessary; like the pilot, overtaken by a storm, who, in order to conduct the vessel to a safe haven, throws his merchandise and provisions overboard.

"I find I have written you a very long letter, which you must now accept as it is. Although I never write a line for the newspaper press, nor a line of my usual nonsense, I every now and then send my effusions to my friends, more indulgent than the public, who read and quote, but do not understand me. I have no intention of going to the Assembly.[1] I have objected, and do object, to our sending up any members, and I have many friends to whom I am sorry to be obliged to send a refusal, but I cannot act contrary to my conscience. I am, besides, born to keep to the pit, and those who would send me on the stage would annihilate me. My nerves are shaken and upset by a mere nothing, and the agitation at my heart carries away understanding and speech ; so that, though I feel I have much I could say, I end by saying nothing. To go there to stammer and play the fool, does not suit me ; and though I entertain no rancour against any living soul, I have felt the bite of the wolf, and have had enough. They now confess we were in the right ; but as I have always remained constant to that moderation with which they reproached us, I will take care not to take up the cudgels again to fight those who wished to injure us. Let us place a stone upon the past, and be better friends than before.

"Remember me to Lello, and do all you can to prevent any one causing a disturbance in the country. Whether our rulers wear a crown or a hat, civil discord is the worst scourge which can afflict a people. Adieu."

[1] The Constituent Assembly, to decide the question of the union of Tuscany with Rome, to which Giusti had been elected by the inhabitants of Borgo a Buggiano, who had remained faithful to their old principles, and were not under the influence of the ultra-democratic party.

To Lorenzo Marini.

"Florence, April 10, 1849.

" MY DEAR LORENZO,

"I must add another long letter to that I wrote to you the day before yesterday, as I am anxious to draw your attention to the evil threads interwoven in the web of that plot which transpires in recent events in Europe.

"Two hostile parties, both equally active and vindictive, had agitated Europe for several years, when Pius the Ninth appeared among us, and when the Revolution of February exploded in Paris ; I mean the party of Carlists, or Legitimists, or Retrogradists ; and the party of Republicans, or Socialists, or Communists. The focus of both these parties, has been, and always is, France, which, if I may so express it, is destined to perform the function of the liver in Europe, of that organ on which depends our digestion, and consequently our good or bad humour. The accession of Louis Philippe was a severe blow to both parties, as, by strengthening himself upon the commercial and industrial classes, he put an end to the practices of the old Court, which included that party who had followed principles suggested by prudence, but which, after a trial of fifty consecutive years, had fallen into disrepute ; principles, which really aimed at throwing back society, then in a state of progression. Satisfied with foiling their opponents by secret plots, they did not dare to show themselves in the light of day, and waited until the faction they hated, yet to whom they gave opportunity and breathing space, should open a way for them to advance. You may remember how frequently it has been said that the Legitimists and Republicans had an understanding with one another; this was so far true, that the two factions were equally sufferers, and equally irritated; and therefore, whilst butting at each other one moment, they united their forces the next to destroy a common obstacle, waiting for the end of the fray to knock one another finally on the head. It therefore fell to the turn of the Communists to give mortal battle to Louis Philippe, in which, if the Carlists did not take part, they looked on, rejoicing. They knew that Communism, which is destructive even of family ties, has not any sound basis, and has to encounter an irresistible repugnance in the feelings of civilized man, therefore could, at the most, only float on the surface for a moment, and would then create disgust and derision, leaving the field barren and in a state of confusion, and thus increasing more than ever the desire for order and wealth. Now, as in everything human there is always a danger of extremes meeting, so it is not uncommon for fear, and the injury caused by an excess in novelties, to induce people to turn round and fall back upon that which is old. And, in fact, the Carlists, after the exposure of the evils caused by Communism, and

after men had seen what harvest was reaped by the supporters of the cannon of June, raised their heads, and
contended for the upper hand. They perceived that the
Republicans could no longer have their way, and they saw
the parties who had suspended a war of blood, preparing
for a war of votes; they were aware that Cavaignac, a
true Republican, and adverse to Communism, was equally
opposed to the Reds and to the Constitutionalists, they
further perceived that it would neither be prudent nor
easy at once to proclaim Henri Cinq; and, in the hope
of dealing a first blow at the new order of things, they
joined the adversaries of Cavaignac to elect Louis
Napoleon: saying, France is by nature monarchical;
the Republic is only a medium by which to pass from
one dynasty to another; the monarchy of battles,
incarnate in the dynasty of Napoleon, cannot easily
be grafted on the country again, in a time in which
peace is demanded at any price; therefore, now is the
time for the restoration of the elder branch of the
Bourbons, or, if nothing better, the opportunity for
an accommodation, by placing the crown on the head
of the Comte de Paris. So much for France; as to
the rest of Europe, which has been in a state of agitation for a whole year, something of the same kind, more
or less, has occurred in every nation. The impulse
given by the Red Republicans roused Vienna, Berlin,
and a considerable part of Germany; it reverberated
in Milan, and carried all Italy along in the great, spon-

taneous, earnest, universal movement, the impulse to which was given in our country by Pius the Ninth, and acquiesced in by all the Princes of the Peninsula ; and yet this movement, from which all promised themselves salvation, has been thrown into disorder, and has deviated from the right course, until we have been driven over the precipice ; and now that our hopes have fallen in the dust, when doubt and disappointment have come among us, the monarchical party have made converts everywhere, and reap their harvest from the overcautious, whilst their opponents have only gleaned theirs from wild fanatics ; and they rest the foundations of their projected restorations on the ruin these last have brought about. As most men of ardent tempers have unconsciously served the ends of the Communists, so the lukewarm now almost as blindly serve the ends of the Carlists, who have a finger in everything. If you ask for proofs—between February and March, 1848, the period of progress, there were persons circulating among us (persons connected with the revolutionary party in Paris) endeavouring to throw discredit on representative government. They were sent here to spread the idea that this kind of government was only intended to check the enthusiasm of the people ; that it could not be reconciled with liberty ; that the sovereigns intended to take back fraudulently that which they had granted to necessity, and so forth : thus, from the commencement, they poisoned the germs of the liberty we had regained, and, by kindling a desire for something better, they made us indifferent to the good we had obtained. On the other hand, after the defeat of the Piedmontese armies in July, 1848, and when more than ever the Mazzinian party was let loose here, and all over Italy, when the Ministers, the Chambers, and every name which could give umbrage or offer an impediment had been knocked over, the mass of the people who took no part in the disturbances, and did not like them, and the Princes who had been ready to grant concessions, all began to be alarmed, and to fear the worst. At this juncture, the Carlists, Legitimist or Retrograde party, for they are one and the same, began to show themselves, and, insinuating themselves by the breach opened by the hostile faction, they fomented the fears of the Princes and of the people. They persuaded Pius the Ninth to take a retrograde step, they induced the Grand Duke to fly, and they now surround them both in Gaëta; and who knows what will be the result? I know little about the Pope, but I can tell you as regards the Grand Duke, that as far back as last December or January, a certain San Marco introduced himself at Court, a man who had been one of the followers of the Duchess de Berri; clever, cunning, *intrigant*, allied in close friendship with others of that party, and who, years before, had striven to make his way to the Pitti, but failed. This man followed the Court to Siena, and this man is with the

Court at Gaëta.   In short, to sum up in a few words what I have said at length, the Carlists allow the Communists to weary out society by tumults, threats, and bloodshed, and when they see men thoroughly disgusted, they persuade them to wish for repose, *in statu quo*. I think both parties have made a false reckoning. There is a necessity for change agitating mankind, felt by all, understood by none ; an imperious necessity, which all, in different ways, seek to find a word to express, a word which has not been hitherto found, but which some day or other will burst forth of itself. Meantime, let us beware of accepting this word from nations differently constituted from ours, and, above all, let us beware of the mad folly of serving the secret ends of persons who are working underground, and laughing at us."

CHAPTER XXI.

MAZZINI had left Milan for Florence, and arrived there just as the flight of the Grand Duke from his capital had thrown the whole country into embarrassment and confusion : Guérazzi and Montanelli accordingly invited the republican leader to a conference, in which they discussed the policy of proclaiming a republic for Tuscany, and immediate union with Rome. Mazzini assured them no time was to be lost to effect this junction, and was supported in his opinion by Montanelli, whilst the third Triumvir, Mazzoni gave a silent assent. Guérazzi alone opposed the measure, plausibly alleging that it was neither just nor reasonable to impose this form of government on the whole State, in order to appease the clamours of a single city, although the Capital ; the less required, since a Constituent Assembly to decide the question by lawful vote had already been determined on. Mazzini, who had, at any rate, the merit of being sincere in his enthusiasm, and without any sinister motive in his acts, continued to urge the necessity of imposing a republic on the Tuscan people, certain that they would learn to appreciate the benefit of such a form of Government, and that even if at first this should occasion some bloodshed, the cost would not be too great for the advantage gained. . Guérazzi, however, maintained his opposition to the measure, and the Council broke up without coming to any resolution. A few hours later, the mob, with Mazzini in the midst of them, crowded the courts and passages of the Palazzo Vecchio, and even forced themselves into the room where the Triumvirs were sitting, demanding an immediate proclamation of a republic. To a speech from Mazzini, Guérazzi replied with bitterness, calling him the greatest calamity to Italy, though afterwards apologizing for this language. He declared if the people would grant him two thousand well-armed and well-tried men, he would not delay issuing the proclamation ! upon which, shouts resounded from all sides, of " We will give you five thousand—ten thousand—thirty thousand ! " A great banquet followed, in the Piazza della Signoria, in the midst of which the bell of the Palazzo was suddenly heard tolling, and the windows of the city blazed with illuminations, whilst trees of liberty were raised, with cheers for the republic. Though the Florentine people looked on in silence at the banquet of democratic leaders and their followers, the members of the political clubs were giving way to loud and exaggerated rejoicings, with extravagant speeches and proposals ; but the general sympathies were inclined

to favour those who advocated referring to a popular
vote to decide the form of Government by which
they were to be ruled. The noisy patriots of the
banquet, however, met with no opposition, as they
proceeded to plant their trees of liberty in every
square of the city.

The example of Florence was followed in the other
cities of Tuscany, but Guérazzi declared that such
demonstrations were unbecoming in a people engaged
in the serious task of changing the Government of a
State ; Montanelli, however, under the influence of
Mazzini, insisted that these expressions of republican
aspirations should be accepted as the desire of the
nation, and be sanctioned by a decree from the
Government. The democratic party accordingly divided
into two factions, that headed by Guérazzi, who was
secretly working for his own ends, though ostensibly
promoting those of the friends of rational liberty and
of popular government, and that led by Montanelli,
supported by Mazzini, who sincerely believed that they
were conferring a benefit on the nation, and securing
the future liberty and independence of Italy, whilst
forcing on the Italian people their own ideas of
a free Government. Guérazzi at last succeeded in
persuading his colleagues to consent to issue a proclamation, that these demonstrations could not decide
the question of union with Rome, which could only
be settled after having been submitted to a legally

appointed Constituent Assembly, composed of the chosen of the nation.

Montanelli, who was eager to emulate the popularity Guérazzi had obtained at Lucca, now offered to lead an army against the Austrians, who were rapidly approaching the confines of Tuscany. As a preliminary step, he visited every town and village, haranguing the people, and, whilst reminding them of the cruelties practised by the enemy, urging them to rise in arms, as they had done before. But the Tuscans had been disheartened by the mismanagement of the army of volunteers who had perished at Curtatone and Montanara, and were little inclined to try the experiment over again, under a Government at war within itself, and therefore inspiring even less confidence than the previous Government, whose neglect had contributed to the loss of so many of their gallant friends and relations. A few companies of light infantry, and a troop of cavalry, with two cohorts of volunteers, were accordingly the whole force which started with Montanelli for the frontiers ; but as the Austrians approached Tuscany, the Piedmontese General, La Marmora, occupied the passes of the Apennines they abandoned, and thus gained possession of those military posts which were most important, in the event of a general rising against the common enemy.

Though Guérazzi refused to hold any further intercourse with Mazzini, the republican leader never ceased urging his own ideas upon the Government. The

Marchese Gino Capponi, in a spirit of conciliation, consented to an interview with him, and tried to convince
him, that to establish a republic in central Italy was at
that moment equivalent to invite foreign armed intervention. Mazzini replied that he was aware of this, but
considered the project ought to be persevered in, and
that the triumph would be more secure when they had
again encountered and defeated the invader. Soon after
this interview with the Marchese Capponi, Mazzini left
Tuscany for Rome, and a few weeks later, the Constituent Assembly, which was to decide the future
government of Tuscany, met in the Cinque Cento Hall
of the Palazzo Vecchio of Florence. Montanelli there
proposed the union of Tuscany with Rome in one
republic, and might have succeeded in carrying this
measure, in spite of the opposition of Guérazzi, had
not the disastrous news of the defeat and flight, rather
than retreat, of Carlo Alberto from Milan, of his second
attempt and failure, with his resignation of the crown
in favour of Victor Emanuel, rapidly succeeding one
another, and finally of Venice being closely besieged by
the Austrians, absorbed every other consideration in
that of the common danger. After a stormy debate in
the Constituent Assembly, Guérazzi, though accused by
the republican party of having been bought by the
Grand Duke, an accusation he indignantly repudiated,
was appointed Dictator, and invested with extraordinary
powers to provide for the defence of the country.

The Director's first act was to persuade Montanelli to leave Florence, as he thus hoped to deprive the opposition of their most able, as well as most honest leader. Montanelli was himself convinced that his presence only added to the embarrassment of the new Governor, without furthering his own cause, and therefore consented to depart for Genoa. He was said to have been sent on a mission to England, but no explanation has been given why he did not proceed farther. As the idea gained ground, that Guérazzi was secretly working for the Grand Duke, those who were favourable to this measure became more inclined to support his administration. A Committee met to compose a letter addressed to the most distinguished citizens, such as the Baron Ricasoli, the Marchese Capponi, Count Serristori, the Advocate Capoquadri, and the Duca di Casigliano, brother of Don Neri Corsini, to the effect, that the country looked to them for preservation, entreating them to unite with the municipality and with Guérazzi, and agree upon the means to be adopted at the present juncture to avoid a foreign occupation, at the same time assuring them that the Prince would trust in their loyalty, and the Tuscan people never forget their names among those who deserved well of their country. The several copies of this letter were enclosed in one envelope, and addressed to the Director of the Post-office, who carried them to the Dictator. Guérazzi, after reading them, sealed and despatched them to those for whom they were intended, adding a request that they would not enter into any secret intrigue, or thwart his schemes for the protection of the country. The Prefect of Florence, hoping to effect a reconciliation with the Constitutional party, and aid in the restoration of the Grand Duke, refused to listen to Guérazzi's assurances that the time had not yet arrived for the reception of the Prince, and held a conference on. the subject with the Marchese Capponi, Count Serristori, and Giuseppe Giusti, when it was agreed that Serristori should proceed to Gaëta, and urge the Grand Duke to issue a proclamation, calling on the Tuscans to return to their allegiance, and that he should resume his throne with the Constitutional Statute of 1848. Serristori accordingly left Tuscany to execute this commission, but the Prince did not condescend to return any answer. Meantime, secret intelligence was conveyed to and from Gaëta, by the Russian Prince Demidoff, whose gold helped to stir up an insurrection in the country in favour of the Grand Duke.

Guérazzi sent agents to France and England, to obtain their mediation to arrest the entrance of the Austrians into Tuscany ; he, at the same time, endeavoured to keep the partisans of the republic, as well as those belonging to the absolute monarchy, in check, and thus smooth the way for the Constituent Assembly to restore the Grand Duke, with such guarantees as he considered sufficient for the preservation of the Constitution. Whether he had any very earnest desire to secure this last condition may be doubted, when, as he himself expressed it, he hoped to play the part of General Monk in Tuscany. He had hitherto professed himself an ardent republican, but his conduct laid him open to the charge of duplicity, and he was mistrusted by men of all political parties in Italy.

Before the day had arrived in which the Assembly was to decide the future government of Tuscany, a street riot frustrated the schemes of the Dictator. A squadron of Livornese, composed of some of the worst characters in Leghorn, arrived in Florence, on their way to the frontiers. They were quartered in the Borg' Ogni' Santi, and from imprudence or from some unknown motive, were detained several days in the city. Their disorderly conduct had already given offence to the Florentines, when it was increased by a second equally disorderly troop of Livornese joining the first, on their way to Arezzo. A report was spread that Guérazzi had brought them to Florence to keep the people in check, and the panic was increased by another report, that the soldiers were about to pillage the town : that very day, the 11th April, Guérazzi sent orders to the Livornese immediately to quit the city ; but before they could depart, a scuffle in a shop where some of the soldiers had refused to pay for articles they had purchased, led to a disturbance, whose magnitude was exaggerated in fresh reports circulated throughout

Florence. Professor Zannetti, as commander of the national guard, hastened everywhere, and used every precaution to restore tranquillity ; but just as the Livornese troops reached the Piazza Vecchia di Santa Maria Novella on their way to the railroad, they were attacked by a furious mob. The soldiers fired in self-defence, which increased the rage of the people, who, in return, fired from the windows of the adjoining houses on the troops. The Livornese commander, Major Guarducci, endeavoured to restrain his soldiers ; and Guérazzi, who was at all times ready to hasten to the post of danger, was immediately on the spot. But he had hardly succeeded in stopping this fray, when the report of a more alarming riot reached him. Some of the soldiers belonging to the infantry regiment quartered in the town, had joined the people in an attack on the Livornese, and, in spite of the efforts of Zannetti, several of the Livornese who had taken refuge in a shop, were massacred. Guérazzi himself narrowly escaped with his life, and during the night which followed, cries were heard of " Death to Guérazzi," " Long live Leopold II. ! "

The municipality met to consider what measures should be taken to restore the peace, and after they had sent a messenger to confer with Zannetti, it was agreed that the Constituent Assembly, the municipality, and the national guard should provide in concert for the protection of the city, and for the return of the Grand Duke. As the illness of the Gonfalonier

Peruzzi deprived the municipality of his assistance, a committee of five of the most distinguished citizens was named to aid with their counsel. This committee consisted of Baron Bettino Ricasoli, the Marchese Girio Capponi, Count Luigi Serristori, the Marchese Carlo Torrigiani, and the Advocate Capoquadri.

Giusti gave an account of the anxious suspense of that day, in a letter to his father, the Cavaliere Domenico Giusti, who was at his residence in Pescia :—

" My dear Father,   " Florence, April 12, 1849.

" A tumult fell out yesterday between the Florentines and the Livornese volunteers. At one moment we thought the city was to be all in an uproar. We were at dinner, and you may imagine the sensation caused by a sound of musketry, which continued perhaps five minutes. There were some dead and wounded, but the affair was no worse. The people, however, continued in a state of agitation, and late in the evening the trees [of liberty] were ordered to be cut down. At the time I am writing, which is about mid-day, the trees are all prostrate, the bells are ringing, and I am told they are shouting in the Piazza for Leopold II. I, who am an enemy to all disorder, and abhor civil discord of whatever shade or colour, keep out of the way. I fear, however, that poor Gino, who would rather remain at home without mixing in public affairs, of which he has had so much bitter experience, will be obliged to come forth again. My love to my mother.

" It is now two in the afternoon. The people are all in revolt ; the Grand Ducal arms are restored, and they are shouting, 'Down with the present government.' The municipality has taken the reins of the State in their own hands, associating with themselves six citizens, among whom are Gino, Serristori, Ricasoli, and Carlo Torrigiani. The national guard are under arms. If no one plays the fool, matters will right themselves without any serious disorder. I wish for nothing except that the country may be preserved from an Austrian invasion ; and we have the means of warding this off. I have received your letter. The order or instruction from the Prefect of Pistoia is useless for me, as I have resolved not to put myself forward in anything. Meantime, keep your mind tranquil about me, and I will write to you with greater ease.

" I have re-opened my letter to make you more fully comprehend the meaning of what has taken place. For three consecutive days the country had shown signs of hollowness• and mistrust, as suspense is insupportable to all, but most insupportable for a people of an exciteable temperament. God grant that the return [of the Grand Duke] may not be more injurious than his departure ! I fear the people who go back, more than those who hasten on. The events from September, 1848, to the present day, should be a lesson for all ; if not, we shall fare worse."

CHAPTER XXII.

WHILST the municipality was engaged in providing for the security of the city, Guérazzi was taking a short repose after the fatigues of the previous day. He woke to find himself displaced, almost alone, and his schemes, whatever they might have been, frustrated. The unreasoning mob believed themselves betrayed by him, and demanded his life; the Republican party were indignant against him for having, whilst in power, abandoned their colours; his personal friends belonging to the Constitutional party, who had never approved of his policy, had lost confidence in his honesty; and the Grand Duke, for whose return he had secretly laboured, was not likely to show favour to a man who had been forced upon him as a Minister, who had since consented to play the part of sovereign in what he considered his dominions, and who now, it was said, made the maintenance of the Constitution a condition for his restoration. Guérazzi appears to have possessed great natural courage, hardened by unmerited suffering in his youth,

which was sometimes displayed in prompt and daring
acts, sometimes in the boldness with which he faced
those before whom a better man would have felt shame.
No sooner was he roused on the morning of the 12th
April, and learnt that the people were again collecting
in vast numbers, than he ordered out the municipal
guards; but counter orders having been given by the
municipality, they refused to obey. The President of
the Constituent Assembly gathered together the few
members remaining in Florence, and persuaded them
to consent to the resolution of the previous night.
Guérazzi, in spite of his natural hardihood, showed a
troubled and anxious expression of countenance, whilst
in a few words, he reproached the Assembly for having
demolished all he had happily accomplished. Indifferent to these remonstrances, they issued a proclamation
to the Florentines, declaring that the Constituent Assembly had resumed the power which they had confided to
the Dictator, and promising to shield the people from the
calamity of a foreign occupation. Guérazzi, finding all
further attempts to retain power vain, consented to proceed to Leghorn, and to use his endeavours to pacify
the Livornese, as that city, it was feared, would be in
a state of insurrection, on account of the assault and
massacre of so many of their fellow-citizens. But meantime, the tumults in Florence had increased, and a
renewal of acts of violence was threatened. Some
of the people were still in favour of Guérazzi, though

the majority were opposed to him. The fury of his
enemies at length rose to such a pitch that he was
advised not to show himself, or else to leave the city ;
but whilst deputies and others fled, he persisted on
remaining in the Palazzo Vecchio, refusing, though
with courtesy, to accept the advice of those who
offered to conduct him in safety beyond the walls of
Florence.

The municipality proposed to convoke the Parliament without delay, and place it on the same footing
as before its dissolution ; but Capoquadri, who was
secretly working in the interest of the Grand Duke,
objected, saying that they would thus deprive the
sovereign of a means to ingratiate himself with his
people. How to dispose of Guérazzi was the greatest
difficulty which presented itself at that moment ; it appeared dangerous now to send him to Leghorn, as his
presence there might create a party in his favour, and
complicate matters still further, by preventing the return
of the Grand Duke, whose presence, provided he agreed
to adhere to the Constitutional Statute, would, they
believed, alone restore order. A proposal was moved
that Guérazzi should go into voluntary exile, and, his consent having been obtained, money was furnished him for
his journey. But the people in the piazza below were
calling for his death, and threatened to break into the
Palace ; they were only tranquillized by the Marchese
Gino Capponi addressing them from a balcony, and

assuring them that the ex-Dictator was in safe custody.

The following morning a rabble of peasants arrived from the country, armed with scythes and hatchets, and carrying the banner of the Grand Duke, shouting, "Death to the liberals," in the name of Pius the Second. To save Guérazzi's life, it became necessary to transport him to the fortress of San Giorgio, behind the Pitti Palace; and the perilous task of conveying him thither was confided to Professor Zannetti and the national guards. Zannetti, accordingly, went to Guerazzi, and persuaded him to consent to this measure, pledging his word that he should be only detained a few days, he himself having been assured to this effect before undertaking the task assigned him.

Guérazzi was confided, in the Fortress of San Giorgio, to the charge of Captain Bonaventura Galeotti, who, instead of treating him as had been expected, maintained, or rather exceeded, all the severe forms of imprisonment used towards criminals, or prisoners of State. None were allowed to approach him, and he was forbidden books or the means of writing, a deprivation never before practised in Tuscany towards untried prisoners. Meantime, disturbances took place in various parts of the country, but the Provisional Government happily succeeded in appeasing all, except that in the city of Leghorn, which steadfastly refused to sanction the recall of the Grand Duke. The Government had sent a deputation to Gaëta to invite the Prince to return, but in spite of this measure, the Austrians began to occupy the frontier towns, and were gradually encroaching on Tuscan territory. Leopold was dissatisfied by an invitation which included a condition for the maintenance of the Statute, and he still hesitated to accept. Reports spread in Tuscany that quarters for the reception of Austrian troops were preparing in Lucca, and Professor Zannetti, though beloved by all parties, and only retaining his onerous position from patriotic motives, received many threatening letters demanding his resignation as general of the national guard, with which demand, rather than be a cause of disturbance, he now readily complied.

The Grand Duke sent, as his representative, to Florence, a commissary invested with extraordinary powers, to prepare for his return by the restoration of internal order and what he termed "a strong Government;" for this end, the commissary was to use the most expeditious means, and such as the present condition of Italy rendered necessary. The Florentine people at once remarked that all allusion to the Constitution was omitted, and, therefore, justly concluded that the means hinted at could only be foreign troops. The bearer of this unwelcome message was no other than the very Count Serristori, who had gone to Gaëta as the representative of the wishes of the Constitutional party, and whose appointment by

the Grand Duke had assured his friends that the
introduction of Austrian troops was impossible.   His
first act was to post up a placard throughout the
city, containing a letter from Leopold, in which a
promise for the restoration of a constitutional form
of Government was somewhat neutralized by the sovereign assuming the title of an " Imperial Prince of
the House of Austria."   A few days later, seventeen
thousand Austrians entered Tuscany, with fifty pieces
of artillery, under the conduct of General D'Aspre,
and accompanied by the Archduke Albert and the
Duke of Modena.   Upon their arrival in Lucca, the
general issued a proclamation, informing the Tuscan
people that he had come to defend the rights of their
legitimate sovereign, and to restore peace and order.
He further exhorted the Tuscans to receive his soldiers
as friends and brothers, and promised to preserve the
strictest discipline, and bring them only happiness and
peace.

This news caused no small consternation in Florence,
where the Provisional Government entered a protest
against the measure, addressed to Serristori, in which
they declared that, when they assumed the direction of
affairs in the name of the Prince, they had pledged
their word to preserve the people from the infliction of
a foreign occupation.   This protest was signed by all
but Capoquadri, who was absent.   The leaders of the
national guard likewise entered a protest against the

arrival of the Austrians.   Serristori, accordingly, sent the Florentine General, D'Arco Ferrari, to Lucca, to confer with General D'Aspre, to inform him that tranquillity was restored throughout Tuscany, with the exception of Leghorn, and to request him to confine his occupation to that city.   General D'Aspre, yielding to this remonstrance, proceeded, with the larger part of his army, to Pisa, on his way to Leghorn.   At Pisa the Austrians met with an amicable reception on the part of a small number of persons—sufficient, however, to enable them to report that their arrival had been welcomed throughout the city.   Meantime, a minority in Leghorn advocated attempting an armed resistance to the invaders.   The municipality proposed capitulation ; and the foreign consuls, from selfish considerations and regardless of the interests of the city, advised unconditional surrender.   But the opinion of the revolutionary party, in spite of the smallness of their numbers, prevailed.   The shops were shut, the bells were rung to call the people to arms, and barricades were thrown across the streets.   The Austrians, however, found little difficulty in overcoming these hasty preparations for defence ; and, after a short but sanguinary struggle, the people fled to the port, pursued by the German soldiery, who, having taken a few prisoners, put them all to the sword.   Wherever firing had taken place from the windows, the victors broke into the houses, and massacred indiscriminately, men, women, and children.

White flags were displayed, to deprecate further vengeance, and the city was seeking some repose, when
the alarm was renewed by the sound of muskets fired
from the cathedral, by which one soldier was killed.
The troops were again called to arms; and five unhappy men found within the church were mercilessly
shot down.   General D'Aspre proclaimed, whoever was
found with arms should suffer the punishment of death,
and every sign of the late revolution was severely prohibited.   He ordered the shops to be reopened, and
trade carried on as usual, whilst commanding the
citizens, through the municipality, to supply his troops
with quarters.

As General D'Aspre now turned to Florence, he proclaimed, from Empoli, that he had been sent by the
Emperor, at the request of the Grand Duke; for which
proclamation he was reproached by Serristori, as the
Grand Duke did not desire his cognizance in this affair
to be made known.   The Austrian soldiers marched
into Florence, with olive-branches in their caps, and
were received by the Florentines in silence.   They were
quartered in the various monasteries, whilst their
general took possession of the fortresses.   That same
day the new Ministers of the Grand Duke arrived.
Baldasseroni had been re-appointed, with De Laugier,
Capoquadri, and others, whose retrograde tendencies or
treachery had won for them the favour of the restored
prince.   The institution of the national guard was at

once annulled, but with promises to the people of its reinstatement at some future time, when the Statute should likewise be restored, and such improvements made as to meet the wishes of the majority. The Grand Duke's approach was announced as that of a father returning to his children after five months' painful separation. He landed at Viareggio, where he was met by the Gonfaloniers, or Mayors of Florence and of Lucca. The next day he reached Lucca, receiving on the way demonstrations of welcome, which were, however, somewhat cooled by the presence of a foreign soldiery. From Lucca he proceeded to Pisa, avoiding Leghorn, and on the 28th July set out for Florence. At Empoli he was met by the Marchese Ridolfi, whom he received coldly; and, on his arrival at Florence, the foreign ambassadors, the ministers, the officers of the Austrian army, with a crowd of courtiers of both sexes, and the representatives of the municipality, came out to receive him. He drove at once to the Church of the Santissima Annunziata, and thence proceeded to the Pitti Palace. The city was illuminated that night, but the rejoicings were in marked contrast from those of the preceding year. The order of merit of St. Joseph, the highest order the Tuscan Crown had to confer, was bestowed on Field-Marshal Radetzky, General D'Aspre, the Archduke Albert, and other Austrian officers; whilst all who had the year before fought for their country at Curtatone and Montanara, amongst them Professor Zannetti, who had attended the wounded and the dying on that field, were deprived of the honours which at the time had been conferred on them by the Grand Duke himself. Such a commencement did not augur well for the promised restoration of the Constitution.

In September, the Grand Duke made a journey to Vienna, to visit his young cousin, the Emperor Francis the Second; and, on his return, the Prefect of Florence issued an order for the elections to a new Parliament, which was considered by the people a proof that the Prince intended to redeem his pledge; but it seems that the Prefect's zeal for the honour of the Grand Duke, to whom he was sincerely attached, had overstepped his prudence, and the Prince with difficulty forgave his presumption.

Guérazzi, who had been left in prison by the Provisional Government, was now put on his trial, which lasted four years, to the scandal of all Tuscany. The Grand Duke meantime concluded a convention with the Emperor of Austria for the maintenance of ten thousand Austrian soldiers in his dominions, for whom Leopold engaged to furnish quarters and provisions, besides acceding to the condition which placed all the fortresses of Tuscany at their disposal. During the three years of occupation, the country had to pay upwards of thirty-six million six hundred and fourteen thousand lire, for the maintenance of these foreign troops, besides being subjected to martial law at the hands of a tribunal composed of Austrian soldiers. Persecutions by arbitrary acts followed, besides numerous executions of innocent persons, and the most galling insults, which the people were obliged to suffer without a hope of redress.

On the 5th May, 1852, the Grand Duke, Leopold II., issued the following proclamation :

" We, LEOPOLD THE SECOND,

" *By the Grace of God, Grand Duke of* " *Tuscany, &c. &c.*

" When in the midst of extraordinary events which were enacting in and out of Italy, we resolved to grant our beloved Tuscany wider political institutions, promulgating the fundamental Statute of the 15th February, 1848, we were not moved thereunto by any other consideration than the desire to preserve the country from the dangers with which she was menaced, to conform our Government to that of neighbouring States, and to contribute by the new system to the greater prosperity of our beloved subjects.

" But the results did not answer our common expectations. We did not derive the hoped-for benefits, nor did we escape from the evils we feared ; our authority was subsequently obliged to yield to the violence of a revolution which at once overturned the Statute, and occasioned Tuscany the most deplorable calamities.

"We were soon afterwards restored, by the courage of those Tuscans who remained faithful to the lawful Government ; and, thanking Providence, who has thus consoled us for the bitterness of exile, we accepted the generous deed, *reserving to ourselves to restore*, notwithstanding our painful experience, *the political order instituted by us in February*, 1848, so that there might likewise be no fear of a repetition of past disorders. Nevertheless, to restrain the machinations of the several factions which were disconcerted, not subdued, by the happy successes of the 12th April, 1849, it was necessary to use extraordinary measures, and thus secure the tranquillity of the State, and provide in an expeditious and efficacious way for the better administration of the country ; we have therefore determined to resume the exercise of our full power, until the general condition of Europe, and the particular condition of Tuscany and of Italy, shall permit the restoration of the system of representative government.

"Meantime very serious events have succeeded one another in Europe. The foundations of society have been more or less menaced, and society has, therefore, been obliged to seek, and still seeks, its safety under the shelter of those principles which allow of the firm and free exercise of authority. No trace now remains of representative government in Italy, and we are convinced that the majority of Tuscans, remembering the peace and prosperity they so long enjoyed, and taught a lesson by unhappy experience, must feel the necessity of trusting for the development of the well-being of the country to the consolidation of power and order, rather than desire to see a form of government revived, which is neither consonant with the institutions of Tuscany nor with the habits of our people, and which proved such a failure in the brief period of its existence.

"Therefore, as the real good of the country requires, and the general conditions demand, that the Government of the State shall be constituted on the same basis with that on which it was conducted until 1848, we, having deliberately arrived at this conclusion, promulgate the following resolutions, assuring the Tuscans that our first and dearest care will ever be, whilst life is granted us, to promote in every way the moral and material welfare of our beloved country.

"Thus may God daily more aid and strengthen the concord and confidence of our much beloved people, since we are convinced that the new political organization of Tuscany, by increasing the prerogatives of those in authority, will increase the burden of our duties. . . ."

The resolutions which followed contained the abolition of the Statute; and thus did Leopold fulfil the

words he uttered to a confidential friend when setting
foot again in Tuscany :—" The Tuscans have rejected
me for their father, they shall have me for their step-
father ; and I will only leave them eyes to weep their
misery."

CHAPTER XXIII.

ON the 22d May, 1849, Giusti wrote to the Marchese Capponi, from Pescia :—

"MY DEAR GINO,

"We have the Germans in Pescia. They poured in unexpectedly this morning, numbering about two thousand, and, it appears, they intend advancing upon Pistoia. I have neither heart nor health to bear the sight of them, and I stay at home in shame and sorrow. We were just going into the country, but fearing they might make a search for arms, or demand a lodging, or something of the sort, we have remained here, as we have no one to give the whole in charge, on whom we could depend.

"It is hard to be obliged to suffer for another's fault, but we are perhaps deserving of punishment. If we had only had a grain of common sense! Meantime, there is 'the devil to pay' in Germany, and I believe they are setting to in earnest. I cannot at all make my way out of it,

A A 2

and I consider the most ignorant are always the most presumptuous ; but that Russia should offer her support to Austria is, I confess, the most intricate problem of all that is presented to us among the facts passing before our eyes. Was it not only to aim a blow at Austria that Russia tried to strengthen herself by her Sclavic population ? Perhaps if the Magyars should be conquered, she will return to the old scheme, or renew the Holy Alliance, or there may possibly spring up some new fungus that will inflict pain, where least expected. Yet there are those who on seeing the arrival of these birds of ill-omen, expect fair weather to return. . . . We shall know the truth some ten years hence, if the storm has not by that time swept us all away. Meantime here we are, sold like a set of blockheads, when we thought that we should have made a sell of all the world."

In another letter of the same month, he alludes to the Marchese Capponi having generously spoken in behalf of Guérazzi, and adds, " I am ashamed that even at a moment like this there should be any who take pride in trampling upon the fallen, and I can hardly believe it true that they afford me this opportunity of declaring that I do not share their baseness."

Writing to another friend, he thus takes a hasty review of the state of feeling produced by the vicissitudes the country had undergone :—

"MY DEAR ——,

"If you wish to know of what stuff the courage of certain persons is composed, you have only to look back a little, and remember the tone of conversation formerly held by those who are now howling most loudly over recent events. Beginning from the time when the law on the Press and other franchises, including the national guard, were first spoken of, you might have heard them turning it all into ridicule, and compare the proposed reforms to mouthfuls thrown to a dog to quiet him ; further, maintaining they were concessions which would have no influence one way or another, and that the people were not ripe for liberty, and would not know what to do with it ; that between the bad faith of the rulers, and the unwilling spirit of the ruled, these measures must necessarily fall of themselves ; and, therefore, they would have had us act like people in a fog—wait patiently to find our way out in time. Thus when the hour arrived for urging the people forward, these courageous persons called out, 'Stop.'

After the publication of the Statute, and when they found they could really speak out, they thought of playing the liberal as authors, smoothing down the people who were on the rise, and shaking off the princes who were on the decline. They were sure not to be the only servile flatterers, as tyranny, whether vested in one man or in the million, is never without its worshippers. The few who attempted to speak out to the multitudes were called the enemies of liberty and traitors to their country; so true is it that there was more talk than substance.

"And now what do you say to the cowardly language boldly hurled against the fallen? Firing away as in a farce, at Montanelli who has fled, and at Guérazzi who is shut up in a fortress. Certain papers may well take the name of insects;[1] but, rather than insects, they appear to me carrion crows, fattening themselves on dead carcases. If *La Vespa* (The Wasp) or the *Stenterello* had stung and ridiculed the Democratic Ministry when they had the wind in their favour, that would have been an act of courage; but where is the courage, where is the delicacy, where is the dignity and generosity, to add to the bitterness of misfortune, even if these men did bring the country to trouble and ruin."

On the 19th June, Giusti again wrote to the Marchese Capponi, from Pescia :—

" MY DEAR GINO,

" I cannot speak of the affairs of our country without shame and grief, and I turn continually for refreshment to scribble, as of old. At times my head gives way, and I feel myself forced to stop; at other times I wish that I could write in characters of fire. I assure you that

---

[1] One of the newspapers of the day was called *La Zanzara*, The Gnat, another, *La Vespa*, The Wasp.

every now and then a bitter and profound sensation of melancholy comes over me, such as I have not felt for years and years.   It is like that which takes the soul by surprise in early youth, when the cruel shears of doubt and suspicion suddenly cut the thread of faith and hope.   Then you almost regret having to live, and virtue itself has no longer that charm which first attached you to life.   And what is this future which is preparing for all of us ?   Seeing good in everything, as I have always done, I feel that I cannot throw myself overboard and despair ; but it would be folly, or worse than folly, not to pause in uncertainty and doubt. Meantime, you cannot imagine into what mistakes all those are led who have not watched the progress of our affairs.   Newspapers, gossip, and the intrigues of all parties, have confused the heads of everybody : after getting a blow by running head foremost, you get another blow by falling back ; one man prides himself in his errors, from not understanding the consolation there is in calling oneself a fool ; and most are boiling over with indignation under a mistaken idea that we could have saved ourselves, and therefore take comfort in calling out : ' I said so. . . .' "

Giusti's published poems end with 1848.   In the summer of 1849 his health became so decidedly worse, that he went to Viareggio, hoping to derive some benefit from the sea-air, but he did not remain there

long, and he writes to the Marchese Capponi, from
Pescia, on the 22nd August:—

" MY DEAR GINO,

" I had to leave Viareggio, because in the course of
a few days I had fallen back in a strange manner.
Next week I shall go to Montecatini, to try everything
before the return of winter.

" This work of Galvani's is very remarkable. I am too
norant of those studies to venture to say more ; but
I read it with a pleasure I have not felt for long. Rome,
a cosmopolitan city from the egg, which all adopt and
all would imitate, is a fact which both natives and
foreigners should consider somewhat more. Without
jesting, I would say that Mazzini tried to restore the
asylum of Romulus ; but the misfortune was that he
found the Vatican in place of the Tarpeian Rock.

" I can imagine your sorrow at the loss of the brave
Colonel Pepe. I am not surprised that he should not
have been able to command in the midst of so many
errors and of so much folly and baseness. The account
Massari has given of the affair is short and incorrect,
but I hope that soon one may arise better acquainted
with the matter than he is, and who will write as
justice and duty demand. I always seem to see Pepe
in his cabin in Florence, or in that garret of the
Locanda dell' Allegria in Naples. He was certainly not
a man of these times. He had a soul like one of the

ancients, sent to live in our days, and had even an excess of virtue for one belonging .to that region down in the South.

" I do not know when we shall meet again, because I do not know when I shall cease from suffering ; but, God knows, I have need of both."

CHAPTER XXIV.

SOON after writing the letter given in the preceding chapter, Giusti came to Florence, where he was seized with milliary fever, one of the most terrible forms of disease incident to Italy, which almost exclusively attacks natives. Though he recovered from this illness, the germs of a lung disease appeared, which finally carried him to the grave. He resided as usual, when in Florence, in the Palace of the Marchese Capponi, from whence his last published letter was written, on the 15th March, 1850 :—

" *To Enrico Mayer.*

" MY DEAR MAYER,

" A few lines to tell you that I am alive, and that I expect to see you here, in the house of Capponi, the first time you come to Florence. You will see that I have learnt to suffer. I served my noviciate in your house—the milliary fever has completed my training.

" If I wish to write to Orlandini, where should I direct my letter? To Leghorn or to Pisa? It is an age since I heard anything of any of you, to whom I owe so much, for so many reasons ; and now that I can myself write, I am anxious to send a greeting to all, one at a time.

" And what is the Signora Vittorina about ? Remember me to her, and kiss the children, who, I suppose, seem to grow beneath your eyes. What a pleasure yours must be, who, having occupied yourself so many years with the children of others, are able now to occupy yourself with children of your own ! It is a real reward which you deserve.

" I embrace you from my heart."

After tracing Giusti's life through the troubled sea of politics, in which, by his writings, he had taken so active a part from the commencement of his career, there is repose in dwelling on the closing scenes of his remaining days on earth, when, amidst great bodily suffering, his intellect continued vigorous as ever. He prepared to enter upon another stage of existence, by study and reflection on the great mind, which, many centuries before, had preceded his in that world where time and space, separating them here, are as nothing. Whilst writing a commentary on Dante, his thoughts were so engrossed by the subject, he could speak of little else, and his friends always found him with his bed covered with books and old manuscripts. This work was never completed, and the fragments which remain, have only recently been published, in a volume containing his inedited writings. He appears in them to allude to the experience of his own life, whilst forming his judgment on the meaning of the great poet, which has been so frequently a subject of dispute.

"Some assert that the scheme of this composition is a dream of the poet, and thus believe they have given us all a satisfactory answer. I suppose it to be a dream, and he himself calls it a vision, but I believe this dream to be founded on truth, and a sublime induction from the known to the unknown, from the present to the future, by one saddened by present evil, and finding himself, as it were, a stranger here ; and who seeks consolation in forming out of this real an ideal world. Say that Plato's Republic is a dream ; say that Cebetus's Table is a dream ; say that St. Augustine's and Campanella's City of God and City of the Sun are dreams ; but you cannot deny that all these great men desired the good of mankind ; and, observe, that in regard to what is possible they are at an infinite distance from Dante, because Dante, instead of aiming at remodelling the world, aimed at conducting civil and religious questions back to their first principles. Macchiavelli himself was under an illusion when appealing to Lorenzo de Medici ; but who would, therefore, maintain that the book of the Prince was not dictated by the conditions of the time in which he lived, and by the mind of a philosopher ?

" Whatever may be the opinion formed of Dante, as a private individual, I believe I may assert, that the poem is not the work of a man influenced by a spirit of party. For a partisan appears to me one who is excited to accuse the opposite party of every crime, and is obstinate in a determination neither to know nor to confess the faults committed on his own side. Now Dante, in his Commedia, neither shows indulgence to Guelph nor to Ghibelline, neither to clergy nor layman, neither to Pope nor Emperor. For one Pope whom he charges with avarice, he charges two Emperors— Rudolph and Albert—with covetousness and cowardice, and invokes the vengeance of God on their descendants. And, if it were true, that he was a furious Ghibelline, so much the greater praise is due to him for having been able to throw off this spirit in his poem.

" After describing how the affairs of Italy were all in disorder, and the people blind or misguided, Dante shows that there is no other way by which to ameliorate the condition of his times than by recalling the Florentines to just principles in politics and religion."

Faith in the goodness and wisdom of the Creator had sustained Giusti in his hope for the renovation of his country, amidst scenes the most hopeless, the most discouraging ; and the same faith did not fail him in the contemplation of his own approaching end. His time was not spent as if in the expectation that death would

change his soul in an instant, either in being or in aim
or that in departing this life, he was to enter upon a
world alien to ours.　As he lived, so he died, filled with
the thought of all that is pure and great and good, and
with that perfect Christian charity which, whilst teaching him to love his fellow-creatures whom he had seen,
led him to love the Father, whom he had not seen.
Writing to the Marchese Capponi in 1845, he expressed
sentiments which appear to have continued with him
to the end of his life :—

"I wish that reverence for that which is above us
should be united with reverence for great men.　Faith
in God, and in our fellow-creatures, go hand in hand ;
and the atheist (if such there be, which I do not
believe) is, of necessity, the first enemy of the human
race and of himself.　For this reason, charity is the
fruit of faith."

Such faith could only be attained by the wisdom of
that true humility which confesses in our disappointed
expectations the limits of human knowledge and foresight, and the immensity of that scheme of which it is
only permitted to man to know a part.

Giusti's last poem was a prayer :—

> " Alla mente confusa
> Di dubbio e di dolore
> Soccorri, o mio Signore
> Col raggio della fé ;
> Sottevalo dal peso

Che la declina al fango,
A te sospiro e piango,
Mi raccomando a te.
Sai che la vita mia
Si strugge appoco appoco,
Come la cera al foco
Come la neve al sol ;
All' anima che anela
Di ricovrarti in braccio
Rompi, Signore, il laccio
Che le impedisce il vol."

During the severe winter of 1850, Giusti was unable
to leave the Capponi Palace. On the 25th March, a
friend who visited him describes him as calm and
happy, speaking of his approaching end. Six days later,
on the 31st March, he was seized with a sudden rush of
blood to the mouth, from the rupture of some vessel,
and he had only time to throw himself on the bed, when
he expired.

The news spread sorrow throughout Florence ; but
the Government made considerable difficulty in grant-
ing permission to the request that public honours
should be paid to his remains. On the evening of the
1st April, the body was conveyed to the church of San
Miniato ; beside the coffin walked, the Gonfalonier
Ubaldino Peruzzi, the Abate Raffaello Lambruschini,
Professor Domenico Valeriani, Professor Giovan Battista
Giorgini, and the friend he loved as a brother, the
Marchese Gino Capponi ; and it was followed by a long

line of mourning friends. Eulogiums on him appeared in the newspapers, and various literary men wrote in his praise, whilst, in September of that year, the Academia della Crusca held a solemn meeting in remembrance of him. The highest honour paid him, however, has been the grateful love and veneration with which his countrymen cherish his name, and which may perhaps have afforded some consolation to his sorrowing parents for the loss of their only son.

The statue of Giuseppe Giusti by Reginaldo Bilancini has been erected on one side of the entrance to the beautiful church of San Miniato. Around where Giusti lies, are the splendid monuments of the art and the wealth of Florence in the days of her republican glory, and from this spot Michael Angelo made the last stand for her expiring liberty. On the pavement below, and down in the crypt, are the more humble memorials to the relations of living Florentines, and the little church is always fragrant with offerings of flowers, strewing the ground so closely that the stranger must walk carefully to avoid desecration; stepping out of the cool shade of that hallowed temple, he looks down on the country of the Poet. Nestling below him lies Florence, her cupola and towers, with the Arno, like a silver thread, winding between her streets; beyond, stretches the wide extent of richly wooded and cultivated plain, with a border of undulating hills, sparkling with villas, towns, or villages, or crowned by some old monastic residence, bearing all the signs of an art-loving, poetical, yet industrious, frugal and social population. Enclosing this lovely valley, and clearly defined against the cloudless blue sky of the sunny landscape, may be traced the grand outline of the Apennines, the distant Carrara mountains and Pisan hills, the heights above Prato and Pistoia, the nearer Monte Morello and the mountains which skirt the valley to Vallombrosa, with the range above range of distant hills leading towards Rome. Such has been the home of Tuscan poets from Dante to Giuseppe Giusti, and such a land and such a people seem well worthy of the leaders Providence has assigned for the accomplishment of their redemption.

The following inscription has been placed below the statue to the memory of Giusti :——

" Qui riposa in Dio le mortale spoglie
Di GIUSEPPE GIUSTI ;
Che dalle grazie del vivo nostro idioma
Trassi una forma di Poesia
Prima di lui non tentata
E con arguto stile castigando i vizi
Senza togliere fede a virtù
Inalzò gli uomini al culto dei nobili affetti
E delle opere generose.
Onde ebbe dall' Italia onore e compianto
Quando nel fiore della virilità
Le fu rapito da insidioso morbo——
Morì in Firenze il XXXI. Marzo MDCCCL.

B B

Il Cav. Domenico Giusti, Padre infelicissimo,
        Deponeva in questo sepolcro
        L'unico figlio maschio
        Sostegno e gloria del suo nome."

————————————

" Here reposes in God the mortal remains
        Of Giuseppe Giusti,
Who from the beauties of our living tongue
        Drew forth a form of poetry
Not attempted by any before him,
And by a lively style reproving vice
Without diminishing our faith in virtue
He raised men to the culture of the noblest affections
        And of generous works :
For this he was honoured and wept in Italy,
        When in the prime of his manhood
He was carried off by an insidious disease.
He died in Florence the 31st March, 1850.

The Cavaliere Domenico Giusti, his unhappy father,
        Has laid in this sepulchre
            His only son,
    The prop and glory of his name."

INDEX.

WORKS BY THE REV. CHARLES KINGSLEY.

CHAPLAIN IN ORDINARY TO THE QUEEN ; RECTOR OF EVERSLEY ;
AND PROFESSOR OF MODERN HISTORY IN THE UNIVERSITY OF CAMBRIDGE.

THE WATER BABIES:

A FAIRY TALE FOR A LAND BABY.

With Two Illustrations by J. NOEL PATON, R.S.A.   Small 4to.   7s. 6d.

WESTWARD HO!

New and Cheaper Edition.   Crown 8vo. cloth, 6s.

TWO YEARS AGO.

New and Cheaper Edition.   Crown 8vo. cloth, 6s.

HYPATIA:

OR, NEW FOES WITH AN OLD FACE.

Fourth Edition.   Crown 8vo. cloth, 6s.

ALTON LOCKE, TAILOR AND POET.

New Edition.   Crown 8vo. cloth, 4s. 6d.   With New Preface.

THE HEROES.

GREEK FAIRY TALES FOR THE YOUNG.

Second Edition, with Illustrations.   Royal 16mo. cloth, 3s. 6d.

ALEXANDRIA AND HER SCHOOLS.

Crown 8vo. cloth, 5s.

THE LIMITS OF EXACT SCIENCE

AS APPLIED TO HISTORY.

AN INAUGURAL LECTURE DELIVERED BEFORE THE UNIVERSITY OF
CAMBRIDGE.   Crown 8vo. 2s.

PHAETHON.

LOOSE THOUGHTS FOR LOOSE THINKERS.

Third Edition.   Crown 8vo. 2s.

MACMILLAN AND CO. LONDON AND CAMBRIDGE.

POPULAR WORKS.

Third Edition.
AUSTIN ELLIOT.
By HENRY KINGSLEY.
2 Vols. Crown 8vo. cloth. 1*l*. 1*s*.

" Mr. Henry Kingsley's novels have so much fulness of life in them, such a strong, bounding pulse, that there are few books of the kind pleasanter to read."—*Spectator*.

Second Edition.
RAVENSHOE.
By HENRY KINGSLEY.
3 Vols. Crown 8vo. cloth. 1*l*. 11*s*. 6*d*.

" Admirable descriptions, which place ' Ravenshoe ' almost in the first rank of novels. Of the story itself it would really be difficult to speak too highly. The author seems to possess every essential for a writer of fiction."—*London Review*.

Second Edition.
RECOLLECTIONS OF GEOFFRY HAMLYN.
By HENRY KINGSLEY.
Crown 8vo. cloth. 6*s*.

" Mr. Henry Kingsley has written a work that keeps up its interest from the first page to the last—it is full of vigorous stirring life. The descriptions of Australian life in the early colonial days are marked by an unmistakeable touch of reality and personal experience. A book which the public will be more inclined to read than to criticise, and we commend them to each other."—*Athenæum*.

Second Edition.
TOM BROWN AT OXFORD.
3 Vols. 1*l*. 11*s*. 6*d*.

" A book that will live. In no other work that we can call to mind are the finer qualities of the English gentleman more happily portrayed."—*Daily News*.
" The extracts we have given can give no adequate expression to the literary vividness and noble ethical atmosphere which pervade the whole book."—*Spectator*.

Twenty-ninth Thousand.
TOM BROWN'S SCHOOL DAYS.
By AN OLD BOY.
Fcap. 8vo. 5*s*.

" A book which every father might well wish to see in the hands of his son."—*Times*.

Eighth Thousand.
SCOURING OF THE WHITE HORSE.
By the Author of " Tom Brown's School Days."
With numerous Illustrations by Richard Doyle. Imperial 16mo. Printed on toned paper, gilt leaves, 8*s*. 6*d*.

" The execution is excellent. . . . Like ' Tom Brown's School Days,' the ' White Horse' gives the reader a feeling of gratitude and personal esteem towards the author. The author could not have a better style, nor a better temper, nor a more excellent artist than Mr. Doyle to adorn his book."—*Saturday Review*.

MACMILLAN AND CO. LONDON AND CAMBRIDGE.

Received May 1. 5. 24 = //

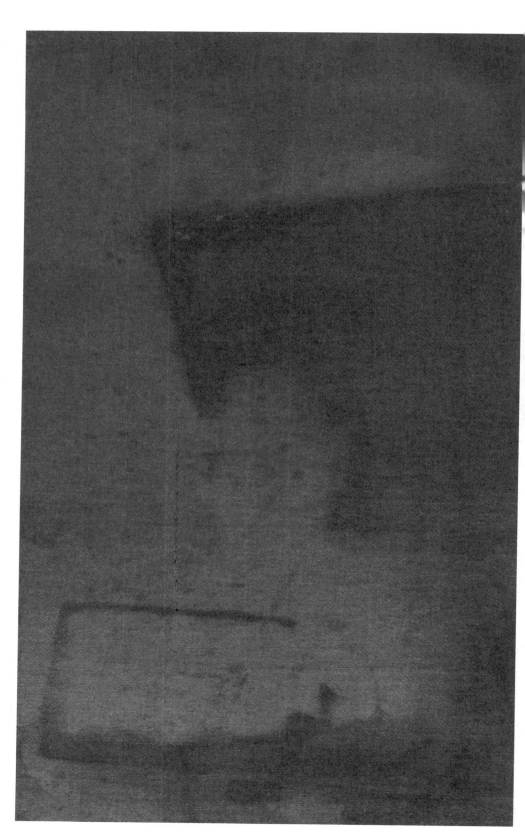

Check Out More Titles From HardPress Classics Series In this collection we are offering thousands of classic and hard to find books. This series spans a vast array of subjects – so you are bound to find something of interest to enjoy reading and learning about.

Subjects:
Architecture
Art
Biography & Autobiography
Body, Mind &Spirit
Children & Young Adult
Dramas
Education
Fiction
History
Language Arts & Disciplines
Law
Literary Collections
Music
Poetry
Psychology
Science
…and many more.

Visit us at www.hardpress.net

CPSIA information can be obtained
at www.ICGtesting.com
Printed in the USA
BVHW040447160819
555988BV00025BA/544/P